THE GREAT NORTH ROAD

The Great North Road

A Guide for the Curious Traveller

Frank Goddard

FRANCES LINCOLN

To Sandie, my wife, who has shared, enjoyed, and on occasion shown great patience, during so much of this exploration of the Great North Road. Happy days!

Frances Lincoln Ltd.,
4, Torriano Mews
Torriano Avenue
London NW5 2RZ
www.franceslincoln.com

A catalogue record for this book is available from the British Library.

ISBN 0 7112 2446 3

Printed and bound in Hong Kong.

9 8 7 6 5 4 3 2 1

BY THE SAME AUTHOR
Lakeland Fells
Foothills of the Fells
The Beeston Trail

CONTENTS

Introduction

This book is an account of a personal journey north through Britain and invites the reader to join the author and his wife as they explore a linear slice of our history and heritage. It records places which remain the highlights of travels and holidays over a period of many years and traces a route which has grown over the centuries to be our most famous and historic road, linking the capital cities of England and Scotland.

The motorway is the nearest thing we have to the fictional time machine. You enter at one junction, leave at another and between these points you travel in a time vacuum oblivious to the lives of those you pass on the journey and to the affairs that have influenced the hinterland of the great grey way. Cities and towns are indicated only by bold blue direction signs and even these are just names to pluck from a time continuum which rarely has meaning for the passenger in the capsules speeding past. In this respect motorways are quite unlike the roads of old which visited ever town and village. It was said that you could tell where you were merely by looking at architecture and building materials – the granite of Aberdeen, mellow limestone in the Cotswolds, gritstone in the Yorkshire Pennines, flints in the chalklands of the south, et al. Roadside buildings, farms, inns, walls and even the bridges you would have crossed or passed beneath wrote a signature on the countryside. But times change. You'll travel a long way on a motorway before seeing much more than concrete.

The Great North Road is one of the most celebrated routes in the world. Its very name has the ring of history about it, a title redolent of Romans and robbers, coaches and highwaymen, though the reality of dust, noise, fumes and stress of the modern A1 is far from the picturebook perception of a grand old name. It may not even be the same route for there is no definitive Great North Road. At any point in history the line would show differences and variations consequently the route in this book is open to argument and very much a personal choice, but it is largely that of the 18th. and 19th. centuries, the one in common use long before its designation was reduced to a pair of primaries, alphabetical and digital. In those few places where our chosen route is able to break free from the A1 it can be quieter although it is hard to find any road that is a real throw-back to the Golden Age of motoring of the 1930s when there were wider spaces between fewer cars on the roads. This is why many diversions along rural byways are described and recommended.

The Great North Road was never simply a link between capital cities. It also acknowledged the need to find the most direct route from the General Post Office in London to its Edinburgh counterpart and it is still at these points that the A1 starts and finishes, though the respective post office buildings no longer provide the services of their high street equivalents. You'd have no success in trying to buy a stamp there! Even the concept of a route for the mails is no longer accurate – I suppose your letter would travel by rail or air in the present day. Yet if you wish to have a useful definition of the Great North Road you can hardly do better than remember it as the post road linking London with Edinburgh.

Neither the Great North Road nor the A1 traces the shortest possible of modern routes. The distance varies according to which source you choose but a combination of the A1 and the A68 over Carter Bar has a smaller mileage and with fine tuning even that may be trimmed. However, if mileage is of no consequence, the fastest route combines the M1 and M6 with the A7 to produce a distance of 413 miles, to quote the Automobile Association's handbook, twenty-two more miles than calculated in this book. However, the 391·6 miles calculated here should not be taken as definitive. This is merely the figure arrived at by measuring the strip map in the following pages and should be taken with a pinch of winter road-salt! The A1 with its bypasses, smooth curves and pure lines would certainly be shorter but these pages often detail an itinerary which avoids the obvious.

The route will change. Roads will be closed, re-routed, made one-way, upgraded to dual carriageway or motorway, even re-named; and there will always be temporary diversions caused by repairs, improvements, re-laying of electric cables, gas pipes, sewers, lorries shedding their loads and, regrettably, accidents. This is not a route for the impatient, especially on diversions down byways where local life must go on. Drive with care. Injudicious application of brakes too soon after the Friesians have crossed for milking can have interesting, even spectacular results.

The itinerary described in the following pages is not the way for those in a hurry. Readers will find themselves involved in possibly the longest journey between London and Edinburgh on record for this is a book for the curious and interested traveller. It is not the road in itself that is the attraction. A modern road is no more than a stretch of tarmac. It has counterparts throughout the world. A road is basically a device for facilitating the passage of people and goods from point A to point B. These points and the multitudinous points between have stories to tell and it is these that make the road interesting. It is only when you lift your eyes from the way ahead that you discover the fascination of The Road. The further you cast your eyes the more fascinating it becomes and if you let your mind rove too you may travel in time. There is history about you on the long miles north.

The Great North Road has been described as unattractive because it passes through undistinguished scenery. Initially this may well be so but it improves as you journey north. Often the countryside is nothing to write home about but there are places along the way where spectacular scenes are within reach. In Yorkshire, for example, the North York Moors and the Yorkshire Dales form horizons east and west while further north you have the incomparable Northumberland coast on your right and the wild rolling hills of the Northumberland National Park on your left. Here and in the Border country ahead even the scene viewed from the road is excellent and it is possible to forget that you are on a major trunk road – if you can ignore the flow of traffic impatient for its destination. Let it pass!

The places we shall investigate, with a few exceptions, will be near our line of travel. They are the making of this road as a route of interest and many of them have had a part to play in its growth. Some sit astride the road. Others are further afield but rarely so far as to make a diversion unreasonable. It is hardly surprising that a journey of nearly 400 miles should take the traveller through or within reach of so many splendid towns and cities. A random half dozen might include Peterborough, Stamford, Grantham, Durham, Newcastle and Berwick-upon-Tweed which were always on the itinerary; and Lincoln and York were destinations on the road to the north during periods of its history.

Often a minor site on a map opens a line of thought that may lead to notes which hardly seem relevant to the Great North Road; the yews at Weston, the plague at East Markham, the Templars at Temple Dinsley; but this is the fascination of travel. Look, note and enquire. It is often surprising what you may turn up.

The descriptions are necessarily brief. Treat them as samples. These are places my wife and I have enjoyed visiting but there is space here for only a few comments. Each piece is no more than a thumb-nail sketch to whet the appetite, hopefully to arouse interest, to provide some indication of whether the place is worth seeking out, to give some idea of its appeal and to provoke further exploration or study.

If you are persuaded to follow in our tracks then buy the guidebook which is always available locally. Most towns are waking up to the value of tourism and are setting out their stalls accordingly. The nearest Tourist Information Centre has rarely let us down; there is always a supply of free leaflets and usually a stock of cheap, attractive and informative booklets. And maps! Failing that, most towns of any size will have a decent bookshop. You soon develop a 'nose' for the right sort of establishment. In smaller towns or villages look for the post office or newsagent. Or ask a passer-by. A query at a sweet shop once led me to a furniture store where there was a nice stack of useful books just waiting for the likes of me to turn up – the proprietor was a local historian with all the material at his fingertips!

If you intend to do justice to the suggested itinerary it is worth joining the National Trust and English Heritage. The fees will be repaid before many miles have been travelled. We have always found membership of these groups to be invaluable – a canny Yorkshire lad can always spot a bargain. Their properties can provide a splendid day out at any time and support is always appreciated. You may be sure that the membership fees are put to good use.

The selection of subjects for illustration is not comprehensive. If every place described was to be pictured the book would be impossibly long and completion time unforeseeable so the choice is subjective. Pictures which may be considered peripheral to the main subject are often drawn to the exclusion of subjects on or adjacent to the main route. It is all a matter of personal choice. If the illustrations provide a flavour of the journey they will have served a good purpose and together with the text should suggest ideas for the adventurous traveller who wishes to explore and learn more about our British heritage. Don't stick with the traffic of the trunk road. Get away from the old planned way and enjoy yourselves.

Happy motoring!

Tourist Information Centres

In the following pages you may find mention of transient attractions which have become history. A passing reference is not a guarantee that a place is still open and for this reason I have generally avoided giving times, dates and telephone numbers; they change from season to season. It is always worth checking in advance and this is where the local Tourist Information Centre can be so useful.

The "TIC" is invaluable. It has alway been our first port of call when visiting somewhere new, both as a source of local information and as a reliable means of finding somewhere to stay for the night. Unfortunately some of the smaller ones are not open from late autumn until early spring. Except in popular areas it would appear that tourists are only expected in summer.

There may be nearly a thousand TICs in Britain. Frequently they are in the obvious place, the railway or bus station, sometimes in a corner of the major car park where they are of most use to travellers coming into town. It is surprising how often they occupy buildings of historic or scenic interest, a sort of advertisement for the services offered within. Just about every town along our route has its TIC, even places that are hardly bigger than a large village. One was a portable structure in a layby in Scotland where there was a splendid and enticing view across a valley to Traprain Law. It was attracting plenty of custom.

Most TICs will hold a list of useful accommodation and will provide a booking service. The ladies (mostly ladies) and gentlemen who will greet you are usually local people - who better to tell you all you need to know, whether it's the way to the local castle, stately home, museum or even the best place to go for lunch, the whereabouts of the nearest post office or where to find the local supermarket. All this and a good stock of guides, maps, local books and often a plentiful supply of souvenirs.

Those folks behind the counter are angels in disguise. They'll greet you with a smile and do their utmost to help you. They deserve a smile and a thank you in return. So don't forget to do just that!

NOTES ON THE MAPS

When the strip map in the following pages was drawn it was as accurate as the author could make it; he had recently re-driven the route for a final inspection of recent road developments, re-alignments and general alterations. However, the upgrading of this major transport axis of Britain, especially where it still coincides with the A1/A1(M), continues apace and inevitably changes will have already occurred between this final check and publication of the book. Before very long the entire length of the A1 as far as Tyneside will be motorway. If the map pages were to be updated on a regular basis the author would be tied to his Great North Road pen for the rest of his life: as each page is hand-drawn even the simplest of revisions would require a great deal of time and effort, certainly more than he can afford with fresh projects in mind.

The information will continue to be reasonably accurate but in detail it will become progressively less dependable as the years go by so it is better to regard the strip map as an historical document depicting the route as it was when the twentieth century gave way to a brand new millennium rather than as a guide for motorists. The mapping will always be of value in locating the places described in the text – which was always the intention. It was done as a personal record of places visited and as such it is very much at the mercy of one man's observations and potential for error – here is an opportunity to acknowledge that there will inevitably be mistakes, oversights and downright blunders. This cartographer is very much an amateur and it shows. But the pleasure was in the drawing. The advice is to use the maps in conjunction with the Ordnance Survey's splendid Landranger series (the relevant sheet is indicated on each page) and for accurate, up-to-date road information to use the latest road maps published by the O.S. and the Automobile Association.

As for the strip map itself, not every road junction is shown, especially in built-up areas. That kind of detail is not really needed. However most junctions and side roads are included, if only to help the reader to identify a position on the road from the car. There are other junctions whose inclusion is purely arbitrary. They may be there for purely cosmetic reasons, to improve the appearance of, or merely to decorate an otherwise bare stretch of road. Yet it may be found that in many places a junction shown in good faith has been closed when the road was upgraded. Please accept this as a fact of motoring life.

Road numbers may not be totally reliable. They may have been when the map was drawn but changes occur more often than you might expect. Since the book was sketched out with its maps a dozen years ago many roads have been re-numbered, usually in conjunction with upgrades or the construction of bypasses. The most radical example was around Tyneside where the original A1 through Newcastle shifted east, then west. The first change was to re-number the A194(M) and sections of the A184 and A108 (now A19!) so that the A1 went through the Tyne Tunnel on its way from Birtley to Seaton Burn. With the completion of the Western Bypass the A1 moved to this modern road and there it remains. Such major alterations always bring changes in their wake. It is a story with counterparts throughout the land (not only along the Great North Road). The latest piece of complicated re-alignment at the time of writing is the arrival of the M1 to join the A1(M) at Hook Moor. There are minor examples all along the way, hardly realised until you try following a road that still exists but has been allocated a different number. It is fair to note that most of these variations are passed unnoticed unless you leave the corridor of the A1.

Distances and mileages are the author's own measurements and in no way guaranteed to be accurate. Maps are generally to the scale of one inch to the mile, except where otherwise indicated, but may be distorted where necessary in order to allow greater detail; and there is some compression at the northern end of the route where it approaches Edinburgh to comply with the demands of space. The area of Greater London is at double the scale, two inches to the mile, to accommodate greater detail. Use of the old imperial measures reflects this traveller's generation and obstinate unwillingness to accept metric linear distances. It sounds less in miles! However decimal fractions have been used in the running totals, being more convenient.

Maps showing diversions into country areas will probably be useful for years to come since changes along byways are less likely. However it cannot be overstressed that the Ordnance Survey's Landranger maps are indispensable assets for the curious traveller and are needed to provide details of the general picture if there is any intention to spend an extended period of time exploring a particular district. The Landranger series of 204 maps covers the U.K. in 25 mile (40km) square sheets at a scale of 1:50 000 (1¼ inches to a mile or 2cm per kilometre). It is a general purpose publication packed with invaluable information including picnic areas, viewpoints, places of interest, rights of way, camping and caravanning sites and general tourist information which, together with accurate mapping, will bring the landscape to life for the enlightened map reader. However, for main road driving the latest edition of a motoring atlas published by the O.S. or the A.A. is a worthwhile buy and may be studied in conjunction with the maps in this book.

These pages tend to be shy on the subjects of parking, one-way streets, pedestrian precincts and the like on the principle that such things change. Parking places often occupy temporarily undeveloped plots of land which can abruptly become prime building sites; one-way streets may be redesignated; this year's thoroughfare may be next year's shopping precinct: omission is surely to be preferred to commission when it is less than useful to provide information which can quickly become out of date. Surely it is better to arrive knowing that local advice must be sought than to be provided with misinformation which could lead to frustration and ill humour.

The maps are drawn and described assuming the journey to begin in London, i.e., from south to north (there is no intention to suggest that we are trying to escape from the Big City) therefore it is natural to read them from the bottom of the page. It follows that all distances are measured and noted in this way. There is absolutely no reason why the guide should not be followed in the reverse direction as long as the reader remembers to make the necessary mental adjustments. Whichever way you follow the route, enjoy your journey.

MAP SYMBOLS. Anyone with a rudimentary understanding of maps will have no need for this key to symbols used on the strip maps. However, they are set out here in order to complete the record.

⌒GNR⌒	The Great North Road.	(coastline symbol)	Coastline.
(road symbol)	Other roads. The less important the road, the more narrowly will it be depicted.	+	Church, abbey, cathedral, chapel, etc.
+++++++	Railway, where relevant.	× or •	Other landmark, i.e., standing stone, building or structure referred to in text.
⊖	Underground Station, in London.	▪	Individual building where relevant, usually as an aid to locating position.
⟶	River, with direction of flow.		

North is invariably at the top. Occasionally there is an overlap from page to page to accommodate detail. Page distance panels may use reference points which are insignificant as you drive by, i.e., individual houses or minor geographical features. Don't worry if you miss them. It's not important (except to the cartographer).

It would be expensive to buy the full complement of Landranger maps to cover the Great North Road but for those folk feeling flush with funds here are the seventeen sheets required:-

66; 67; 75; 81; 88; 93; 99; 105; 111; 120; 121; 130; 141×; 142; 153; 166; 176.

×Note. Our road impinges only on the north-east corner of sheet 141 but it is useful as a guide to the adjoining area, especially as it covers Stamford.

THE EVOLUTION OF THE NORTH ROAD

The true ancestor of the Great North Road is Ermine Street which linked Roman London with military centres at Lincoln and York, generally east of our own route but the two coincide between Alconbury and Colsterworth. The route reached York via a ferry across the Humber estuary, not the most convenient choice for an army on the move so the route was eventually superseded by a new road from Lincoln which visited forts at Doncaster and Castleford. North from York they engineered another major road, Dere Street, as a supply route to the frontier at Hadrian's Wall. This is closely followed by the Great North Road between Boroughbridge and Scotch Corner but thereafter Roman antecedents of our modern road become scarce. The Romans maintained their roads but when they departed so did the maintenance men so only useful trade routes, packhorse ways and monastic tracks were sustained.

So it remained until 1555 when, with heavy wagons playing havoc with rudimentary road surfaces, the Statute of Philip and Mary required parishes to look after their through roads but there was little improvement in communications. At the death of Queen Elizabeth Sir Robert Carey rode the 392 miles from London to be first with the news at the Court of James VI of Scotland, an exceptional journey given the roads of the day. It is asserted that he reached Edinburgh in less than three days, starting at ten o'clock on the Thursday morning to arrive on Saturday evening as the King was about to go to bed. After acceding to the throne as James I of England in 1603 the new King introduced a Post as far as Berwick-upon-Tweed to facilitate despatches between the two countries. The posts rode the eastern route out of London, now called the Old North Road, through Ware to Alconbury thence mainly close by the line of our present road except that they diverted east in Yorkshire through Northallerton.

In 1677 Thomas Gardiner, Controller of the Inland Office, had a survey prepared which included maps of the principal post roads. This was two years after Ogilby's "Britannia" had been published so Gardiner's maps may owe something to this previous set of road maps. Gardiner's draughtsmen produced plans of six mail routes radiating from London, terminating at Yarmouth, Dover, Plymouth, Bristol, Holyhead and Edinburgh - the earliest plans to specifically include the Post Road between London and Edinburgh. It visits York and Northallerton but by and large matches our own line from Alconbury onwards.

The Great North Road between London and Alconbury was developed towards the end of the 17th. century as an alternative to the mud and flood of the original way, a sort of Great North Bypass. It used existing routes, particularly between London and Hatfield. Even so, the newer route was not without its problems, especially in the soft clays north of Baldock where locally there was no stone for repair work. In wet seasons or winter this was 'the great slough', a morass of wheel-churned mud which must have been in the mind of John Bunyan when he wrote of the Slough of Despond in his "Pilgrim's Progress." A Bedfordshire man, he would have known the place well.

In 1663 tolls were enacted at Stilton and on the Old North Road at Caxton and Wadesmill so it may be claimed that the age of the turnpike began on the North Road. But it was not until the 18th. century when the Turnpike Era was well and

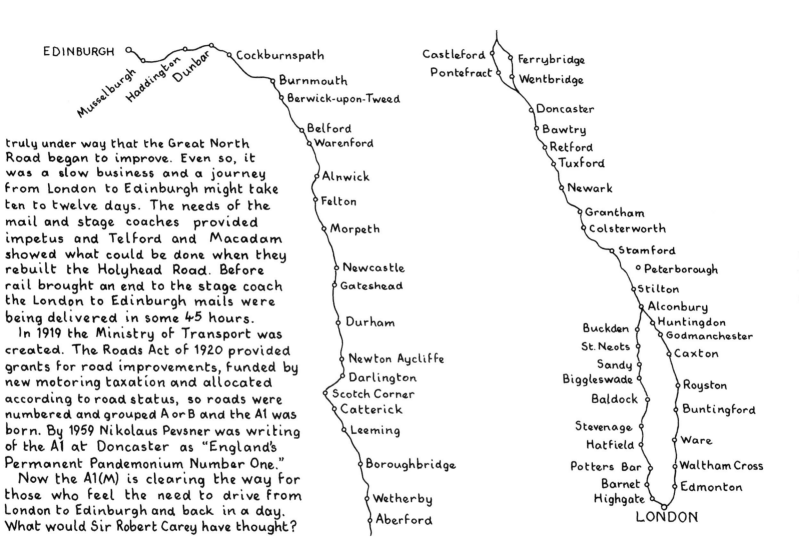

EDINBURGH

Musselburgh
Haddington
Dunbar
Cockburnspath
Burnmouth
Berwick-upon-Tweed
Belford
Warenford
Alnwick
Felton
Morpeth
Newcastle
Gateshead
Durham
Newton Aycliffe
Darlington
Scotch Corner
Catterick
Leeming
Boroughbridge
Wetherby
Aberford

Castleford
Pontefract
Ferrybridge
Wentbridge
Doncaster
Bawtry
Retford
Tuxford
Newark
Grantham
Colsterworth
Stamford
Peterborough
Stilton
Alconbury
Huntingdon
Buckden
Godmanchester
St. Neots
Caxton
Sandy
Biggleswade
Royston
Baldock
Buntingford
Stevenage
Hatfield
Ware
Potters Bar
Waltham Cross
Barnet
Edmonton
Highgate

LONDON

truly under way that the Great North Road began to improve. Even so, it was a slow business and a journey from London to Edinburgh might take ten to twelve days. The needs of the mail and stage coaches provided impetus and Telford and Macadam showed what could be done when they rebuilt the Holyhead Road. Before rail brought an end to the stage coach the London to Edinburgh mails were being delivered in some 45 hours.

In 1919 the Ministry of Transport was created. The Roads Act of 1920 provided grants for road improvements, funded by new motoring taxation and allocated according to road status, so roads were numbered and grouped A or B and the A1 was born. By 1959 Nikolaus Pevsner was writing of the A1 at Doncaster as "England's Permanent Pandemonium Number One."

Now the A1(M) is clearing the way for those who feel the need to drive from London to Edinburgh and back in a day. What would Sir Robert Carey have thought?

APOLOGY

There is plenty of scope for error in a book of this nature and despite all my efforts it will be a miracle if I have not achieved a few mistakes of one kind or another. In some cases they may be the result of carelessness - a word missed here, a letter omitted there. Distractions in a busy household are always a problem but there can be no complaints about the typesetting: it's all handwritten. More serious will be errors of fact which others better qualified (local folk, for instance) will be quick to spot. For such gaffes I duly apologise. Please feel free to make corrections, or even additions, in the margins or wherever space allows. Surely you will find plenty of snippets of information worth adding. Put your name on the title page - let's make this a team effort! The only regret is there will not be sufficient space to do justice to such late research. A better idea is to carry your own notebook; a small loose-leaf binder would be ideal. Start volume two.

I have re-read the text and made corrections, where possible without having to re-draft a whole page. Some readers may see it as a challenge to locate such corrections, usually done using simple cut-and-paste techniques. Occasionally, impossible errors have led to desperate tearing of paper and such hair as I have left. In fact the book could have been produced quickly and easily by handing over the work to a professional typesetter or even by using computer-driven home dtp software which would have allowed seamless alterations. Modern technology allows full control over page layout to an extent that only the expert would spot the amateur's lack of skill and judgement.

I repeat, it could have been done that way but not with as much satisfaction. The book has been produced for personal pleasure, being drawn and written as a hobby (admittedly with an eye to possible publication) and the thought of electronic production methods was never considered. That said, it must be admitted that after the first few pages a computer was used as an aid to page design. There is much to be said for being able to shift things around to see how it all fits together before setting text and pictures down on paper. It is a great time-saver and the author is not completely computer illiterate. But plenty of editing still took place before the layout was committed to the page, as would be seen by anyone able to set eyes on the original drafts. And even with such an aid (cheating, some might say!) a surprising number of pages reached the waste paper basket as I felt my way to the most satisfactory arrangement, the final design that you will see in this book.

Again, there will be mistakes and for these I plead guilty. Please accept my apology.

THE GREAT NORTH ROAD

King Edward Building: p18

Gateshead Millenium Footbridge. pp. 127 and 173.

The Great North Road in Stamford. pp. 55 to 57.

The Border near Lamberton, p.151.

WHERE FIRST?

As we stand in King Edward Street with the King Edward Building behind us the question arises: "Where First?" The initial instinct may be to visit the cathedral that peers invitingly over the roofline on the right. But St. Paul's is not on the route (not that such trifles are going to influence us overmuch on the way north.) Anyway, it is fair to assume that St. Paul's Cathedral has already been inspected during any preliminary schedule of exploration. The problem is that if we start diverging from the itinerary in the midst of London's profusion of treasures, before even crossing the road, we will never get away from the City at all. This is to be a journey along the Great North Road. London is London and its exploration is a separate enterprise, guaranteed to last a lifetime.

So, "Where first?" The A1 begins at the junction of St. Martin's-le-Grand with Newgate Street, the A40, but the Great North Road for the purposes of this book is the post road between the G.P.O. in London and the G.P.O. in Edinburgh, which is why we are standing by the King Edward Building. It is no longer the G.P.O. but it was opened as such five years after Edward VII laid the foundation stone in 1905 and when this book was begun it still fulfilled that function. Prior to the King Edward Building's assumption of the role the Central Post Office was in St. Martin's-le-Grand and the Great North Road would truly have begun as the A1. But in the pre-railway days of the early 19th. century Lombard Street Post Office held postal pre-eminence and the mail coaches left in a daily flurry of excitement from there.

Curiously, an earlier King Edward is associated with the King Edward Building's site for in 1553 Edward VI founded Christ's Hospital here, where Grey Friars Monastery had previously stood. Of interest, too, is the fact that a specimen of the old Roman wall of Londinium survives on this spot. The Romans also started here! In the circumstances it would seem a good idea to turn around and go inside to see the National Postal Museum which at present (1994) uses part of the building. A look at the history of the postal services would make an appropriate beginning to our odyssey.

That done, where next? Our choice was to say "Goodbye" to the statue of Sir Rowland Hill, cross the road and go into Postman's Park. The postmen's garden fills a tiny space where there was, until 1880, a graveyard. Read the information board for the history of this charming green oasis. You may enter from King Edward Street and exit to join Aldersgate Street as it takes the baton of the A1 from St. Martin's-le-Grand. You are on the Great North Road. But it's probably time for lunch so first pause in the park to eat your sandwiches. We did.

Only a fool would endeavour to explore the Great North Road in London by car when there is a facility virtually tailored to take the hassle out of the process ~ the London Underground. All places south of Barnet described in these pages were explored by leaving the car at High Barnet Station and purchasing One Day Tickets. The Northern Line shadows the road closely enough for our purpose, with excursions onto the Piccadilly Line for Holloway Road and the Victoria Line for Highbury and Islington if necessary, though not all stations are needed. We would emerge at one and walk to another as appropriate. It is certainly a good way of getting to know those places off the tourist track that local folk well appreciate.

If time can be found for a visit to St. Paul's Cathedral, do take the option of paying the fee to climb to the top of the dome. This necessary support for cathedral funds is worth every penny, in fact cheap at the price. The Whispering Gallery may be the initial attraction but the view from the highest platform is superb, not least in picking out the route to Highgate. Highly recommended, but not for those who suffer from weak hearts or vertigo.

The broken line on the inset map shows the probable position of Roman city and fort walls in this area. Extant remains within the Post Office perimeter are shown unbroken.

KING EDWARD BUILDING
to HOLLOWAY ROAD
2.5 miles

Holloway Road (A1)
Highbury Station Road
GNR
Highbury & Islington
Canonbury Road
Upper Street
Essex Road
ISLINGTON
Upper Street (A1)

To accommodate the greater detail of London's urban sprawl for the benefit of explorers on foot, the maps on this and the succeeding three pages are at double the scale generally used in the book. The purchase of a London street map and guide is advocated.

Pentonville Road
Angel
City Road
GNR
Goswell Road
Roseberry Avenue

Aldersgate Street
London Wall
Aldersgate Street (A1)
Little Britain
Postman's Park
King Edward Building
King Edward Street
Angel Street
Gresham Street
St. Martin's-le-Grand
Newgate Street
St. Paul's
Cheapside
St. Paul's Cathedral

Clerkenwell Road
Barbican
Old Street
Fann Street
Beech Street
Long Lane
GNR
Aldersgate Street (A1)
London Wall

Pentonville Road/City Road, above, begun in 1836, was at the time effectively the northern boundary of London.

LANDRANGER MAP 176

HIGHGATE

Coleridge

The London Clay is overlaid by the Bagshot Sands of which, in the north of London, only isolated outcrops remain. Highgate is evidence of this for the village within a city sits on a hill which reaches to some 400 feet above sea level. Here is the first indication that we are leaving London with tracts of open land at nearby Parliament Hill and Hampstead Heath, and splendid views over the City. Half a mile west of Highgate is Kenwood House, noted for the Iveagh Bequest of paintings by, amongst others, Rembrandt, Gainsborough, Reynolds and Turner – and also for its summer concerts beside the lake. Kenwood is an English Heritage property. Another open space is Highgate's Waterlow Park where Lauderdale House has Nell Gwyn associations.

Highgate Hill leads to the village where the tollbar was the first "high gate" on the Great North Road, though it became more dedicated to local traffic after Archway Road was constructed at the beginning of the 19th. century. If you choose the exercise of climbing the hill on foot you will probably make a start from Archway Underground Station. Highgate Hill is a test of wind and limb but there is an excuse for a breather at the halfway mark if you make the short diversion to the viaduct over Archway Road for the view back across London. By the time you reach the Duke's Head, the old coaching inn on Highgate High Street, you will appreciate the efforts of the horses in hauling coaches to a height approximately level with the top of St. Paul's Cathedral. For some years from 1884 a cable tramway made life easier for pedestrians.

Highgate is known as the place where Karl Marx is buried. His grave is in the Eastern Cemetery but the Western Cemetery is perhaps the more fascinating and may be visited by guided tour. Well known personalities at rest in the shadow of Marx's fame include Christina Rossetti, George Eliot, Jacob Bronowski, Michael Faraday and the Sir Rowland Hill whose stony likeness saw us off on our journey. There is an entrance fee to both graveyards, which are maintained by the Friends of Highgate Cemetery who provide lists of graves to seek out.

WORKERS OF ALL LANDS
UNITE

KARL MARX

Samuel Taylor Coleridge spent the last 18 years of his life resident here (1816-34) and is buried in St. Michael's Church. One has the feeling that apart from the cars, which if not in transit command every available spot for parking, and the modern dress of the numerous folks going about their business or just following the tourist trail, Highgate could hardly have been different in Coleridge's day. This was a residential outpost of London in the 18th. century and the impression of Georgian England remains in the architecture of many of the streets. Highgate is still, in essence, a village.

Holloway Road brought coaches to the foot of Highgate Hill and the first step up from the soft clays of the London Basin. The ill-maintained roads of the early coaching era were eroded by the passage of wagons, pack horses, driven animals and pedestrians as well as coaches, so that in winter or wet weather generally the pummelling of wheels and feet played havoc with the surface. In dry conditions the dust would blow clear resulting, in extreme cases, in a road surface that brought the coach roof below the level of the surrounding countryside. Such roads earned the name of "hollow ways" for obvious reasons and in this instance the name lives on in the road and the district through which it passes.

The first thing to catch your eye at the bottom of Highgate Hill will be the Whittington Stone on the left hand pavement, marking the place where legend tells that Dick Whittington heard the sound of Bow Bells bidding him return to London. The inscribed stone was set up in 1821 but his sculpted cat has been sitting on it only since 1964.

Highgate's North Road and North Hill replaced an earlier route in the 14th. century. Until then the way had meandered through Colney Hatch and Friern Barnet. It may still be followed by way of Southwell Lane, Muswell Hill Road, Colney Hatch Lane and Friern Barnet Lane.

In the early years of the 19th. century, had you travelled out of London along Holloway Road, your coach would have been passing fields devoted in the main to growing the hay needed by London's huge force of working horses.

Holloway Road is a tautology – "way" and "road" historically have the same meaning. It's like saying "Hollowroad Road."

Aylmer Road (This is the A1)

A1000 GNR

A1

Muswell Hill Road

Highgate

North Hill

North Road

Southwood Lane

HIGHGATE

Highgate Cemetery

Archway Road

Hornsey Lane

St. John's Way

Highgate Hill

Highgate Dr.

Archway

GNR

UPPER HOLLOWAY

Junction Road (A400)

LOWER HOLLOWAY

Parkhurst Road (A503)

Seven Sisters Road (A 503)

Holloway Road

A103

Holloway Road

Arsenal Football Stadium ¾ mile.

GNR Road

Drayton Park

Highbury & Islington

A1

LANDRANGER MAP 176

Arsenal Football Stadium ¾ mile.

FINCHLEY COMMON

There is a lot of land between East and North Finchley and it was land that the "gentlemen of the road" knew well. That title has the ring of romance about it but this is a romance that owes much to popular fiction of yester-year. There is nothing romantic about being robbed, on a highway or anywhere else.

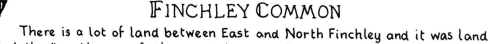

Finchley Common, east of the old village of Finchley, with plenty of hawthorn and birch scrub, was a good place for highwaymen to lurk in wait for coaches as the teams of horses were recovering from the stiff pull out of London. It must have been with a degree of apprehension that coachmen and their passengers crossed the Common.

Most of the stories of those highwaymen of old were culled from broadsheets produced for sale at executions, purporting to detail the deeds of the unfortunate wretch given the starring role. As there was no reliable documentation these broadsheets were largely works of fiction but they had a ready market, meeting a demand in much the same way as do programmes at present day sporting events.

Stories of highwaymen, like those of the Robin Hood legends, often suggest a code of honour, generosity to the poor and a gallantry which in most cases would be far removed from reality. Such names as Dick Turpin and Swift Nick Nevison represent real men but tales of their exploits owe much to popular historical novels of the 19th. century when Harrison Ainsworth gave Turpin his Black Bess.

The most famous criminal to be apprehended at Finchley Common was not a highwayman. This was Jack Shephard who, after serving six years of his apprenticeship as a carpenter decided that an 18 year old lad could find far greater profit in crime. After a four year career of notoriety he was caught - and escaped - four times. On his fifth breakout from Newgate he headed up the North Road and was on his way across Finchley Common when the law caught up with him. On 18th. November, 1724, he was hanged at Tyburn before a reputed crowd of 200,000. The broadsheet sellers must also have made a killing that day!

Our route has now become the A1000, Aylmer Road having claimed the A1 as its own. But our own date with history is along East Finchley High Road; let the A1 go where it will.

When street nameplates proudly announce 'Great North Road' or 'High Road', as they do in Finchley, you may be sure that you are on the right track. Yet these names hide an earlier history. Prior to the early 14th. century the way north lay further east but travellers' complaints of "deepnesse and dirty passage" led to a re-routing between Highgate and north of Friern Barnet. This took the road across the wastes of Finchley Common with its attendant perils. It now also crossed lands belonging to the Bishop of London: note evidence of his title in the street name "The Bishop's Avenue." The Bishop was pleased to grant his permission. By 1318 he was charging tolls!

Though Finchley Common was enclosed in 1816 you may see an occasional remnant hawthorn here and there. The largest open space remaining is occupied by the St. Pancras and Islington Cemetery and, across the North Circular Road, sports grounds and allotments. This cemetery is not quite in the Highgate league but T. H. Huxley, the biologist, and Lord Northcliffe of newspaper fame are buried here.

An indication of the size of Finchley is the fact that it is served by five stations on the Northern Line: East Finchley, Finchley Central, West Finchley, Woodside Park and the spur to Mill Hill East. We found Woodside Park a useful base at which to leave the car on occasion.

Avenue House in Finchley's East End Road is near Finchley Central though some distance from the Great North Road. There are some fine trees in the grounds but they are hardly the reason for the house to gain a mention here. Its appeal, to someone who enjoys dabbling with pen and ink, lies in its associations with "Inky" Stephens, the ink pioneer, who came to live here in 1874 and whose father developed the inks that helped to make the modern fountain pen popular.

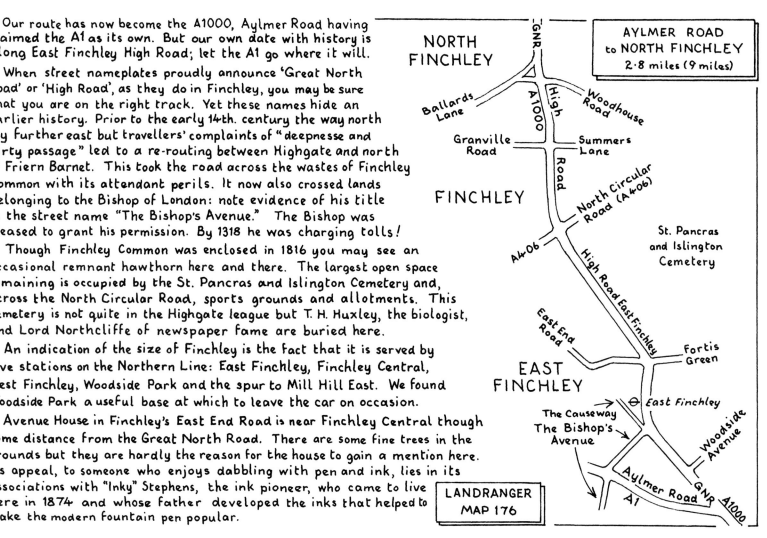

AYLMER ROAD to NORTH FINCHLEY
2·8 miles (9 miles)

LANDRANGER MAP 176

WHETSTONE

Traffic heading north out of London has had a long history of passing through Whetstone, the north road having existed here long before the early settlement came into being. Whetstone was not born until the road from the capital was diverted across Finchley Common, a redirection which was completed by 1350. Settlements at Colney Hatch and Friern Barnet lost their prime positions on a trade route and the innkeepers, wheelwrights, harness makers and blacksmiths, whose livelihoods depended upon a steady flow of traffic, gradually migrated west to the junction of the older road with the new to enjoy better commercial opportunities beside a thriving thoroughfare.

Friern Barnet's new location was the West Town, soon to be documented as Wheston (1417) and Whettstonestrete (1439); but it was Whetstone in 1488. Outside the Griffin Hotel stands an old stone known as The Whetstone. Which came first, the town or the stone, is debatable though it is easy to see how names of place and stone became closely associated. The stone's original purpose has been the subject of minor speculation. Place names elsewhere which include the element "whet" are usually linked to the suggestion of stones for sharpening blades. However, there was a Fayre Cross hereabouts in the 15th. century and the stone is most likely its stump. In this truncated state it has probably served as a mounting block, being situated outside the inn and beside the toll gate until tolls ceased to be charged and the bar became redundant as roads were opened to free traffic after the dissolution of the Turnpike Trusts in 1862.

From its birth Whetstone has always been a busy place. Some ninety long distance coaches a day were counted through in 1835. At about the same time Pickfords, the carriers, grazed up to 200 horses in fields locally and maintained a horses' hospital. Transport and trade were the name of the game.

TOTTERIDGE.   We found this delightful spot almost by accident. Due to inaccurate information we searched for St. Andrew's Church in Whetstone before locating it about a mile and a half west of the bustle of the Great North Road, along Totteridge Lane. The reason for this interest was knowledge of a 1000 year old yew tree that shares the graveyard with members of the Pepys family.

Having located St. Andrew's we realised that we had discovered a gem of a church which warmly welcomed us by glowing in a spotlight of pre-dusk sunshine. This church of 1790 keeps an earlier bell turret of weatherboard and presents a distinctive picture at a bend in the lane as you reach Totteridge, a village which lines a couple of miles of road across open spaces of pleasant parkland where the game of golf is a prime attraction.

St. Andrew's

When the coaching era reached its zenith you might have expected as many as 150 coaches to be using the highway through High Barnet every day. This traffic would have been complicated by vast quantities of beef and mutton on the hoof being driven in to feed London's hungry multitude.

However, the flow would not all have been bound to and from the north. The Holyhead Road branched off at Hadley and much of the trade and transport would have had its origins in the Midlands, North Wales or Ireland. This presents a scene of activity to compare with the present day. Dust and noise were annoying roadside communities long before the term 'environmental polution' was coined.

Pricklers Hill and Barnet Hill are not a problem for modern cars but this long haul must have been hard work for the teams of horses in the days when horse power meant exactly that. Life may have been made easier in 1720 when the road from Whetstone and Barnet to Potters Bar became one of the earlier sections of the Great North Road to be turnpiked. But improvement in road surfaces was slow in coming. Until McAdam's and Telford's pioneering efforts of a hundred years later, roads tended to remain disaster areas.

The Whetstone was moved to its present site round about 1870. Previously it stood much nearer the Griffin Hotel, which occupies the site of an old manor house. Road re-alignments are nothing new, not just a symptom of late 20th. century progress. Look around for evidence of changes made to accommodate modern traffic flow.

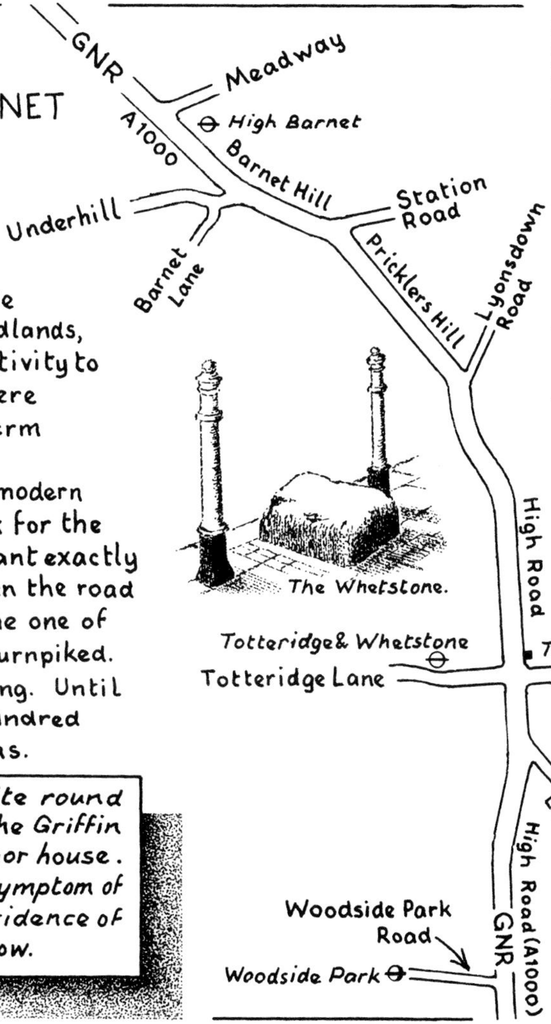

BARNET

WOODSIDE PARK ROAD to BARNET HILL
3 miles (12 miles)

The Griffin.

Friern Barnet Lane (below) is the northern end of the ancient route from Highgate.

The Whetstone.

The Griffin and The Whetstone

WHETSTONE

LANDRANGER MAP 176

DEATH OF THE KINGMAKER

On a misty Easter morning, 14th. April, 1471, the Wars of the Roses came to Hadley Green and the Battle of Barnet raged astride our North Road. The militarily astute King Edward IV deployed his Yorkist army of some 10,000 men in three sections facing north against a force of 15,000 of the Earl of Warwick's troops, drawn up in similar lines.

Edward's younger brother Richard, Duke of Gloucester, attacked Warwick's left flank while the Earl of Oxford led the Lancastrian right flank – from behind a hedge which still exists on the local golf course – and drove Lord Hastings' men back into Barnet. His triumphant troops scented victory and set about looting the town. When Oxford gathered the remains of his force and returned through the fog he came up against his own Duke of Somerset's front line which was contesting Edward's attack in the centre. To cries of "Treason!" Lancastrian fought Lancastrian.

As the Lancastrians gave way Warwick sought his horse, left in the rear. He was overtaken, recognised and clubbed to death. Warwick is remembered as the "Kingmaker" for having been instrumental in setting Yorkist Edward IV on the throne before supporting the Lancastrians of Henry VI against Edward.

The battle is superimposed upon modern roads:–

Warwick fell here ✗ A1000
LANCASTRIANS
Hadley Highstone
A1081
Oxford | Somerset | Warwick
Hastings | Edward | Richard
YORKISTS
BARNET A1000

HADLEY HIGHSTONE. An obelisk commemorating the Battle of Barnet stands at the junction of the A1000 and Kitts End Road. It was set up in 1740 by Sir Jeremy Sambrooke of Gobions. This also marks the junction with, originally, the pre-Telford Holyhead Road. Another example of Sir Jeremy's work may be found at Brookmans Park where in about 1754 he built a brick gateway to part of the estate, his 'pleasure grounds.' The arch remains but the house and park have gone.

TO HATFIELD VII MILES

The name of Potters Bar is not a hint at the turnpike age,
s may be thought. It was recorded far earlier, in 1387, as a
te on the highway where it entered private lands belonging
   descendants of Geoffrey de Pottere who was noted as
ving nearby in South Mimms in 1294. Swanley Bar and Bell Bar, a few
iles north, have similar origins. Until the coming of the railway (1852) Potters
ar was a sleepy village astride the north road but the new station brought
asier access to London and a community of commuters was born.

The modern Holyhead Road - the A5 - leaves London as the Edgware Road,
e Roman Watling Street, but the London end of Thomas Telford's great
oneering turnpike road began at Barnet and has now become the A1081. Before
lford's time the route to Holyhead bifurcated from the Great North Road at
adley Highstone where it may now be followed as Kitts End Road.
he new Holyhead Turnpike Road was completed and open by
30 and was Telford's great triumph of road engineering.

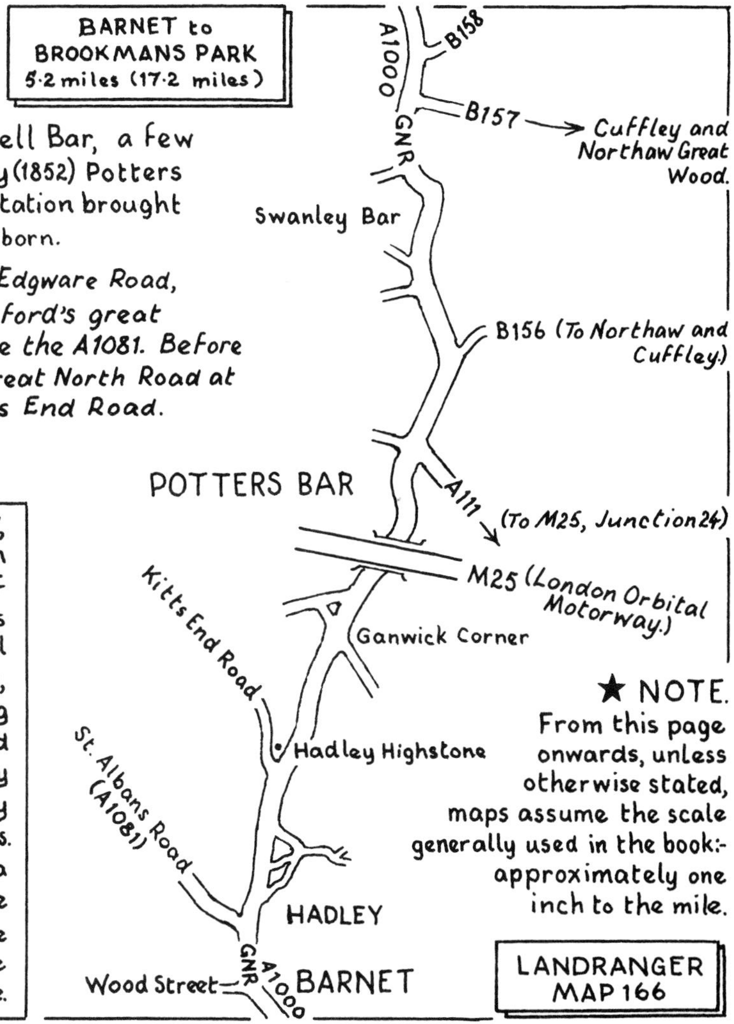

North-east of Potters Bar, a couple of miles along the B157,
is Northaw Great Wood. This is a remnant of the forest which
in medieval times stretched across a large part of
Hertfordshire, typically the estate lands of such men as
Geoffrey de Pottere. It was a countryside in which the local
nobility would enjoy their pleasures of the hunt. Now,
tiny introduced muntjac deer along
with badgers, squirrels, foxes and
a large population of birdlife may
enjoy a safe haven in harmony
with the trees and wildflowers.
The modern hunter, armed with a
camera, is able to wander the
reserve along footpaths and nature
trails. For the less energetic there
are picnic areas and a visitor centre.

Muntjac deer.

A1000
B158
B157 → Cuffley and
Northaw Great
Wood.
GNR
Swanley Bar
B156 (To Northaw and
Cuffley.)
POTTERS BAR
A111
(To M25, Junction 24)
M25 (London Orbital
Motorway.)
Kitts End Road
Ganwick Corner
St. Albans Road
(A1081)
Hadley Highstone

★ NOTE.
From this page
onwards, unless
otherwise stated,
maps assume the scale
generally used in the book:-
approximately one
inch to the mile.

HADLEY
GNR
A1000
Wood Street
BARNET

LANDRANGER
MAP 166

HATFIELD

This town was a regular stop for coaches and the Eight Bells was well enough known to Charles Dickens for him to use it for a scene in 'Oliver Twist.' Hatfield's history dates back to Saxon days but in 1948 it was linked with Welwyn Garden City and designated a New Town.

For many the attraction is Hatfield House, built by Robert Cecil, 1st. Earl of Salisbury, at the beginning of the 17th. century. However, if you have any sense of history, the adjacent Old Palace is the place to see. This is the remnant of that Hatfield Palace which Henry VIII set aside as home for his children, Edward, Mary and Elizabeth, each in turn to rule England. Cecil preferred a newer style but the demolished brickwork was re-used in the present house. The 15th. century great hall with its fine oaken roof trusses and splendid curved wind braces preserves a taste of the history of a fine old building.

It was in the grounds of the Old Hatfield Palace that Elizabeth was at rest, sitting beneath an oak tree reading, when news of her accession reached her. Thereafter, not surprisingly, she spent little time at Hatfield.

The Old Palace, Hatfield.

WELWYN GARDEN CITY

Sir Ebenezer Howard's progressive ideas in town design, of providing good accommodation with plenty o space and greenery, first saw light of day in Letchwort (1903), but Welwyn Garden City (1919) is better knowr for its tree-lined streets, good quality housing, landscape parkland, the separation of residential from commercia areas and for its easy access to London, this is a splendi example of the best in 20th. century town planning.

Stanborough Park, on the River Lea between Welwy Garden City and Hatfield, provides a wealth of outdoo recreation for local folk – boating, angling, children' activities, swimming, a nature trail and the Reedmarsh Nature Reserve for birdwatchers. The only criticism is th proximity of the motorway but the amenity's popularit ensures a happy atmosphere so that on a sunny summe weekend all the adjacent traffic is hardly noticed.

John Tradescant the Elder began his career as a gardener as gardener to the Cecils at Hatfield. In 1609 he went overseas collecting plants for the new gardens. The earl died in 1612 and Tradescant moved on. He and his son introduced countless plants to our English gardens though not all were collected by themselves. Yet many were, and most of them were of greater importance than the one that bears their name, the popular houseplant we know as Tradescantia. *See note, right.

Geology has always influenced routes. The River Lea, passing between Hatfield and Welwyn Garden City, cut through the glacial boulder clay exposing a stratum of limestone which ensured a well drained strip of land along the valley flanks and provided a dry route to Luton (the B653).

Crossing the valley was a different matter. The lie of the land and seasonal conditions across the boulder clay were not conducive to a natural line. The road between Hatfield and London had been in regular use from the days when the Old Palace was built, because of its royal associations, but travellers heading for the north used Ermine Street. The direct link through Hatfield and Baldock was not conceived until the 17th. century.

The Great North Road between Hatfield and Alconbury was developed from a hotchpotch of local roads, especially noticeable between Hatfield and Welwyn where it was never direct, as you will discover if you try to trace the original route. This is no longer possible by car. At one point the Great North Road suffers the ignominy of reduction to a footbridge over a railway! (At ☀, right.)

• TRADESCANTIA. (SEE LEFT) BEFORE ANYONE WRITES TO ENLIGHTEN ME, I DO REALISE THAT VARIETIES OF TRADESCANTIA ARE GROWN AS HARDY OUTDOOR PERENNIALS IN ENGLAND. THERE'S ONE IN MY GARDEN.

St. ALBANS is near enough to be a recommended detour. The ancient Roman city was a British settlement before it became one of the largest and most important towns in Roman Britain: Verulamium. It achieved the rank of municipium, granting its population the rights of Roman citizenship, unique in Britain. The restored Roman theatre is worth a visit. St. Albans Abbey occupies the site where St. Alban, the first British martyr, was executed. The direct route to London was Watling Street and Telford's new Holyhead Road joined it here to ensure that this was a city well endowed with good coaching inns.

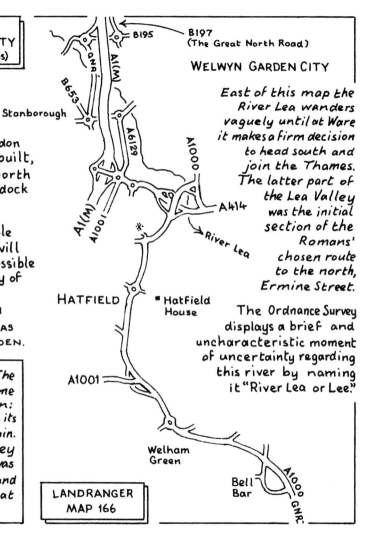

BELL BAR to
WELWYN GARDEN CITY
6·3 miles (23·5 miles)

B197
(The Great North Road)

WELWYN GARDEN CITY

East of this map the River Lea wanders vaguely until at Ware it makes a firm decision to head south and join the Thames. The latter part of the Lea Valley was the initial section of the Romans' chosen route to the north, Ermine Street.

The Ordnance Survey displays a brief and uncharacteristic moment of uncertainty regarding this river by naming it "River Lea or Lee."

Stanborough

HATFIELD

Hatfield House

Welham Green

Bell Bar

LANDRANGER MAP 166

WELWYN

At Welwyn, for the first time since London, our route coincides with a valid Roman way, that from Verulamium (St. Albans) to the Roman town at Braughing. At Woolmer Green it joins another Roman road to continue to Stevenage. In 1927, with the construction of the Welwyn By-pass, the Great North Road ceased to pass along its High Street and take a dog-leg turn to the right into Church Street. The resulting improvement in quality of life can easily be understood. Now the A1(M) of 1972 bears the brunt of the through traffic. There can be no doubt about where the original trade route made its entry; the name London Road is evidence enough. It enters the village down a steep hill, reaching the High Street at the White Hart, opposite which there is an interesting old R.S.P.C.A. sign on a wall referring to treatment of horses by drivers

The Wellington.

as they negotiated the hill. The so-called romance of the road meant nothing to the teams of horses. The Wellington, then known as the Swan, did fine business as a coaching inn, greeting travellers from the north as they entered the village along Church Street, as did the White Hart, happy at the approach of coaches from London. Welwyn remains a pleasant village with many neat old houses, well tended by its proud residents. It has a history worthy of investigation.

For a splendid description of the roads hereabouts see the booklet "Roads" by Tony Rook in the series "Hertfordshire Histories", obtainable locally.

The White Hart.

George Bernard Shaw.

AYOT ST. LAWRENCE. The O.S. map shows a high incidence of Ayot as a placename in the vicinity with Ayot St. Peter, Ayot Bury, Ayot Green and Ayot Place. Some names may refer to single dwellings but the Ayots St. Peter and St. Lawrence are large enough to own churches. There is an Ayot Greenway but this is a modern walkers' way which uses an old railway track. Ayot St. Lawrence was the home of George Bernard Shaw from 1906 until 1950 when he died, aged 94. He renamed his house, which had been The New Rectory, Shaw's Corner. Now owned by the National Trust and open to the public, it is a substantial yet simple house with an ample garden. Shaw often found peace to write in his revolving summer house but regrettably security problems mean that this may no longer be furnished as Shaw knew it.

WELWYN GARDEN CITY to KNEBWORTH
6 miles (29·5 miles)

The Digswell Viaduct carries the main railway line to the north across the River Mimram. It is regarded as one of the great architectural feats of the railway age. Built in 1850 and with 40 spans of 30 feet, it reaches 98 feet above the river and is 500 yards in length. A year later Queen Victoria's royal train used it on the way to Balmoral but the Queen was not amused. She had the train halted in order to make a less intimidating crossing using the familiar coach and horses before resuming her journey by rail. Blondin, whose exploits on the high wire displayed more nerve, was bolder. He used this valley for practice.

Digswell Viaduct.

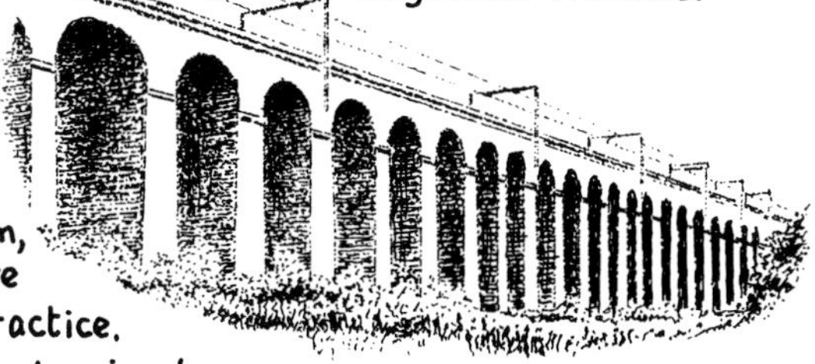

Roman remains at Lockley's were excavated prior to the building of the A1(M) motorway and revealed a bath house of some importance. It has been preserved in an arched vault beneath the new road. The site is open to the public. Check locally for current opening arrangements.

Much of the original road alignment around Welwyn has been obscured by later developments.

At the foot of the hill leading into Welwyn is a reminder of the days when horsepower meant exactly that. There is an old enamel sign, placed by the R.S.P.C.A:

PLEASE SLACKEN HAME OR BEARING REIN
WHEN GOING UP HILL
COMPLAINTS OF CRUELTY TO BE FORWARDED
TO THE SECRETARY AT HEADQUARTERS

Interestingly, the sign begot a smaller sign beneath it:

£1 REWARD WILL BE GIVEN TO ANYONE
GIVING INFORMATION LEADING TO A CONVICTION
FOR DAMAGING OR DEFACING THIS NOTICE

Knebworth
Old Knebworth
A1(M)
GNR
B197
Woolmer Green
Oaklands
B656
Minor roads to Ayot St. Lawrence, 2½ miles
WELWYN
Lockley's
Digswell Railway Viaduct
Tewin
River Mimram
B1000
Sherrardspark Wood
WELWYN GARDEN CITY
A1000
B197
GNR
A1(M)
LANDRANGER MAP 166

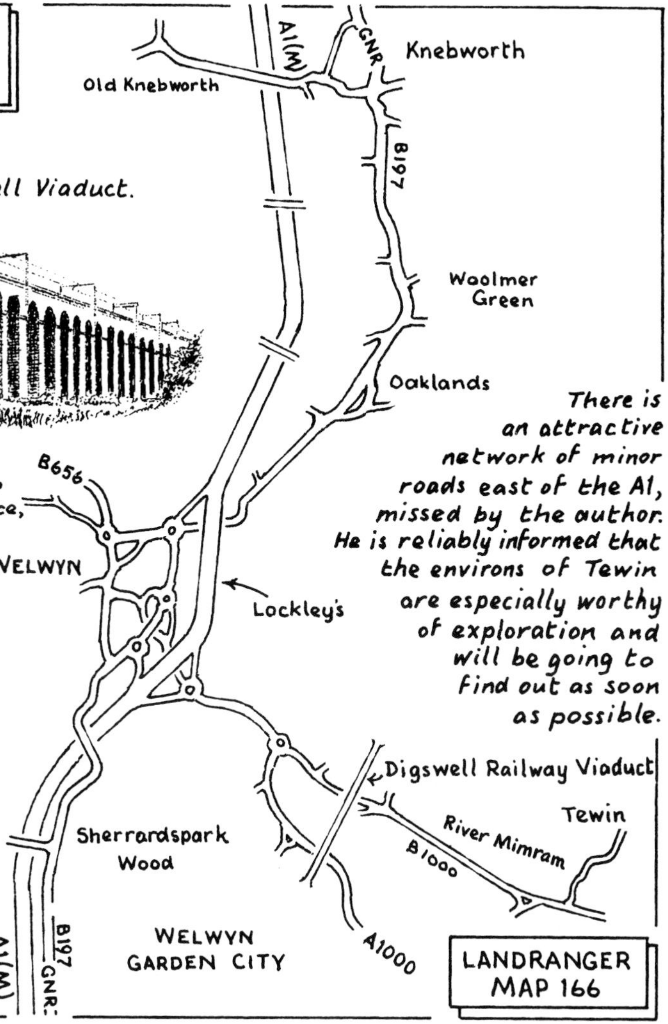

There is an attractive network of minor roads east of the A1, missed by the author. He is reliably informed that the environs of Tewin are especially worthy of exploration and will be going to find out as soon as possible.

STEVENAGE

Old Stevenage has a High Street, wide and attractively lined with trees, which was the Great North Road. It is closely by-passed to the west by two dual carriageway roads and the A1(M) but was itself a medieval by-pass of the first settlement that grew up around the parish church of St. Nicholas. By the 13th. century business had migrated half a mile to the trade route with the population in close pursuit so that this became the focal point of the Old Town.

The New Town was the first in England to be so designated (in 1946) and the centre was finished and thriving in 1957. This is a good example of modern town design with shops, leisure facilities and parkland in Fairlands Valley to provide boating, angling and walks but the town is not the sort of place to excite any visitor not interested in modern architecture and planned development. There is much to be said for the casual style that only comes with centuries of non-planning. We quickly turned to the Old Town - and promptly managed to get lost in driving through the new one though the two live in close juxtaposition. So much for planning when it is disorganised by re-routing of roads!

KNEBWORTH HOUSE AND COUNTRY PARK.

Knebworth: the house from the herb garden.

The building seen here is largely Victorian Gothic but the original house, of which the great hall remains, was built in the late 15th. century since when it has remained the home of the Lytton family. It is open to the public during the summer months and provides interest and entertainment for the whole family. The gardens are noted for having been redesigned by Edwin Lutyens (1909) with a delightful herb garden by Gertrude Jekyll. The settlements at Old and New Knebworth are now separated by a concrete moat - the A1(M) - spanned by a concrete bridge.

Temple Dinsley, two miles south-west of St. Ippollitts, was a property of the Knights Templar. This Order of Chivalry was founded c1118 by Hugh de Payns and Godfrey of St. Omer to defend the routes to holy sites. Their full title of 'Poor Knights of Christ and the Temple of Solomon' arises from one of their bases near the Temple of Solomon in Jerusalem. Their traditional dress was originally a white habit but later a red cross at the shoulder was added by order of Pope Eugenius III. By the 13th. century the Templars had become a rich aristocracy of knightly birth whose fighting force included a class of sergeant brothers and one of lightly armed horsemen known as Turcoples who required no knightly birth but did not sport the red cross. The Order was dissolved in 1312 and its property transferred to the Knights Hospitallers.

BENINGTON. Some four miles to the east is a village of charm approached by way of a winding country lane. The village green, the willow-hung pond, the old timbered cottages, a fine old church and a welcoming inn (the Bell) combine to delight the visitor. There was once even a castle, a thing of folk memory for it was demolished as long ago as 1212. However its site is occupied by the house and gardens of Benington Lordship where we may admire an all-season planting of roses, rock plants, herbaceous borders, a water garden, shrubs and a kitchen garden. Do not imagine the impressive gate arch to be a remnant of the original castle: this is a folly of 1832.

Check opening times, currently summer Sundays, Wednesdays and bank holidays.

Gateway Folly at Benington.

KNEBWORTH to GRAVELEY 5.5 miles (35 miles)

The road north from Stevenage to Biggleswade was turnpiked in about 1720 which date is contemporary with the road we used between Whetstone and Barnet, noted earlier.

St. IPPOLLITTS. This hamlet is barely a couple of miles west, just south of the road to Hitchin. A curious name – the church is dedicated to St. Ippolyts. There were two saints of this name, one reputedly suffered the sentence of being dragged to death harnessed to wild horses, as was the Greek god Hippolytus, son of Theseus, falsely accused of raping his stepmother. The Greek for horse is hippos (think of *hippo*potamus, the river *horse*). There is certainly an association with horses at St. Ippollitts. The Knights Templar of Temple Dinsley came along riding their faithful steeds for a blessing prior to their departure on the Crusades and cut crosses on a pillar in the south aisle. It is also said that all horsemen passing through the settlement were required to take their mounts into the church to be blessed. Perhaps this was a commercial ruse on the part of the priest who would probably have had his collection box, or its medieval equivalent to hand. He would most likely have needed his shovel at the ready too, but it would be good for the vegetable plot.

LANDRANGER MAP 166

To Hitchin (3 miles) & St. Ippollitts (1½ miles)

A602

Graveley

Stevenage Old Town

A1072

A1155

STEVENAGE

A602 →
To Benington Lordship Gardens (4 miles). Turn left from A602 along minor road in a mile – (beside golf course).

Knebworth House and Country Park

Knebworth

BALDOCK

Baldock is a busy working town but a place of character with a proud community spirit. There is evidence of iron age settlement hereabouts and the Romans also put down temporary roots. The medieval town came into being in the mid-thirteenth century when the Knights Templar were granted land and established the borough which became Baldock. The settlement became a market town with a typically wide main street which in time took on the role of the Great North Road. That road is still a busy thoroughfare and there can be real problems at the bottleneck where Hitchin Street joins White Horse Street at the northern end of High Street. It needs little imagination to visualise the traffic situation as it must have been before the A1(M) by-pass was slotted between Baldock and Letchworth. Nearby there is a street name, North Road, connecting Western Way and Icknield Way, which suggests an earlier alternative to the congestion of White Horse Street. There must have been real problems when the fire service was called into action: the Victorian Fire Station was on this corner, a handsome building of warm brick which is currently the Baldock District Council Building. Escape the traffic turmoil by strolling down Church Street from this junction to inspect St. Mary's with its distinctive spike steeple.

The Victorian Fire Station.

HITCHIN

Baldock, Letchworth and Hitchin are almost close enough to be taken for a single town by a casual driver passing through along the A505 but Hitchin has so far retained its separate identity by maintaining a buffer zone of open space to the east. Proud Hitchin had a great medieval market and still has two weekly market days, Tuesday and Saturday. The area was known for its local cottage industry of straw plaiting and in the 19th. century Hitchin market was a trading centre where straw was purchased and returned as plaits for sale.

LETCHWORTH

The garden city that formed the blue-print for Welwyn Garden City was begun in 1903 and by 1905 there was held an exhibition of "Cheap Cottages," 114 dwellings designed by different architects in different styles. Not one of them was priced above £150. If you wish to see what a "cheap cottage" looked like, study the area between Newells Road and Icknield Way. The First Garden City Heritage Museum is housed in the original architects' office close by and should be visited for an appreciation of modern Letchworth's birth and development.

Since Welwyn the line of the road has been one that was pioneered by the Romans, certainly in its later stages. It was usable although in great need of repair even before the Great North Road was developed and helped to provide a reasonable alternative to the Old North Road across the Chiltern Chalk to Baldock. North of here soft clay was always a problem. The road was described by Daniel Defoe, reporting on his travels through England, as 'being so impassable that coaches and travellers were obliged to break out of the way....... rather than plunge into sloughs and holes that no horse could wade through.'*
Landowners whose property adjoined the road would take the opportunity to raise funds by charging tolls for carts and coaches that sought to make such detours across their land. As always, circumstances bred the opportunist.

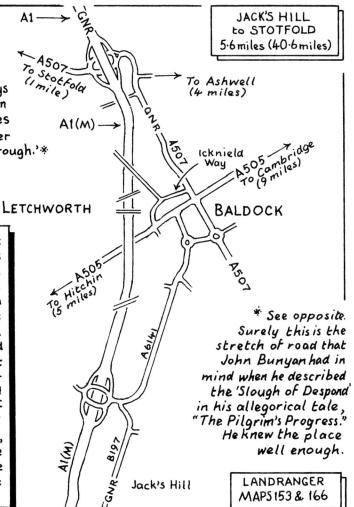

JACK'S HILL
to STOTFOLD
5·6 miles (40·6 miles)

* See opposite.
Surely this is the
stretch of road that
John Bunyan had in
mind when he described
the 'Slough of Despond'
in his allegorical tale,
"The Pilgrim's Progress."
He knew the place
well enough.

LANDRANGER
MAPS 153 & 166

THE ICKNIELD WAY. At Baldock we encounter one of the oldest named roads in England. It runs from Wiltshire, crosses the Thames near Goring, passes along the escarpments of the Berkshire Downs, traces the Chilterns into Norfolk and near Wells-Next-The-Sea arrives at the coast. It unifies a series of shorter tracks which used the chalk belt for ease of passage but no doubt Britain's ancient tribes found this link between the sea and the pagan religious sites of Wiltshire very convenient. In later years it proved very useful as a drove road. The Romans never developed it but it has been incorporated into many a modern highway as, for instance, parts of the A505 east of the A1. It is also preserved as a street name in Baldock, Letchworth and Hitchin. One of its most famous landmark monuments is the White Horse of Uffington, which could be contemporary, but its own name, the Icknield Way, has never been satisfactorily explained. There is now a modern Icknield Way long distance leisure walking route which of necessity has to divert in places from the historic line: no one enjoys tramping tarmac in the wake of heavy traffic.

ASHWELL

This charming village is in Hertfordshire - but only just for Bedfordshire is little more than a mile to the north and the stream that rises here as the River Rhee soon takes the name of Cam as it crosses the boundary into Cambridgeshire barely half a mile east. The early settlers noted the infant river's source by an ash tree and the name of Ashwell was born. It is now a place of some size with a number of timber framed houses and a fine 14th. century church dedicated to St. Mary. This splendid building attracts many visitors, often drawn in search of a collection of medieval graffiti carved upon the internal walls of the tower and elsewhere. Amongst many scratchings is reference to the plague of 1349/50, reflecting the fact that the pestilence visited Ashwell with devastating effect. One detailed drawing represents the Old St. Paul's Cathedral, the one lost in the Great Fire of London in 1666.

BIGGLESWADE

The River Ivel was once navigable between Biggleswade and the sea and the town prospered with the ensuing trade. The Romans had a ford across the Ivel here and this supplied the stimulus for a settlement which eventually became the town of today. The area has long been noted for its market gardening and more recent development in the field of light engineering has provided the basis of much local employment. As with all small towns there is probably much more to the place than a casual visit will reveal and I am sure that our short visit did not do it justice. We wandered round the small but busy market place where there is a timber-framed Market House and a Victorian Town Hall which no longer fulfils that civic function. After calling at the church we strolled down the dusty Short Mead Street to the river and wandered back beside the Ivel, a haunt of anglers, to Mill Lane.

This site has been occupied since the Bronze Age and traces of Roman villas have been found nearby. The Icknield Way passed through here and the modern walkers' route, the Icknield Way Path, visits the village. There is a small museum which is normally open on Sundays and holidays.

Farming has long been the most important land use though the village is now partially a commuter base and is getting itself on the tourist itinerary. When we visited we were attracted to a splendid tea shop on the High Street where we not only enjoyed a finely brewed pot of the beverage that cheers but were drawn into enthusiastic conversation with a knowledgeable proprietor and departed clutching a selection of choice teas, including his own blends. A visit to Ashwell is highly recommended, especially for tea buffs.

Guild House, Ashwell.

Ashwell's Village Museum.

Some 200 years ago - between 1781 and 1794 - the Hon. John Byng regularly travelled the Great North Road on horseback. It is a commentary on the unreliable standards of hospitality of the day that he travelled with his own sheets to avoid the risk of catching a chill by sleeping in a damp bed. Pneumonia was almost certain to be fatal, a fact we tend to forget in these days of antibiotics backed up by intensive care. He would send a servant ahead to arrange accommodation for himself and his horses. One of his favourite overnight stops was at the Sun Inn at Biggleswade.

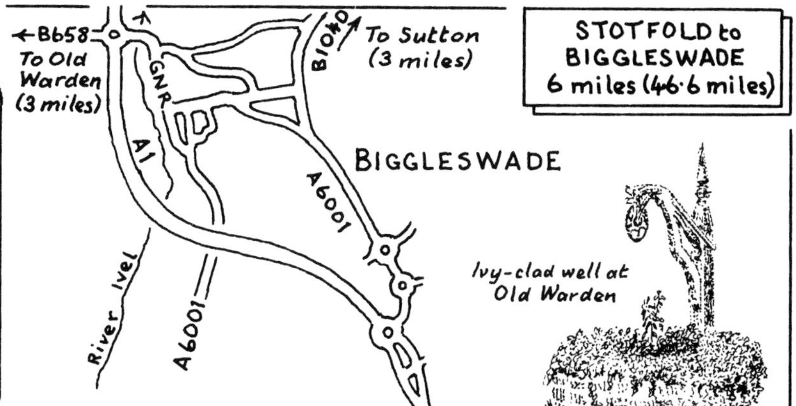

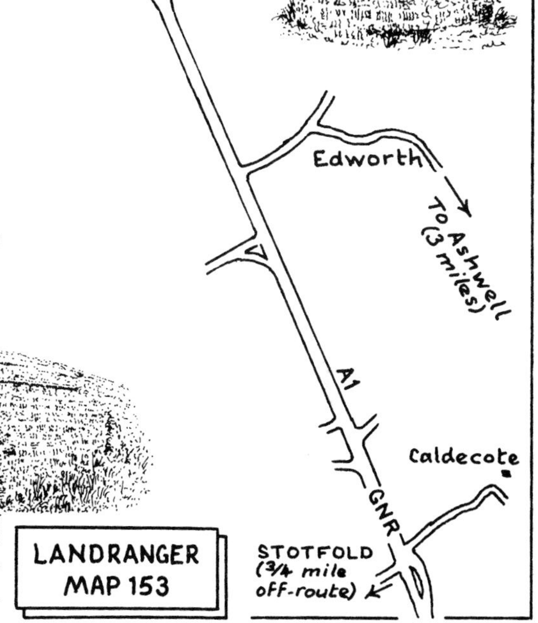

Barely threequarters of a mile east of our route, overlooking a shallow valley, stands the little church of St. Mary Magdalene, now disused and currently in custody of the Friends of Friendless Churches. This and the associated manor house are the remaining evidence of the lost medieval village of Caldecote whose parish was one of the smallest in Hertfordshire.

Some three miles west of Biggleswade is Old Warden, a picture postcard village to beat all picture postcard villages. Here is a community where pride shines in every house, cottage and garden. We found it almost too good to be true - like one of those homes where the presence of a house proud wife makes you afraid to touch anything lest you leave a fingerprint! Nearby is Old Warden Aerodrome and the Shuttleworth Collection of old aircraft.

Three miles north-east of Biggleswade at Sutton is a double pointed-arched packhorse bridge beside a ford, worth a visit if you wish to try an alternative approach to Sandy (next page) along the B1040 and B1042.

Packhorse Bridge at Sutton.

← B658
To Old Warden
(3 miles)

B1040
To Sutton
(3 miles)

GNR

A1

River Ivel

A6001

A6001

BIGGLESWADE

STOTFOLD to
BIGGLESWADE
6 miles (46.6 miles)

Ivy-clad well at
Old Warden

Edworth

To Ashwell
(3 miles)

A1

GNR

Caldecote

STOTFOLD
(3/4 mile
off-route) ←

LANDRANGER
MAP 153

JOHN BUNYAN

This is John Bunyan country. Bunyan was born at Elstow, near Bedford. His father was a tinker and the young John travelled around the district with him, helping out and learning the trade. He became involved in the Civil War as a supporter of Parliament  and, until his marriage in his twenties, he lived the free and easy life of any young man of his time. He joined the Congregation in Bedford which became the Bunyan Meeting and soon discovered his talent as a preacher. At the end of Cromwell's Protectorate the preaching of the Congregations was forbidden but Bunyan refused to acknowledge the ban and spent the next twelve years in prison where he was able to write many books, including the spiritual allegory "The Pilgrim's Progress". After a second period as a prisoner he continued writing and travelled widely as a popular preacher of the gospels. He must have been extremely familiar with the roads of Bedfordshire, Hertfordshire and Cambridgeshire and would have experienced the problems of travel on the Great North Road during his many journeys to and from London.

Worth visiting is the village of WILLINGTON, astride the A603 between Sandy and Bedford where, at the end of a quiet road, a stretch of open grassland holds a large and most imposing oblong dovecote with adjacent stables (National Trust), remnants of a former manor house complex, with John Bunyan associations (he slept in a loft of the stables, finding time to carve his name on a fireplace).

Willington Dovecote.

Willington Stables.

Searchers of literary references may be drawn to the churchyard of St. John in Cockayne Hatley (go through Potton and join the B1040 north to turn right along a minor road by Potton church). Here are two for the price of one, to the memory of Margaret Henley, aged five, and her father William Ernest, respectively models for world famous fictional characters, Wendy of "Peter Pan" fame and Robert Louis Stevenson's Long John Silver.

BEDFORD, the county town, is approximately seven miles west of the A1 at Sandy. The wide sweep of the Ouse, with its embankment and public gardens, is a dominating feature. For enthusiasts, the Bunyan Meeting Free Church and Museum are a must – but also visit Elstow, just south of the town, where the site of his birthplace is marked by a stone. Elstow Green, the Moot Hall, Elstow Abbey and Elstow Cottages – restored as Bunyan would have known them – provide a flavour of Bunyan's Bedfordshire.

Admirers of the King of Swing will perhaps remember that during the Second World War Glenn Miller was stationed near Bedford. There is a commemorative plaque at the Corn Exchange.

BEESTON (near Sandy) is one of several places of this name in England. It is a placename that takes my fancy for I was born and still live in one of them. The name has two elements from the Old English: "béos" (bent-grass) and "tún" (farmstead or small settlement). The bents grow abundantly on dry heaths or sandy soils, but also in damp places. The settlers who built the farmstead from which this village grew chose a flat site near the River Ivel which must have been subject to flooding – but don't forget the clue provided by the nearby town whose name hints at a quick-draining sandy subsoil.

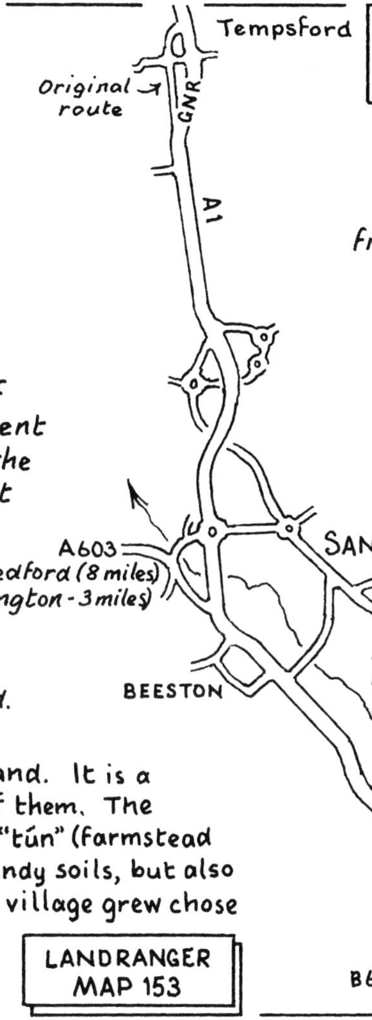

Tempsford

Original route →

A1

GNR

BIGGLESWADE
to TEMPSFORD
5.5 miles (52.1 miles)

The small town of Sandy is known to the ornithological fraternity as the place where the R.S.P.B. lives. At Sandy Lodge (along the B1042) there is a shop, bird sanctuary and a nature trail – plus, of course, the headquarters offices.

A603
To Bedford (8 miles)
(Willington – 3 miles)

SANDY

To Potton (3 miles)
B1042 →

Sandy Lodge
(R.S.P.B.)

BEESTON

River Ivel

RSPB

A1

GNR

BIGGLESWADE

B658

A6001 →

LANDRANGER
MAP 153

Page 39.

ROXTON

We came to this pleasant village drawn by reports of a wooden church. It was worth the effort. Roxton Congregationalist Chapel has a thatched roof with a tree-trunk veranda and at first glance looks nothing like a church. The Lord of the Manor, Charles Metcalfe, converted it from a barn in 1808 and in doing so produced a unique and utterly charming house of worship. It is lovingly cared for and rests peacefully in grounds that have the appearance of a well-tended garden.

We examined and enthused over it in the company of a couple who had been in the habit of calling at Roxton to enjoy the local pub lunches but were early on this particular day. The inn had yet to open its doors. In filling time prior to the filling of stomachs they were wandering aimlessly about the village and were surprised to find this shy delight, previously unknown to them despite their frequent visits to Roxton. On their recommendation we also tried the pub lunches. Great!

Roxton Chapel.

St. NEOTS

We first crossed the Ouse bridge into St. Neots many years ago. Over 300 years earlier, in 1648, a party of Royalists contested the crossing with followers of the fellow who was born some nine miles up the road in Huntingdon, Oliver Cromwell. Oliver's lot won.

This is another settlement to have grown up on the banks of the River Ouse. The Anglo-Saxons had a monastery here in the tenth century where they preserved the venerable bones of a Saxon monk, St. Neot, as a relic. After the Norman Conquest a new priory was founded on the same site. It continued to attract pilgrims and formed the nucleus of the community which became St. Neots. After the Dissolution the priory buildings fell into decay and were dismantled. The site is now occupied by a car park, appropriately down Priory Lane.

When the priory disappeared this was already a busy town which attracted the trade of the Great North Road for, although the route was across the river, the bridge always attracted travellers into the thriving market place. The 19th. century railway brought further development.

Eaton Socon, west of the river, sits astride the road to the north and was a more obvious coaching stop than St. Neots. Now they fit neatly into the space between the new A1 and the railway and are near enough to London for a later population to see them as commuter country; but they are supported by their own light industries. Yet there is a firm link with times past. Islands Common in St. Neots is even now controlled by the Association of Common Rights Proprietors and, though its duties no longer include the annual allotment of farming strips in an open field system, cattle are still grazed on The Common.

TEMPSFORD sits peacefully on the old Great North Road, happy to benefit from the bypass. It seems to be a village that history has also passed by but appearances can be deceptive. In 921 a.d. the Danes chose this site where the Rivers Ouse and Ivel meet as a defensive position against the Saxons. Edward the Elder, son of King Alfred, was unimpressed and when he captured it he slew everyone there, man, woman and child. It was ninety years before the Danes were back to take revenge, burning down the small township. There is a defensive site, Gannock's Castle, probably nothing to do with the tenth century conflict. The earthworks seemed hardly worth the effort of the search - I gave them a miss in favour of the neat church of St. Peter.

We meet the River Great Ouse at its confluence with the Ivel at Tempsford and follow it closely for some miles north. This waterway, which approaches the sea at King's Lynn, is one of the great rivers of England and, at 156 miles or thereabouts, is fourth in length after the Thames, Severn and Trent. Between Bedford and Huntingdon it lies within the compass of our explorations. In this stretch it falls nearly seventy feet to the level of the Fens whereupon man has taken a hand in helping it on its journey seawards by making its waters navigable. The entire river system has a catchment area of well over 2000 square miles.

EATON SOCON has proudly preserved a tiny 19th. century lockup. This is one more town (or is it a village?) with Dickensian associations - the good Charles is said to have stayed at the Old Plough Inn. The Ouse Valley Way (26 miles for walkers) starts here.

TEMPSFORD
to St. NEOTS
5·1 miles (57·2 miles)

51 MILES FROM LONDON

TEMPSFORD

The Old Lock-up.

The plaque on the old lockup reads:
"The Eaton Socon Gage. This ancient lock-up was built in 1826 for the confinement of local malefactors. Restored in 1963 it is now in the care of the Bedfordshire and Huntingdonshire Naturalists Trust."

LANDRANGER MAP 153

BUCKDEN TOWERS

The Great Tower is the most impressive remnant of the palace that occupied this site when it was a residence of the bishops of Lincoln. This structure of bold brick stands three storeys high in a corner of the grounds and is defended by outer and inner gatehouses, the latter also of three storeys. These and some of the curtain walls are basically 15th. century, built to replace an earlier palace - which had succeeded previous buildings destroyed by fire in 1291. They are not open to the public though it is possible to enter the grounds to the inner gatehouse for an appraisal of their strength.

The first bishop known to have had a house here was Sir Hugh of Lincoln, whose statue stands just beyond the inner gatehouse. It is inscribed "St. Hugh. Bishop of Lincoln and Lord of Buckden Palace, 1186-1200." Included in the composition is his swan. The story is told that when he was installed as Bishop a singularly ferocious swan arrived and became the scourge of the local populace. It was eventually caught and presented to the new Bishop who tamed it so that it became his pet.

The main house is predominantly Victorian. The outer

The Great Tower.

gatehouse incorporates a book shop. Buckden Towers passed into the possession of the Claretian Missionaries in 1956 and they set about the restoration of the complex and built the new Roman Catholic church dedicated to St. Hugh. This is now the centre for Catholic life in the parish of Buckden.

PAXTON PITS are north of Little Paxton between the River Ouse and the busy A1. Water-filled following the extraction of gravel, they are managed as a nature reserve and include an S.S.S.I. (Site of Special Scientific Interest). A walk along the riverside, part of the Ouse Valley Way, shows what can be achieved in the aftermath of industry. Apart from leisure walking, all the usual water-based activities may be enjoyed by local folk.

GRAFHAM WATER. In the 1960s the wide green vale of Diddington Brook was dammed to produce a reservoir of some 2000 acres, now linked with other reservoirs in the region (i.e. Rutland Water) to supply some one and a half million customers. It has also been marketed as a tourist attraction for those who like to take their pleasures on and around water. Reach it, if you are so inclined, by following the B661 west from Buckden.

BUCKDEN. As early as 1086 the village of Buckden is known to have belonged to the Bishop of Lincoln for in the Domesday Survey of that date the manor was held as his property. Apart from a few dwellings there was a church, a mill and a patch of woodland. The road from London to Lincoln passed through the village and as that became the Great North Road its importance grew so that in the height of the coaching era Buckden was a well known posting station. The White Horse Inn, pictured right, proudly proclaims itself an 18th. century coaching house. It did not have a monopoly in the trade - but note a sign of modern times in the cultural change that has been brought to one of the others which had become an Indian restaurant and Tandoori take-away when we visited Buckden.

The White Horse Inn, Buckden.

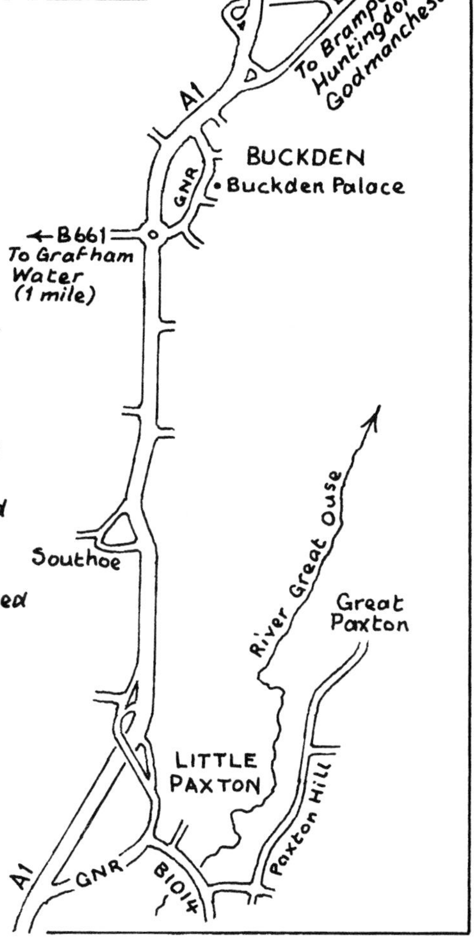

LITTLE PAXTON.* Travellers with nimble minds will be quick to observe that if Paxton deserves the adjective 'Little' then there should be a Great Paxton around somewhere. There is. It is across the river on Paxton Hill and is probably the more impressive village. It has a fine old church - Holy Trinity - and pleasing thatched cottages with views that have been described as among the most beautiful in Cambridgeshire. If you can spare the time to drive up there note the river Great Ouse as a watery highway and the flooded gravel pits alongside, now maintained as a nature reserve. There are lessons in geography to be learned here.

Great Paxton is also smaller than Little Paxton, which seems surprising until you consider their relative positions, one on a hill, the other at its foot. Little Paxton, in the valley, could hardly expand until the marshes were drained but then, like Topsy, it grew while its name remained unchanged. Its situation was on the Great North Road (now by-passed) and consequently better placed for trade. It remains so - just look at the paper mills beside the river.

* In retrospect, maybe this is the wrong title. There is more about Great Paxton than Little Paxton so perhaps "The Paxtons" would have been better?

LANDRANGER
MAP 153

The Old North Road finally calls at Godmanchester, Huntingdon and the Stukeleys before it is joined by the Great North Road at Alconbury Hill. This was Ermine Street, although the two do not exactly match all the way from London; for example, as far as Ware medieval travellers tended to prefer a more passable hillside route to the old and disintegrating Roman way. On the modern road map the Old North Road approximates to the A10 as far as Royston and the A1198 to Godmanchester. Despite original intentions to present a section on this precursor of the main route to the north in the manner of the rest of this book, pressure on space prevents such detailed treatment. Yet it is worth considering brief sketches of the highlights as an incentive to those who wish to explore for themselves. This alternative has much to commend it for the traveller who is familiar with the Great North Road route so far described. The towns along the Old North Road are quite as well worth seeking out as those on the western itinerary. The list begins, logically, in London with villages fully assimilated within the urban spread.

STOKE NEWINGTON. Daniel Defoe attended school and also wrote his most famous classic, "Robinson Crusoe," here.

TOTTENHAM. The manor was once owned by Robert Bruce, the Scottish king – seek out the Bruce Castle Museum. The resident kings of Tottenham now hold court at the stadium of Tottenham Hotspur Football Club.

EDMONTON. Charles Lamb lived the final years of his life at Lamb's Cottage and is buried in All Saints churchyard. John Gilpin began his famous fictional ride here. (See Ware, below.)

ENFIELD. A market town where John Keats was a pupil at the Grammar School. Royalty hunted Enfield Chase; now more available to commoners as a country park (Trent Park).

WALTHAM CROSS. The cross is one of the Eleanor Crosses. This one is still there, much restored and isolated amid the traffic on an island enclosed by walls of functional modern architecture that contrasts starkly with the work of the imaginative medieval masons. These abbreviated notes leave no space for a drawing, much to the relief of the illustrator.

WALTHAM ABBEY, a couple of miles to the east, is where Eleanor's body was rested before continuing on its journey to London. The cross marks the junction of this diversion to the abbey. In Sun Street the Greenwich Meridian is set in the paving so you may place one foot in the eastern hemisphere and the other in the west, if that sort of thing appeals.

CHESHUNT. The size of the old village may be gauged by the length of its High Street, one mile at least. London's Temple Bar of 1672, built to replace the wooden gate to the city burned in the Great Fire, was re-erected here in 1888. There are recurrent plans for its return to The City.

HODDESDON. Nearby, to the east, was Rye House where in 1683 the assassinations of Charles II and his brother (James II to be) were plotted. Careless planning led to the deaths of only the plotters. Rye's Gatehouse remains.

WARE. A pleasant town on the River Lee and a good centre of historic interest. In 1553 Lady Jane Grey was here proclaimed queen and began her brief nine days of rule that linked the reigns of Edward VI and Mary I. Shakespeare's "Great Bed of Ware" is now in the Victoria and Albert Museum. Scott's Grotto will appeal to troglodytes. John Gilpin's ride, told in William Cowper's frolicsome poem, ended at Ware.

STANDON. Just off route but notable for an event that occurred on
15th. September, 1784, is this Hertfordshire village. On that day the
young Italian, Vincenza Lunardi, brought great wonder into the lives
of the local populace by arriving in a most unorthodox fashion, for the age.
He travelled the 24 miles from London by air in England's first manned hydrogen
balloon flight, a perilous device for avoiding the mud and pot holes of the Old North Road!
PUCKERIDGE. This was an important junction for the Romans. Ermine Street
and Stane Street (from Colchester) crossed at the Roman town half a mile north.
BRAUGHING. The Roman town was just to the south, on Ermine Street. Braughing,
its descendant, is by-passed by the Old North Road but it is a fine village with splendid
examples of Hertfordshire's vernacular architecture. In the 16th. century Matthew Hall's
coffin was dropped on the way to the graveyard; he was obviously not as dead as his doctors
declared for the shock revived him. The next time he took the road to church it was to be married.
BUNTINGFORD. Ermine Street approaches the River Rib with the honest line of a true Roman
road before, a mile beyond the crossing, making an abrupt turn to the north with its sights set on the
horizon. There is a bridge now; the town's name suggests a more primitive original crossing.
ROYSTON. Almost 1000 years ago a Lady Roisia from nearby Newsells had a stone cross
erected to mark the junction of Ermine Street and the even older Icknield Way; hence
Roisia-stone, which in the process of time has evolved into Royston. It's a good story, and
a stone does exist which may well be the base of the eponymous lady's cross.
WIMPOLE HALL. The site of the largest and finest mansion in Cambridgeshire
was no doubt chosen in part for its position beside the road to London. Together
with its extensive parklands this National Trust Property almost demands a visit.
CAXTON GIBBET. The scaffold is a gaunt reminder of the days when highwaymen
were strung up and left to rot as a warning to their fellows and supposedly to re-assure
honest travellers but there were always candidates to replace the mouldering bodies.
PAPWORTH EVERARD. The words "Papworth Village Settlement" on the Ordnance
Survey map give some indication of the size of the hospital.
GODMANCHESTER & HUNTINGDON are near the main route and covered overleaf.

Alconbury Hill
Little Stukeley
Great Stukeley
Alconbury
Huntingdon
Godmanchester
GNR
Papworth Everard
Caxton Gibbet
Wimpole Hall
Royston
Buntingford
Braughing
Puckeridge
Standon
Ware
Hoddesdon
Cheshunt
Waltham Abbey
Waltham Cross
Enfield
Edmonton
GNR
Tottenham
Stoke Newington
LONDON CITY

Plantagenet House.

Godmanchester:
three
of the
older
buildings,
entirely
typical.

The Gables

The White Hart Inn.

Cromwell

It would be a shame to speed on to Alconbury without having turned aside to Godmanchester and Huntingdon. Turn off through Brampton where Samuel Pepys once lived (see across). The house is privately owned.

GODMANCHESTER

The 'chester' in the name reveals Roman origins, as a civil settlement rather than a fort, and it retains an original pentagonal street framework. Here is a town which has largely escaped the insensitivity of modern industrial and residential development. If the locals need to avail themselves of a shopping centre they must cross the River Ouse to Huntingdon. The old dwellings are a delight and form the basis of a conservation area. Words cannot do justice to the place. Godmanchester should not be missed.

HUNTINGDON

As you cross the old bridge over the Ouse from Godmanchester, be not surprised to see its alignment change at the halfway point. The story is told that in 1332 teams began the construction from each bank and the workmen of Godmanchester met their counterparts from Huntingdon almost coincidentally mid-stream, an instance of the medieval town planning - or lack of it - that accounts for so much of the character of Britain's architectural heritage and townscapes. The old bridge is overshadowed by the modern one demonstrating, if need be, how lack of consideration or lack of feeling for the past accounts for so much that is to be deplored in modern *planning*. This by-pass also takes a chunk out of Huntingdon's castle mound. The castle had a short history; it was dismantled in 1172 but the impressive earthworks remained inviolate until the age of the railway. Now they have also suffered the unsympathetic assault of the new road. A major attraction for visitors to Huntingdon lies in its Cromwell associations. The future head of state, the Lord Protector, was born here in 1599 and attended the Grammar School (as did Samuel Pepys). The school building is the remaining part of a monastic infirmary hall and now houses the Cromwell Museum.

Travellers who have come thus far and think the way has been busy will find a severe shock awaiting them as they translate their northward progress from the map to the real thing on the road. All the traffic that has accompanied them along the Great North Road from London is joined by a new throng from the Old North Road (the A10/A1198) plus an eager contingent of continental container traffic flowing along the A14 from the docks at Felixstowe. This mêlée merges at the inverted funnel of the Alconbury junction in a calamitous cacophony of cars, coaches, container trucks, cumbersome juggernauts, caravans and their countless consorts in an endless line of chariots, the sight of which on their Ermine Street would have put more fear into the Romans than Boadicea and the Iceni ever did. Here the need for an upgrade to motorway standards was paramount. Avoid these horrors (but not the noise!) at least as far as the approaches to Peterborough by using the local access road, B1043, which shadows the A1(M) on its eastern side, effectively the line of the Great North Road. Drive through the Alconburys or branch east to the end of the A14.

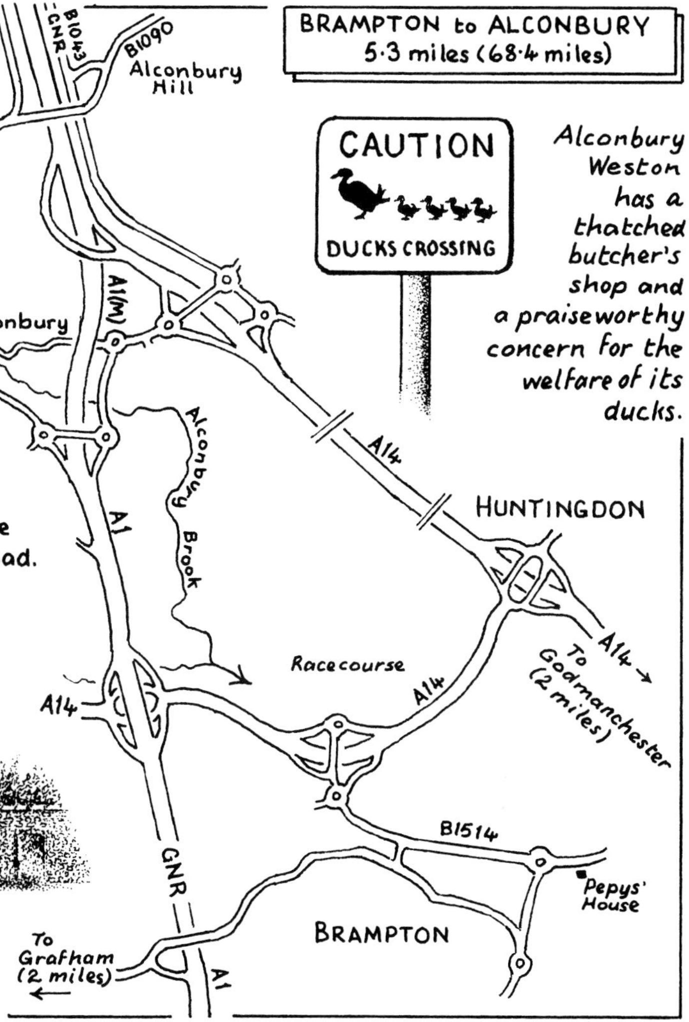

BRAMPTON to ALCONBURY
5·3 miles (68·4 miles)

CAUTION
DUCKS CROSSING

Alconbury Weston has a thatched butcher's shop and a praiseworthy concern for the welfare of its ducks.

Alconbury Hill

Alconbury Weston

Alconbury

A1(M)

Alconbury Brook

A1

A14

HUNTINGDON

A14 → To Godmanchester (2 miles)

Racecourse

GNR

B1514

To Grafham (2 miles) ←

BRAMPTON

A1

'Pepys' House

PEPYS' HOUSE

IN 1644 ROBERT PEPYS OWNED THIS HOUSE AND FROM IT HIS NEPHEW SAMUEL FOR A WHILE ATTENDED HUNTINGDON GRAMMAR SCHOOL. IT PASSED TO SAMUEL'S FATHER (1661-1680). HERE THE GREAT CLERK OF THE ACTS, DIARIST AND LATER SECRETARY FOR THE AFFAIRS OF ADMIRALTY VISITED AND STAYED.

TO BE VIEWED BY APPOINTMENT ONLY

Pepys' House and the plaque at the gate.

LANDRANGER MAPS 153 & 142

THE FENS

On this section you are riding a significant geographical boundary. The flat expanse to the east is the Fens, a landform that covers more than 1000 square miles, reaching almost from Lincoln to Cambridge and pointing a finger of Fenland at Sawtry. It was for good reason that Ermine Street, later the Old North Road, swung west to find the fringe of the wetlands where they were joined by the Great North Road at Alconbury. Historically roads may have been difficult of passage but there were limits which had to be recognised.

Windpump at Wicken Fen.

In times past the Fens was a region of almost impenetrable swamp. In effect, here was a shallow bay of the sea which had gradually silted up. Marine deposits left at high tides checked rivers which in turn deposited silt and resulted in fresh water swamps that in due course allowed the formation of peat in depths of up to fifteen feet. In this landscape any rise of fifty feet is a mountain. Such elevations provided sites for settlement and before the fenlands were drained afforded refuge for robbers - or sanctuary for men of God.

Drainage began with the construction of embankments before the Romans arrived but it was their engineering skills that led to the building of causeways and dykes, both of which meant an improvement in communications. But when the Romans left maintenance came to an end and the fenlands reverted to inland sea and marsh.

With the coming of the Normans religious settlements such as Ely began to reclaim land again but not until the seventeenth century did reclamation begin in earnest. Drainage windmills, as many as 2,000 by one estimate, gave the region a distinctive signature. Wind power was superseded by steam which, in turn, gave way to diesel and electricity. Not surprisingly there were objectors to the drainage schemes, those whose livings depended upon the special character of the wetlands, the fowlers, fishermen and the sedge cutters, but the value of the rich new land was recognised and soon the farming interest was calling the tune with the production of wheat, sugar beet, fruit and the cultivation of bulbs.

Now only one working windpump remains *in situ*, the weatherboarded pump on National Trust land at Wicken Fen, though at the Museum of East Anglian Life, Stowmarket, a rescued windpump has been re-erected. Wicken Fen, some 25 miles east of the A1, is not on this itinerary though worth a visit when you are in the vicinity.

The merest glance at the O.S. map reveals this to be a special landscape. Nature does not design her watercourses in direct lines and a vast area of Landranger Sheet 142 is a chequerboard penned in blue. This is the land of the zero contour. There is one a mile and a half east of Sawtry - it continues within a mile of Stilton (next page) - a full 35 miles from The Wash and nearly ninety miles west of the sea at Lowestoft. You can walk at sea level here without having to check the tide tables.

A brief glance at the average road map will suggest little to detain any motorist along this section and a passenger peering through the window will confirm that the countryside hardly excites interest. That may well be so but a study of the Ordnance Survey map will show that the area has a history, even if it is no longer obvious on the ground.

South of Sawtry notice the houses named Toll Bar Cottages,* a clear indication of their origin beside this turnpike road. Further south is the legend *Manorial Earthworks*, the lost manor house being that of Coppingford. You will find moats at Coppingford, Grange Farm, Woodwalton, Bruce's Castle Farm and near Glatton – and this without looking more than perhaps a couple of miles from the Great North Road; search further and you will find more.

A Cistercian Abbey (1147–1536) existed two miles south-east of Sawtry, remembered in the name of Abbey Farm. The drain here is still named Monk's Lode and to the south lies Monk's Wood. This wood is a National Nature Reserve, as are Woodwalton and Holme Fens, but visits to these special sites are only allowed by permit. Near the abbey site, across the railway, look for a motte and bailey and a church standing in pastoral isolation.

The tutored eye will find far more evidence of days past but the O.S. map is always a source of information and repays even the amateur's careful study.

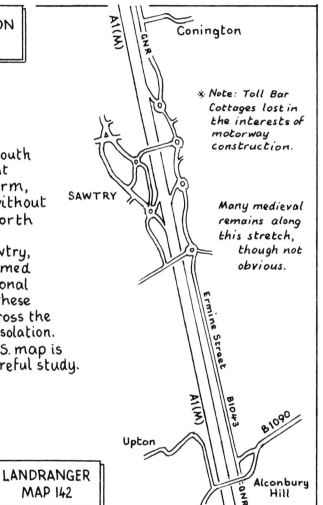

ALCONBURY HILL to CONINGTON
5.1 miles (73.5 miles)

Conington

⁎ Note: Toll Bar Cottages lost in the interests of motorway construction.

Many medieval remains along this stretch, though not obvious.

SAWTRY

Ermine Street

A1(M)   B1043   B1090

Upton

Alconbury Hill

LANDRANGER MAP 142

SAWTRY. William Sawtry (usually "Sawtre" in history books) was born here. He was a Lollard, one of the "poor priests" who were followers of Wycliffe, and achieved fame as the first Christian martyr to be burned in Norman England, at Smithfield in 1401.

Sawtry is a pleasant village with some 17th. century cottages and an old lock-up standing on the village green.

STILTON

Stilton was always a staging post on the Great North Road and though now by-passed by the A1 its proud traditions remain. No ordinary coaching stop, Stilton. This is where a celebrated cheese from the Leicestershire area was brought to be collected by the London-bound coaches. London folk asked for the cheese from Stilton not knowing, or not caring, of its true origins and the name endures. At the Angel a Miss Worthington made a name for herself selling the cheese. The inn faces its competitor, the Bell, across a now unnecessarily wide road.

The Bell.

The Angel.

THE CHEESE

Stilton cheese is traditionally known as the King of Cheeses. Blue Stilton is at its best between November and April, it should have a strong, lingering taste and between the veins the colour should be rich and creamy.

The rind is crusty and top quality Stilton will have been matured slowly for perhaps nine months to a year, so that the blue veins grow to perfection. It is the immature cheese that is sold as white Stilton. This still has a delightful creamy flavour and a good aroma but lacks the tang of the connoisseur's cheese.

There is a tradition of soaking in port, especially if it has dried out – Mrs Beeton recommended using port, sherry, Madeira or even old ale – but this does no justice to the cheese, being a camouflage to the distinctive flavour.

Eat your Stilton with plain biscuits or fresh, crusty bread and enhance its piquancy with a glass of full-bodied wine or a good port or sherry.

You will know when you are approaching this page. Its advent is announced by the tall tower of All Saints' Church at Conington – visible from afar.

There is now no cross at Norman Cross but the name recognises the existence of an Eleanor Cross at this point, one of twelve that were set up to mark the resting places of the cortège of Edward I's queen on its journey to London after her death at Harby in Lincolnshire, in 1290.

During the Napoleonic Wars prisoners were held at a number of sites, Norman Cross being perhaps the largest. A prison was built here in 1796 to house captive Frenchmen, of whom some 1800 died, which says much about the conditions that prevailed in these places.

Off the A15, a couple of miles from the A1 at Norman Cross, is the village of Yaxley, a pleasant backwater with some black and white thatched cottages, a thatched inn, a village green and a pump. It was the interesting name that drew us there in the first place. It is derived from the Old English word for cuckoo, *geāc*, which together with *leāh*, meaning woodland or a woodland glade, produced a sound which has come down through the centuries as the modern pronunciation. Say them quickly and see!

North of Norman Cross the bend in the Great North Road marks an obvious change in alignment in the parent Ermine Street. The two remain in reasonable partnership hereabouts.

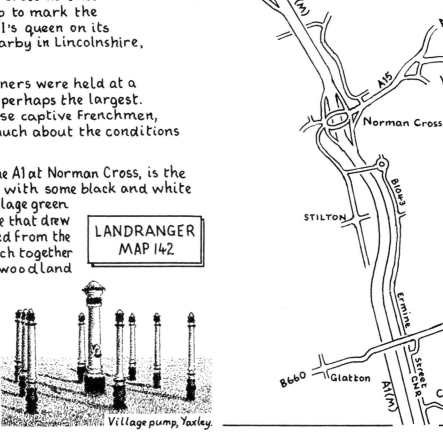

LANDRANGER
MAP 142

CONINGTON to A1139
5·3 miles (78·8 miles)

Village pump, Yaxley.

PETERBOROUGH

The Great North Road by-passes Peterborough but the city holds a key position 'twixt Midland and coast, as it does on the way north, and the development of the railways brought growth. The brick industry centred on Fletton had much to do with 20th. century expansion and since 1967 the New Town has doubled the then population of 81,000.

Yet Peterborough is a city of ancient origins. Its venerable cathedral was not first on the scene. A Saxon abbey was founded in 654 a.d. and sacked by Danes in 870 a.d. Fire destroyed its replacement and the present building was begun in 1118. It is without doubt one of the finest Norman cathedrals in the country.

Medieval Peterborough grew up naturally at the western gate of the abbey, around the market place which was renamed Cathedral Square when the market moved to Broadway in 1963. Facing the West Gate is the splendid old Guildhall of 1671, one of the city's most memorable secular buildings. Behind and pre-dating it by some 270 years is the Church of St. John the Baptist. Nearby are Miss Pears' Almshouses which are not quite as old as they appear having been to a great extent rebuilt in 1901, funded by a legacy from the lady whose name they now bear. It is quite obvious that they are now almshouses in name only. The Square is a good place to study your guide and plan an exploration of this fine old city.

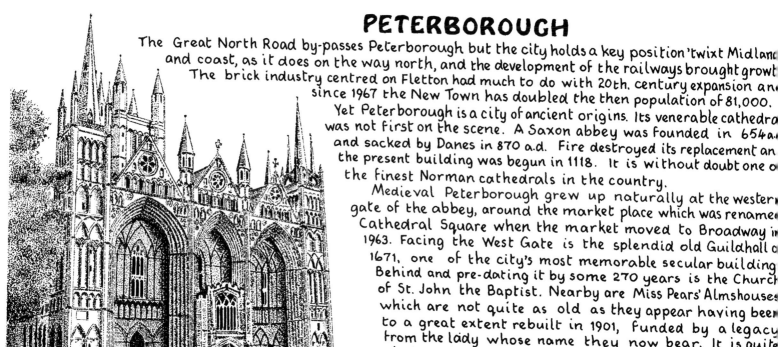

Peterborough Cathedral.

NENE PARK. Peterborough is lucky to have this country park with its centre piece of Ferry Meadows stretching from the A1 to the city itself. Outdoor leisure is the theme with camping, watersports, pony riding, golf, fishing, nature trails and reserves, and adventure playgrounds for the young. Facilities for the disabled are not forgotten. You name it – it seems to be there! Just check with the park wardens. Energetic readers may like to park at Wansford and walk the Nene Way into Peterborough. Others may choose to do the same journey in style and with a dash of adventure by using the Nene Valley Railway which can usually provide steam or diesel hauled trains in season, usually weekends from March to December, but with a fuller service in summer. Check the timetable.

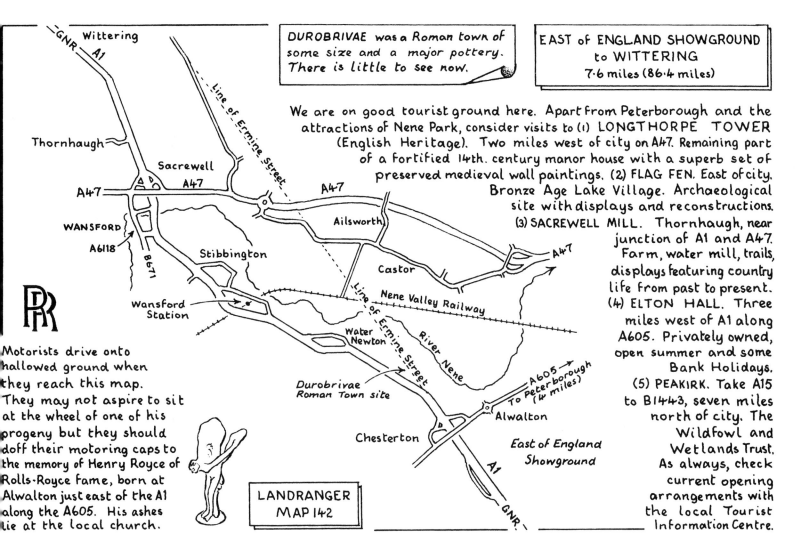

DUROBRIVAE was a Roman town of some size and a major pottery. There is little to see now.

We are on good tourist ground here. Apart from Peterborough and the attractions of Nene Park, consider visits to (1) LONGTHORPE TOWER (English Heritage). Two miles west of city on A47. Remaining part of a fortified 14th. century manor house with a superb set of preserved medieval wall paintings. (2) FLAG FEN. East of city. Bronze Age Lake Village. Archaeological site with displays and reconstructions. (3) SACREWELL MILL. Thornhaugh, near junction of A1 and A47. Farm, water mill, trails, displays featuring country life from past to present. (4) ELTON HALL. Three miles west of A1 along A605. Privately owned, open summer and some Bank Holidays. (5) PEAKIRK. Take A15 to B1443, seven miles north of city. The Wildfowl and Wetlands Trust. As always, check current opening arrangements with the local Tourist Information Centre.

Motorists drive onto hallowed ground when they reach this map. They may not aspire to sit at the wheel of one of his progeny but they should doff their motoring caps to the memory of Henry Royce of Rolls-Royce fame, born at Alwalton just east of the A1 along the A605. His ashes lie at the local church.

LANDRANGER MAP 142

Wittering
GNR A1
Thornhaugh
Sacrewell
A47   A47
WANSFORD
A6118
B671
Line of Ermine Street
Stibbington
Wansford Station
Ailsworth
A47
Castor
Nene Valley Railway
River Nene
Water Newton
Line of Ermine Street
Durobrivae Roman Town site
Chesterton
Alwalton
A605 To Peterborough (4 miles)
East of England Showground
A1
GNR

BURGHLEY HOUSE

This house is the finest shop window imaginable for local stone from the historic quarries of Barnack and is arguably the largest and most splendid example of Elizabethan architecture in the country. It has belonged to the Cecil family since the first Lord Burghley devoted thirty-two years to its design and construction. There have been alterations over the years, notably those made by Capability Brown in the 18th. century. When called in to landscape the gardens his brief included the re-design of the South Front and the construction of various out-buildings. Yet surely Elizabeth I's favoured adviser would have no difficulty in recognising the house he gained so much pleasure in planning.

Connoisseurs of art will enjoy Burghley's fine picture collection and many people who never have aspirations to visit a stately home will know the parkland in television guise as the setting for the annual Burghley Horse Trials.

The West Front.

Stamford is the hometown of the celebrated conductor, Sir Malcolm Sargent, actually born away from home when his parents were on holiday. But he is buried here in Stamford.

If Sir Malcolm was one of our greatest musicians, then another 'resident' of a Stamford graveyard can surely lay claim to the title of England's greatest ever man. Weighing 52 stones and 11 pounds when he died on a visit in 1809, it required 22 men to lower Daniel Lambert's coffin into his grave in St. Martin's churchyard!

Tolethorpe Hall, a couple of miles north of Stamford on the byway between Great Casterton and Ryhall, is a 16th/17th. century manor house, greatly altered inside. It is home to the Browne family whose forebear Robert held ideas which were instrumental in the foundation of Congregationalism. It is also home to the Stamford Shakespeare Company which holds a summer season in a fine open-air theatre in the grounds. The house may be open seasonally.

The Great North Road crossed the River Welland at Stamford's Town Bridge but the Roman crossing was a quarter of a mile west of this. The line of Ermine Street passes near Barnack coinciding with 600 yards of minor road where the T-junction for Barnack represents a change in alignment. The line continues through Burghley Park and beyond the river rejoins the Great North Road (B1081) as it approaches Great Casterton. The modern A1 is aloof to all this as it takes a smooth curve to the west.

The A606 provides the most direct route to Rutland Water. This vast man-made lake almost encloses a low lying ridge between two adjacent valleys so that Hambleton now is practically an island, boosting the shore line to some 27 miles. With so much water about it is hardly surprising that all the usual water-based leisure activities are to be found in abundance, including a pleasure cruiser which operates in season. Cycle hire is available – should you wish to test your legs round those 27 miles.

WITTERING to GREAT CASTERTON
5·5 miles (91·9 miles)

Tolethorpe Hall
GNR A1
Tickencote
Great Casterton
GNR
B1081
A6121
A16
← A606
A606
STAMFORD
To Rutland Water (4 miles) & Oakham (10 miles)
B1443
A6121
River Welland
Burghley Park
A43
GNR B1081
Line of Ermine Street
Barnack
Wittering Airfield
A1 GNR
Wittering

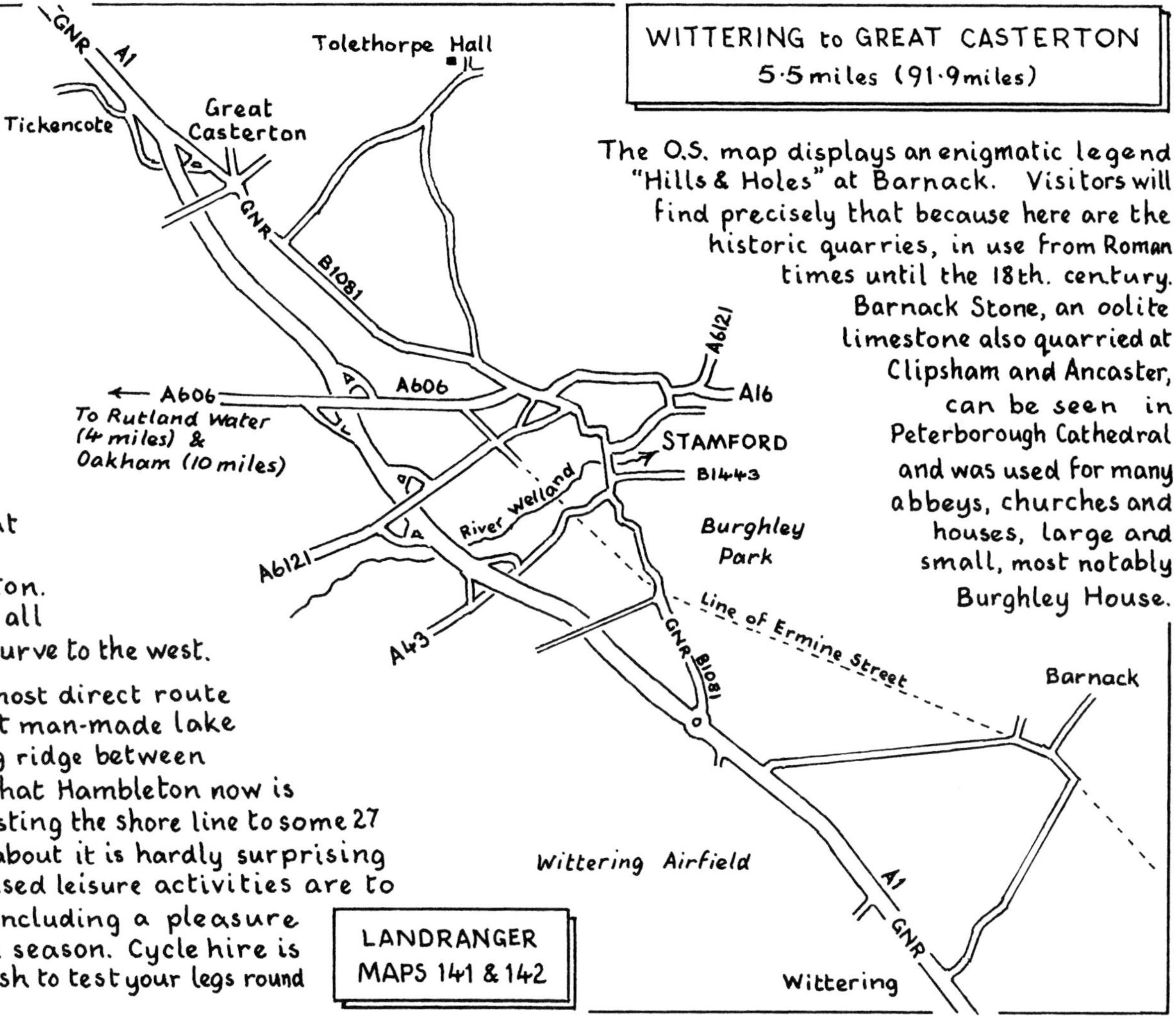

LANDRANGER MAPS 141 & 142

The O.S. map displays an enigmatic legend "Hills & Holes" at Barnack. Visitors will find precisely that because here are the historic quarries, in use from Roman times until the 18th. century. Barnack Stone, an oolite limestone also quarried at Clipsham and Ancaster, can be seen in Peterborough Cathedral and was used for many abbeys, churches and houses, large and small, most notably Burghley House.

STAMFORD

The stone town of Stamford has been called "one of the two or three most beautiful towns in England" and I see no reason to dispute that. There is no doubt that it demands two pages of this book ~ not that such attention will do it justice but at least we can acknowledge some very special qualities.

Stamford has over a thousand years of known history. Here was the only point in miles where the River Welland could be forded and it was consequently the focus of many pre-historic tracks. By the time of the Danes it was the capital of the Fens, one of the Five Boroughs of Danelaw. Stamford was recorded in Domesday Book and in 1254 Henry III granted its Charter. This period saw the foundation of many religious houses; there have been monasteries, priories, friaries and religious hospitals, including the medieval Browne's Hospital Almshouses and Chapel of 1475, open to the public and worth a visit.

Wool brought prosperity in the Middle Ages and affluent merchants displayed their wealth by building churches. Five of the original fourteen remain, their proud towers and spires embellishing the medieval street pattern. St. Mary's especially demands attention. Its 13th. century tower is surmounted by a soaring 14th. century broach spire which grasps your gaze as you enter St. Mary's Street from Sheepmarket.

In the 16th. century Queen Elizabeth favoured her Chief Secretary of State with the Manor of Stamford. As Lord Burghley he built Burghley House south of the river and it is thanks to the patronage of this family that much of the medieval town has been preserved for appreciative 20th. century eyes.

With the upsurge of trade from the 17th. century onwards Stamford, as a key point on the road to the north, knew fresh prosperity. Fine coaching inns

The view down Barn Hill.

Originally the Shambles, now the Library.

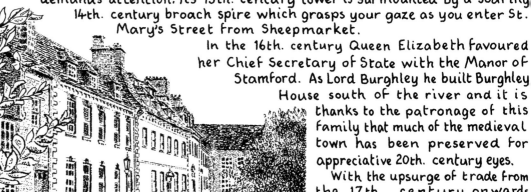
A corner of St. George's Square.

The Town Bridge over the River Welland.

All Saints Church.

catered for travellers, some of whom, notably Dickens, stayed long enough to describe a town so obviously pleasing to their eyes. By the Georgian Period professional men and wealthy merchants were building houses that still grace many of the streets.

The railways and the industrial revolution left Stamford largely untouched but the Victorians continued to build, always with the unifying continuity of Cotswold limestone. The mellow warmth of this material endures in the memory and it is Stamford's good fortune that a long finger of this rock reaches cross-country into Lincolnshire.

Stamford is one of the high points on the journey north. Go into the Tourist Information Bureau and purchase a few guides - there is a splendid selection. And while you are there seek accommodation for a few days and give the place the attention it deserves.

A corner of Browne's Hospital.

THE COUNTY OF RUTLAND

We are now passing Rutland which historic county, temporarily mislaid during the final quarter of the twentieth century, we enter as we leave Stamford. Re-organisation in 1974 linked it with Leicestershire in a move that many folks, especially residents, rightly found hard to accept. Twenty years later the Local Government Commission for England acceded to local pressure and returned England's smallest county to the fold. Rutland is about 18 miles by 15 miles in extent, the boundaries enclosing some 150 square miles. In this predominantly agricultural landscape the highest ground is to the west, rising to nearly 600 feet. The Great North Road crosses the eastern half of the county which is effectively a low sloping plateau of between 200 and 400 feet where limestone makes a significant contribution to the architecture giving a special flavour to the village scene. It is worth finding time to explore a few of Rutland's country lanes to absorb some of this village character. If you venture as far as the county town of Oakham visit the surviving great hall of the castle, one of the finest aisled halls in England, and see the collection of horseshoes presented by visiting royalty and nobility, including both Queens Elizabeth I and II.

GREAT CASTERTON, our first village in Rutland, lies on the Old Road north of Stamford with which it shares relief from the pounding of persistent traffic that now takes a diversionary sweep west along the Stamford bypass.

The Romans needed no bypass. Ermine Street went this way and it is likely that in those days the place was of much greater importance. In 1959 the Roman town revealed itself because the very dry summer allowed cropmarks to show its outline, and also that of a 4th. century villa. Earlier in the occupation there had been a fort which had provided the focus for the later civilian development. The modern name is a direct link with the old time Romans: "caster" (= "castrum") as always signifying the presence of a fort.

There is not much to see, just a few earthworks visible from a side road north-east from the crossroads before you rejoin the A1. Instead, go look at the delightful little church of Saints Peter and Paul, taking care to avoid courting couples down the lane. There must be something romantic in the air of Great Casterton. Peasant poet John Clare met his future wife here whilst working as a labourer on a farm, the girl he immortalised as "Sweet Patty of the Vale."

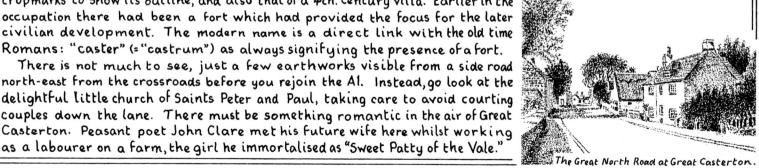

The Great North Road at Great Casterton.

Secluded TICKENCOTE, barely half a mile from the A1, attracts church connoisseurs for its late Norman chancel arch of five orders. The old mill is now a house, happy in its riverside setting.

EMPINGHAM is quite a large village but has all the characteristics of finest Rutland. Remains of Roman buildings were uncovered near Rutland Water.

EXTON's cottages of limestone and thatch line the village green. It is an estate village, typical of Rutland. The old Elizabethan hall now exists only as a scenic ruin, burned down in 1810. Its replacement dates from 1852.

COTTESMORE was made famous by its hunt, Rutland being part of England's most renowned fox-hunting country, the Shires. Cottesmore and Greetham tend to be dominated by the nearby airfield.

BURLEY-ON-THE-HILL is known for its superb country house (never to be confused with that other Burghley, near Stamford). This Palladian style mansion is the finest in Rutland, commenced in 1694. Enjoy the view of it through the avenue of trees from the Oakham road beside Rutland Water.

Across the A1 is the Lost Village of PICKWORTH. It was hit by the plague in 1349 and later. It also suffered in 1470 when the Battle of Losecoat Field raged between here and the Great North Road. The adjacent woodland of Bloody Oaks must surely take its name from the event? Pickworth is now a scattering of isolated buildings where the lone arch of the one time parish church standing in a field provided inspiration for John Clare to write his poem, "Elegy on Ruins of Pickworth."

At STRETTON we move on from this map but do first take a look at the little church with its simple Norman arched south doorway.

GREAT CASTERTON to STRETTON
6·4 miles (98·3 miles)

GNR
A1
Stretton
Ram Jam Inn
B668
To Cottesmore (3 miles) & Burley (5 miles)
Ermine Street
Clipsham

To Pickworth (2 miles)
Bloody Oaks
To Empingham (2 miles) & Exton (4 miles)
Great Casterton
A1
B1081 GNR

LANDRANGER MAPS 130 & 141

Clipsham is a limestone village where the mellow stone is only part of its charm. Yet the local rock has had a part to play beyond this picture-postcard community. After the House of Commons suffered air raid damage during the war it was to Clipsham that they turned for a suitable, attractive and durable stone when the time came to rebuild. The quarries, a mile to the east, have long been a source of good building material which may be seen in many of the ancient colleges of Oxford as well as in cathedrals, churches, mansions and simple cottages across this region.

For many years the sideboard in our dining room displayed a wizened, prune-like object. This had been an apple. It held pride of place because my daughter had picked it from beneath an apple tree in the grounds of Woolsthorpe Manor, the birthplace of Sir Isaac Newton. Though the tree concerned was not the one permanently linked with Newton's work on the theory of gravity it is reputed to be grafted from the original, which fell down in 1820.

Woolsthorpe Manor, a National Trust property, is a 17th century stone-built yeoman farmer's home bought by Newton's father, a prosperous farmer, in 1623. Young Isaac was born on Christmas Day, 1642, shortly after his father's death and might well have been expected to take over the family farm but his uncle, the rector at Burton Coggles, recognised an outstanding intellect and ensured that the boy went to study at Cambridge. From then Newton spent little time at Woolsthorpe, apart from an extended visit in 1665 when the university closed down because of the ravages of the plague and he retreated home to study. Originally the roof sported three dormer windows but internally the house is little changed since Newton's day.

Sir Isaac Newton (1642-1727)

Woolsthorpe Manor.

The hamlet of Woolsthorpe adjoins the larger village of Colsterworth. Together they span the valley of the infant River Witham. Colsterworth church is where Newton was baptised and it has a sundial cut by the lad when he was nine years old and showing rather more interest in practical activities than in his academic work at The King's School, Grantham.

At Colsterworth we are a couple of miles east of the historic boundary between Lincolnshire and Rutland. North of the village the Great North Road and Ermine Street at last go their separate ways and the post road does not follow another Roman route until Bawtry, save for a passing liaison with the Fosse Way at Newark.

If the weather encourages a picnic or, better still a walk, there are two Forestry Commission properties nearby which provide picnic sites and nature trails. For Twyford Wood take the A151 across the A1 east of Colsterworth (1 mile). Morkery Wood can be reached by driving south along the by-road to South Witham and then east underneath the A1 (5 miles).

At Morkery Wood we are re-entering Lincolnshire, South Kesteven to be precise, after a most memorable preliminary introduction to the county at Stamford. This is a region of rolling countryside and woodland noted for its villages and towns of stone. Stamford is the most famous example but there are many places adjacent to our route that will repay a leisurely visit and provide memories of pale stone houses and churches that gleam in the sunlight.

You may like to come to Sir Isaac Newton's birthplace through SOUTH and NORTH WITHAM, the first villages north of Rutland, an approach which certainly has advantages over the traumas of the A1.

A dozen miles east along the A151 is BOURNE, on the fringe of the Fens, reputed to be the birthplace of Hereward the Wake who provided some of the last Saxon resistance to the Normans in this region. It is certainly the place where William Cecil, Lord Burghley, was born (see Stamford).

On the way to Bourne is CORBY GLEN, notable for the 14th. century wall paintings in the parish church, re-discovered during restorations in 1939 and said to be the most extensive in England. The village is historically linked with sheep and still holds an annual sheep fair, first held in 1239.

South of Corby Glen is SWAYFIELD where the church has an Early English tower; south again find the hillside village of CASTLE BYTHAM and nearby is LITTLE BYTHAM set around the tower and spire of its church dedicated to St. Medard, a 6th. century French bishop.

All this is splendid farming country, full of quiet byways, not forgotten but awaiting unhurried exploration.

MORKERY WOOD
to COLSTERWORTH
5·1 miles (103·4 miles.)

LANDRANGER
MAP 130

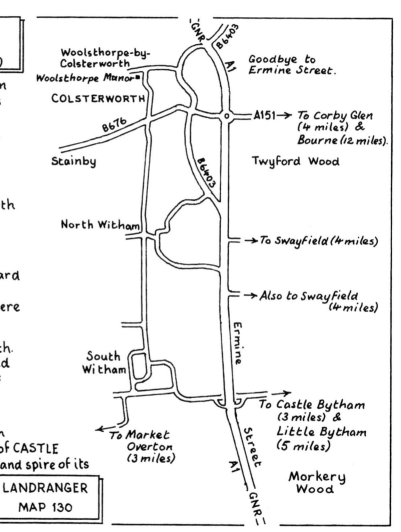

LINCOLNSHIRE VILLAGE CHURCHES

Most of Lincolnshire's village churches delight the eye and there is a fine collection around Grantham. The group presented here is to the South and offers a pleasing tour but there is no need to restrict yourself to the illustrated four – let the Ordnance Survey's Landranger Map be your guide. Do choose a sunny day when the silvery stone of these villages is displayed to advantage. Sadly, the church in our modern world is not proof against vandals and thieves. You will be lucky to find one open, which is a pity. Interiors are what enthusiasts like to see.

Little Ponton.

Great Ponton.

LITTLE PONTON. This village is tucked away from the world in the seclusion of the valley of the Witham, between the A1 and the railway but hidden from each. The curious little church is without a tower but has a bell in an alcove in the west wall. It is dedicated to St. Guthlac.

GREAT PONTON. If you approach from the Great North Road you are upon this fine church before you realise it – round a bend, past the stepped gables of Ellys Manor House, and there it is. The splendid tower dominates this largely Perpendicular church.

BASSINGTHORPE. If you visit no other village you must on no account miss this one. The little church, dedicated to St. Thomas a Beckett, has a small and stubby broach spire and looks like everything a village church should be. Many of these churches stand in close proximity to an attendant manor house and here it is just such a juxtaposition that makes the scene memorable. The house, its upstairs oriel window peering at the church with avuncular concern, is a building of grace. Its tall, ornamental chimneys and stepped gables are perfectly in scale with its companion across the tiny graveyard. Don't forget your camera!

STROXTON. All Saints Church with its neat saddleback tower stands isolated in a setting of fields. Walk along a field lane beside a farm to reach it. Tiny Stroxton (it's pronounced 'Strawson') has just a few houses, a hall and a pond.

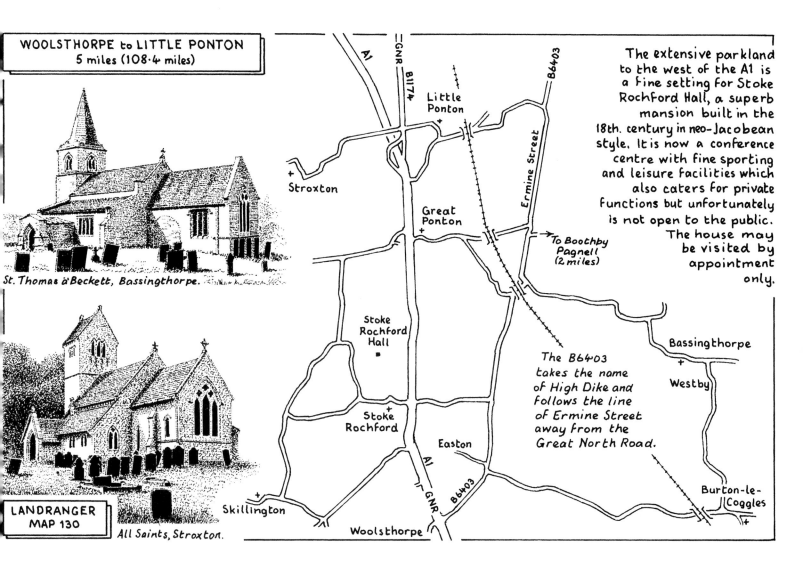

WOOLSTHORPE to LITTLE PONTON
5 miles (108·4 miles)

LANDRANGER MAP 130

St. Thomas à Beckett, Bassingthorpe.

All Saints, Stroxton.

The extensive parkland to the west of the A1 is a fine setting for Stoke Rochford Hall, a superb mansion built in the 18th. century in neo-Jacobean style. It is now a conference centre with fine sporting and leisure facilities which also caters for private functions but unfortunately is not open to the public. The house may be visited by appointment only.

The B6403 takes the name of High Dike and follows the line of Ermine Street away from the Great North Road.

A1

GNR

B1174

B6403

Ermine Street

Little Ponton

Stroxton

Great Ponton

To Boothby Pagnell (2 miles)

Stoke Rochford Hall

Stoke Rochford

Bassingthorpe

Westby

Easton

A1 GNR

B6403

Skillington

Woolsthorpe

Burton-le-Coggles

GRANTHAM

The Parish Church.

Many visitors link Grantham with our first female prime minister and will happily follow the finger posts to her birthplace. Yet this old market town is more than Margaret Thatcher. Its history dates back to Domesday Book when it was a Royal Manor. As a borough it celebrated its quincentenary in 1963. The modern town has lost some of its surface fascination because "improvements" have swept away the character of several older streets, but much of the flavour of an earlier Grantham may still be found if you ignore the late 20th. century changes.

The 282ft. tower and spire of the Parish Church of St. Wulfram has been a beacon to travellers since around the year 1300 when it was completed as part of alterations to the original Norman church. The cathedral-like proportions of the interior are emphasized by its width and help to make this as impressive a parish church as any in the land. Behind the church is Grantham House (National Trust).

Beside the churchyard is King's School, the 16th. century Old Grammar School which Isaac Newton attended. His statue stands upon the town green in front of the Victorian Guildhall, on the site of an Eleanor Cross which was destroyed during the Civil War.

As you walk about the town look for the stone conduit in the market place. It was built in 1597 to safeguard water conveyed from springs at nearby Gonerby.

Of the two major coaching inns the George Hotel, mentioned in 'Nicholas Nickleby', retains a refurbished frontage but has otherwise suffered at the hand of developers whose choice is to promote shopping - but look for the archway provided for the entry of coaches.

The Angel and Royal, established by the Knights Templar, is now a member of the Trust House chain but still looks the part. Though the front is 15th. century this remains one of the oldest inns in the country and has given shelter to King John, Richard III, Charles I and Edward VII.

Other worthy inns include the half-timbered Blue Pig and the Beehive, whose inn sign is a genuine beehive fixed (firmly one hopes, remembering Newton) in the branches of a lime tree. And if you need to work up a thirst, take a walk by the river or follow the 'Gingerbread Way' round the town.

Admirers of great houses in landscaped parkland will find themselves spoiled for choice hereabouts.

Belton House (National Trust) is three miles north of Grantham along the A607. Paintings, porcelain, silver and woodcarving provide interesting viewing, as do personal mementos of Edward VIII and the abdication. Children will enjoy the adventure playground. Special events may include Belton Horse Trials (usually April) and open air concerts.

Further away but not to be missed is Belvoir Castle, the seat of the Dukes of Rutland since the days of Henry VIII. The castle has been repeatedly rebuilt and improved to give a blend that links medieval with modern. Originally William the Conqueror gave all the land visible from this height to Robert de Todeni, his standard-bearer, who considered the view and, with justification, thought the name "Belvedere" most suitable. This became Belvoir but if you wish to impress the locals, say "Beever."

Between Belvoir and Grantham is Harlaxton where the startling façade of Harlaxton Manor exemplifies the architectural extravagance of the 19th. century. It is owned by the University of Evansville, Indiana, which looks after its European Campus with the care it deserves. The house is not open to the public but is available as a conference and function centre, though the formal gardens are open in season. They are at present being restored. This project, which may well last into the 21st. century, began with the flavour of an archaeological dig as it uncovered paths, stairways, stone seats, ornaments and walls.

LANDRANGER
MAP 130

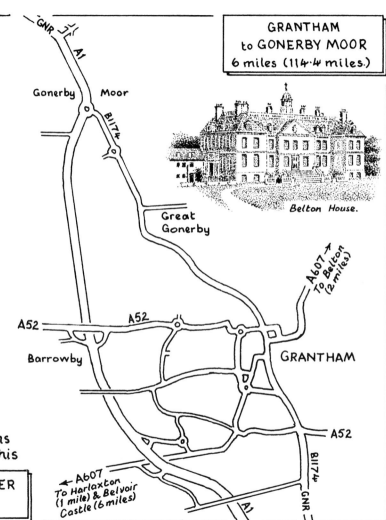

GRANTHAM
to GONERBY MOOR
6 miles (114·4 miles.)

Belton House.

Exploring A Few Byways

I remember a long and agreeable sunlit afternoon spent exploring Lincolnshire byways north of Grantham, between the Great North Road and the main line railway, where limestone spires and towers of churches announce their villages like illuminated capitals of a medieval manuscript; the lovely warm stone of St. Mary's, Marston, where a sundial sitting tall on its cylindrical column is a homely companion to the scatter of gravestones; Hougham set in pastoral tranquillity, so close to Marston as to make you wonder at the need for two churches, yet remember that each manor shared religion but not place of worship; All Saints at Westborough concluding the wide lane of a cul-de-sac village; the impressively proportioned St. Peter's at Claypole, its tall tower supporting a slender crocketed spire of pale shining stone almost fluorescent in the sunlight barely a mile from the Nottinghamshire border; individually pearls, collectively a necklace strung along the valley of the youthful River Witham, a treasure of rural Lincolnshire.

Dry Doddington.

But perhaps the unforgettable memory above all others is the tiny eccentric spire of Dry Doddington as it came abruptly into view, dominating the countryside in a way quite at odds with its size. The church rests on a miniature hill, hardly more than an ambitious mound, to make the most of its neat broach spire, proud enough to stand alone on the village green with a merely vestigial fence to defend the door arch. Its builders, showing great confidence in the power of the Lord, set their church on the Lincolnshire clay with scant regard for the need to provide sound foundations. The tower and stubby spire have a pronounced list away from the body of the church so that one may well imagine the patrons of the village inn, at the foot of the slope, blithely stepping into a moonlit world after an evening of conviviality and immediately vowing never again to allow their favourite tipple past their lips. This was one church we found open, but only because preparations were being made for a wedding.

Sundial at Marston.

Approximately a quarter of a mile south of the junction of the A1 with the B6326 is Shire Bridge over Shire Dyke, the boundary between Lincolnshire and Nottinghamshire. We are now entering Robin Hood country, according to tradition. The inhabitants of South Yorkshire have their own traditions.

A long mile west of the A1 along a byway from Long Bennington is the site where the Three Shire Oak grew, this being the spot where Lincolnshire meets the boundary between Nottinghamshire and Leicestershire. Nearby is the pretty village of Staunton-in-the-Vale, the vale being that of Belvoir.

If you continue south from the Three Shire Oak you will find the large village of Bottesford in the heart of the Vale of Belvoir, overlooked by Belvoir Castle. The link is more than just the view. The Lords of Belvoir have always had an affection for the village and especially the spired Church of St. Mary where eight earls have been laid to rest. The parishioners must negotiate the monumental splendour to take their places in the pews. The practice is no longer current, which is perhaps as well.

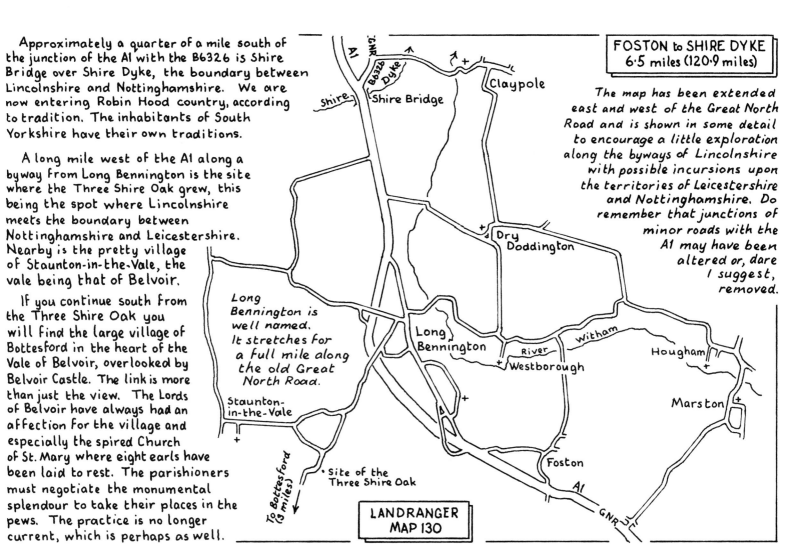

FOSTON to SHIRE DYKE
6·5 miles (120·9 miles)

The map has been extended east and west of the Great North Road and is shown in some detail to encourage a little exploration along the byways of Lincolnshire with possible incursions upon the territories of Leicestershire and Nottinghamshire. Do remember that junctions of minor roads with the A1 may have been altered or, dare I suggest, removed.

Long Bennington is well named. It stretches for a full mile along the old Great North Road.

LANDRANGER MAP 130

Site of the Three Shire Oak

To Bottesford (3 miles)

NEWARK

Situated at a significant crossroads, where the road from the south encountered the Fosse Way and the barrier of the River Trent, Newark enjoyed the title "Key to the North" even before the Normans arrived. It was the Saxons who named the town Newerche (New Work – "Work" being a defensive enclosure) which suggests that there must already have been established some kind of defence or settlement on the site.

William the Conqueror gave Newark and its environs to the Bishop of Lincoln whose successors built the castle and planned the town within a line of defences that enclosed the present central area. If you walk from the river along Lombard Street, branch north at Carter Gate to Appleton Gate and turn back towards the river at The Mount you will be approximately tracing a medieval perimeter which contained the market place and the splendid church of St. Mary Magdalen, 222ft. long, with its memorable 237ft. spire. Such impressive architecture reflects the wealth that wool brought in the middle ages.

The Olde White Hart.

The castle has an imposing river frontage where the western curtain wall largely survives despite slighting after the Civil War. It continues on the north to connect with the gatehouse. Though little else remains it is easy to appreciate the castle's position of strength at the river crossing, indeed the gateway to northern Britain.

By the 18th. century Newark held an important position on the North Road with coaching inns to cater for travellers and increasing trade. As you wander round the town note especially the White Hart, in the corner of the market place, with lines of terracotta saints on the studs of its 15th. century framework. But there is so much more to see. We found Newark fascinating, always ready to surprise, for just as you decide that modern development has much to answer for there comes yet another revelation to lead you further. This is not a town to pass in a hurry.

The Queen's Head.

The A1 bypass disguises the complexities of the River Trent, conveying the unsuspecting motorist north without knowledge of the problems that this crossing held for an earlier generation of travellers.

There had been a ford at Newark since before recorded history and the earliest documented bridge was already some 350 years old when it was swept away by floods in 1486. Its replacement served well - with occasional reconstruction and necessary repairs - until the present late 18th. century bridge was built.

The river flowing beside the castle is a branch navigation. The Trent proper takes a more northerly course, spanned by a bridge at South Muskham, making an island which is traversed by the Great North Road.

The route over this low-lying area was subject to regular flooding so that it was quite easy for travellers to lose the line and ride off the road when it was under water. John Smeaton was commissioned to devise a causeway between the bridges and this was completed in 1770. Daniel Defoe was impressed by this feat of civil engineering: "the greatest of the kind ever executed in England." It still serves local traffic well.

LANDRANGER MAP 121

BALDERTON
to SOUTH MUSKHAM
6.2 miles (127.1 miles.)

B6325 GNR.
A1
A616
South Muskham
Winthorpe
A46 To Lincoln
River Trent
A17
Great North Road
A46
Foss Way
B6166
A617
A46
B6166
To A17
River Devon
NEWARK -ON -TRENT
New Balderton
B6326
Balderton
A1
GNR.
B6326

Newark-on-Trent is the full title but the author has never met anyone who habitually used anything other than plain Newark.

The A616 leads to Ollerton, Edwinstowe and the Sherwood Forest Country Park. (See next page.)

Not surprisingly the barrier of the Trent was of great strategic importance during the Civil War, control of both bridges being fiercely contested. Scottish troops threw up an earthwork near the Muskham bridge and with a touch of nationalistic fervour called it Edinburgh. (Or were they merely homesick?)

LINCOLN

A visit to Lincoln should be on everyone's itinerary - one of our finest cities is so easily missed in the headlong rush along the A1. It rests on a limestone ridge some 200 feet above the Lincolnshire plain. This was chief of the Five Boroughs of Danelaw and later the Normans appreciated its importance - but much earlier than this the Romans recognised its defensive position and established a fort. They brought Ermine Street through Lincoln where Newport Arch is the only Roman gateway bridging a currently used English public road.

Lincoln is worth a visit for the sake of its cathedral alone. Only York Minster and St. Paul's are larger. Walk through the Exchequer Gate and be inspired by the West Front. Go inside and be enthralled by the magnificence of its architecture. Do not forget to contribute to its upkeep. And go on, be an imp. Buy the guide. It's worth every penny!

Lincoln may also be remembered for its castle, for many other old buildings, and the fact that its museum has a copy of Magna Carta, one of only four. Only the supremely fit will forget Lincoln's Steep Hill. But boldly confront the challenge and experience history in the form of fine timber framed buildings.

Newport Gate.

SHERWOOD FOREST

From Lincoln it is possible to see Sherwood Forest on a clear day. In the 13th. century you would have seen 200 times as much of the "Shire Wood" and most of the intervening ground would have been woodland too. Sherwood was a Royal Forest, much favoured by King John - he died in Newark Castle - and you will find the ruins of King John's Palace at Clipstone, used as a hunting lodge when he was enjoying sport at the expense of the local deer. Nearby, find the 19th. century Archway Lodge with carved figures representing the heroes of legend.

As you travel the A616 to Ollerton watch for the signpost, right, to Laxton and make a detour along this byway. Nowhere else in the land will you find a village that retains and displays its medieval origins as does Laxton. The Enclosure Acts did not touch this tiny part of England and its three great medieval open fields are still farmed as in days even before the Normans arrived.

Strip farming in Laxton is true living history. The stories of Robin Hood are legend, perhaps based on elements of truth, but undocumented and therefore suspect. Yet you cannot enter Sherwood and ignore the fabled outlaw and his merry band. Find out about Robin and the rest of Sherwood's story at the Country Park and Visitor Centre, Edwinstowe, before heading north along the A614.

> At Newark a decision will have to be made:-
> 1. Continue north.
> 2. Take the A616 to Sherwood.
> 3. Follow the A46 to Lincoln.
> If in doubt, postpone the initial option and agonise over the two on this page.

These few miles are dominated by the River Trent, the railway and the Great North Road, all major arteries for transport. The villages of North Muskham, Cromwell, Carlton-on-Trent and Sutton on Trent are now closely by-passed by the A1 but in their day were bustling places astride a busy road.

The river is tidal to the lock at Cromwell and the low lying ground has resulted in the Trent changing its course in the past. In the 16th. century Holme was on the west bank but movement of the river did not isolate it from North Muskham because the communities were enterprising enough to construct a ford which allowed carriages to cross in up to four feet of water. When the river was deepened to improve navigation this and other fords were lost although many were replaced by ferries. The ferry between Holme and North Muskham continued until the Second World War.

Near Cromwell the Romans had a bridge. The bases of the piers survived until 1884 when the river was deepened. At the time of writing Cromwell had a privately owned museum of dolls and childhood accommodated in the Old Rectory.

Carlton-on-Trent is memorable for its old smithy with an outsize horseshoe designed in brick relief around the entrance. The blacksmith held an essential position on the coach road and here lived one who believed in the power of advertising. The old coaching house, the Bell, is now Park Farmhouse.

The Trent is third in length of English rivers, made navigable from the sea to Burton-on-Trent in the 18th. century, with sea-going vessels transhipping goods at Gainsborough. There is still traffic along the river but with only a shadow of its former share of trade. Why must we suffer roads that are choked with traffic and fumes alongside a river virtually designed by nature to carry unlimited loads, its potential wasted?

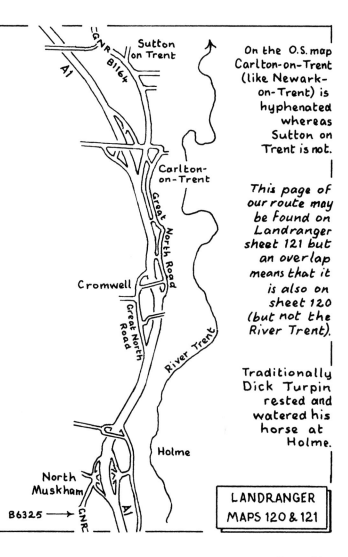

On the O.S. map Carlton-on-Trent (like Newark-on-Trent) is hyphenated whereas Sutton on Trent is not.

This page of our route may be found on Landranger sheet 121 but an overlap means that it is also on sheet 120 (but not the River Trent).

Traditionally Dick Turpin rested and watered his horse at Holme.

LANDRANGER MAPS 120 & 121

PLAGUE AND THE GREAT NORTH ROAD

The village of East Markham was not always on its present site. An outbreak of the plague in 1609 resulted in the deaths of 115 people, over a quarter of the population. The survivors rebuilt their village north of the church, the site of the medieval settlement being indicated by the irregular surface of adjacent fields.

The Black Death swept the known world between 1346 and 1351, reaching England in 1348. There were further epidemics, including the Great Plague of London in 1665, until the disease died out in Britain in the 19th. century as we became aware of cause and methods of control. This pestilence is transmitted by fleas found on rats, particularly black house rats which come into greater human contact than the shyer brown sewer rats, and is carried by these vermin and their parasites in grain ships and other forms of transport and various goods in transit.

There seems little doubt that the Great North Road, along with other roads, played a significant role in the spread of the plague in England. The scourge reached the tragic Derbyshire "Plague Village" of Eyam in a package of textiles from London. The recipient, a tailor, found the cloth to be damp and dried it before a fire. Within a few days he was taken ill and died shortly afterwards. East Markham must have been stricken in much the same way.

The symptoms of this fearful disease are well described in the apparently innocuous little nursery rhyme, "Ring-a-ring o'roses,"

Ring-a-ring o'roses - the rash and spots that disfigure the skin.
A pocketful of posies - pomanders of herbs, a supposed disinfectant.
Atishoo, atishoo - shivering, sickness, sneezing, symptoms as of a chill.
All fall down - death!

Half a dozen miles from East Markham we find that East Retford's church register noted a prescription of Thomas Gylby (vicar 1701-1751): "In ye time of ye plague, let the person either infected or fearful of ye infection take a pennyworth of dragon water, a pennyworth of oyle olive, Mithrodate 1d. and treacle 1d., then take an unyon and fill it full of pepper, w'n you have scraped it, then roast it and after that put it to ye liquor and strain and drink it in ye morning, and if you take ye same at night lay soap and bay salt to your feet and sweat upon it and with God's blessing you shall recover." Perhaps an example of faith healing?!

Tuxford Windmill.

Old lockup, Tuxford.

The B1164 is the Great North Road. The proximity of the A1 and the main line railway in a panorama of electricity pylons does much to suggest a working landscape. Indeed, four sets of power lines cross our road between Sutton and Tuxford. Yet if you can exclude this workaday world from your mind there is much to please. Try to call at Sutton, Weston and Tuxford, elements in a string of interesting villages north of Newark. Tuxford qualifies as a town and has a tiny brick lockup of 1823, a warning to troublesome travellers. Weston's church with its needle-sharp spire takes the eye from afar but you lose sight of it as you pass through the small avenue of close-packed yews leading to the door!

Apart from the need to cross and re-cross the A1 at Tuxford and Markham Moor, our route steers a line well clear of that modern upstart from Sutton until past Adwick le Street. Here we ride the historic way through Retford and Doncaster. However, you will need to join the juggernauts if you have your sights set on Clumber. Take to the A1 at Markham Moor and in half a dozen miles you can meet up with the defectors to Sherwood as they return to the fold along the A614 from Ollerton and Edwinstowe.

The yews at Weston are youngsters. It is said that yews were always grown in churchyards to provide a ready source of wood for the archer's bow. This may be true but many are so old that they predate the church, often marking an existing, pre-Christian sacred site. A register of the country's yews shows nearly 400 to be over 1000 years old and there must be many more. The oldest is Tayside's Fortingall Yew with a reputed 9000 year tag, exceptional maybe, but perhaps the oldest living thing on earth?

Markham Moor

West Markham

East Markham

TUXFORD

← A6075
To Sherwood Forest (9 miles)

Weston

Sutton on Trent

LANDRANGER MAP 120

CLUMBER PARK

Until 1707 Clumber Park was part of Sherwood Forest. It was then enclosed as a hunting park for Queen Anne. The first house was built some sixty years later when the river was dammed to make a lake. A century later the house burned down but its replacement lasted only sixty more years. 20th. century upkeep proved too expensive and in 1938 the house was pulled down leaving just the fine Clumber Chapel and outbuildings around the old stableyard at the centre of the present leisure facilities.

Clumber Park, now maintained by the National Trust, is a very popular resort for townsfolk of the Nottinghamshire region and is one of the Trust's most visited properties. Half of the parkland is forest, including commercial plantations, but there are 1,000 acres of managed woodland which provide a rich wildlife habitat.

For visitors the inevitable shop is always popular, as is the restaurant. Nearby are the walled kitchen garden, a tools exhibition and the Clumber Conservation Centre. Events include horse trials, open air concerts and theatre. There is plenty of opportunity for those who like to walk but, with nearly 4,000 acres to explore, perhaps the best way of getting around is by taking advantage of the cycle hire arrangements.

The lake at Clumber.

RETFORD

I grew up thinking of Retford as East Retford, a station on the line from King's Cross which told me that home in Leeds was getting nearer. But there is also a West Retford across the River Idle. The collective name of Retford seems acceptable.

If we wish to be true to the original Great North Road we should not be visiting Retford at all. In the early 18th. century the Old London Road passed two miles to the west, taking all the trade with it, but the good townspeople arranged a diversion by Act of Parliament in 1766. The 20th. century has now put the A1 four miles west, but that's another story.

Retford received its charter in 1246 and the spacious market square retains the vitality of a market town on Thursdays and Saturdays. Walk away from the bustle of the market along Churchgate to find the imposing Parish Church of St. Swithun. Not a great deal of the medieval structure remains but this building makes a striking contribution to the town centre – as, in a much smaller way does the church's defender, a Russian cannon captured at Sevastopol in 1855.

If you have time, visit West Retford and see St. Michael's Church where the tower and crocketed broach spire are joined with surprising originality. And lest the folk of Ordsall feel left out remember this village is a proud member of the trio that have come together as Retford.

As we pass along the Great North Road through Gamston and Eaton towards Retford it is worth reflecting that as ever, our route is not necessarily the one used by travellers of old. As noted on the facing page the 'official' route in use before 1766 was two miles to the west. This became known as the Old London Road but it is no longer an option available to us. Its early stages are now obscured by Retford Airport and although most of the rest exists as minor roads there is one section of about a mile (pictured above) that is hardly more than a farm track, though I have seen motorists who care little for the suspensions of their cars use it as a short cut between the A620 and the B6420.

The Chesterfield Canal was engineered by one of our finest canal architects, James Brindley, but much of the construction went ahead under the supervision of his deputy, John Varley, between 1771 and 1777. The canal linked Chesterfield in Derbyshire with the River Trent at West Stockwith, near the Nottinghamshire border, a length of 46 miles, including 65 locks and two tunnels, and like the re-aligned Great North Road a few year earlier it brought new trade to Retford. It was taken over by the Sheffield and Lincoln Junction Railway in 1846 but as the railways became more efficient it was allowed to decline. In 1903 the Norwood Tunnel collapsed so that Chesterfield was cut off from the Trent and the canal ceased to have any useful commercial future. The narrow-boats peculiar to this water were known as 'cuckoos'.

James Brindley

LANDRANGER MAP 120

West Retford

A638

GNR

Chesterfield Canal

A620

B6420

The Old London Road

RETFORD

MARKHAM MOOR to WEST RETFORD 6 miles (145.3 miles)

The Rivers Meden and Maun combine to form the River Idle. The Idle is Retford's river. Near the town centre it passes beneath the Chesterfield Canal which flows across a small aqueduct. Some ten miles further north, at Bawtry, this river becomes navigable through the Trent to the sea.

River Idle

Eaton

Gamston

A638

A1

River Rockley

River Maun

River Meden

GNR

Markham Moor

BLYTH

When the modern A1 moved west to join the Blyth road it acknowledged an historic variation. Blyth stands on what was a regularly used highway to London. Perhaps the eastern route through Scrooby developed to facilitate the mail coaches' need for speed. It is more direct. However, Blyth is by-passed by the A1 and retains its village character. There is a long village green to the south of which is the Hospital of St. John the Evangelist, built in the twelfth century for the care of lepers. It became derelict but was restored in the 1960s and is now in residential use. Blyth grew around the gates of an abbey and the Priory Church of St. Mary and St. Martin is based on the nave and aisles of that priory. It preserves a feeling for its Norman origins. There is a smaller green at the church gates where in 1988 was placed a fine carved wooden plaque to commemorate the 900th anniversary of the priory's foundation.

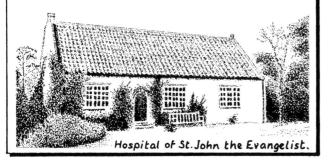

Hospital of St. John the Evangelist.

SCROOBY

This village is remembered in England and America as the place where many of the religious separatists who eventually settled in Massachusetts met in the home of William Brewster. The group was known as the Pilgrim Church and Brewster was a Ruling Elder. There is a tradition that Brewster lived at Manor Farmhouse and it seems most likely that he and many of his Puritan friends worshipped at St. Wilfrid's Church.

The Pilgrim Fathers found it necessary to leave this quiet corner of provincial England in order to find freedom to worship according to their own principles, first settling in Holland before moving on to America where, in 1621, they named the new colony after their final port of call before crossing the Atlantic, Plymouth.

Today's pilgrims are tourists who travel to, rather than from, Scrooby as part of a history tour which includes Austerfield and Gainsborough Hall in Lincolnshire.

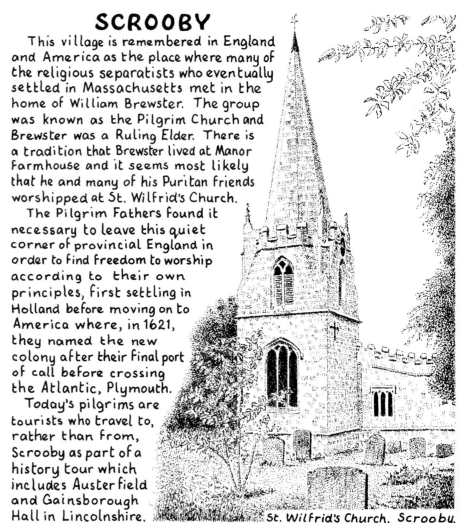

St. Wilfrid's Church, Scrooby.

From the time of Queen Elizabeth Tudor the office of
Postmaster General (or "Master of the Post Generall") had been
in use although the title appears to have been recognised by
statute only from 1657 when a Bill for settling the postage of
England, Scotland and Ireland provided for the establishment of
one General Post Office and one Postmaster General, appointed by
Letters Patent issued by the Lord Protector and his successors
(it being the time of Cromwell's Protectorate).

The early postal service came about to promote the relay of the
king's messages but, human nature being what it is, the temptation
to carry personal mail was great and messengers were willing to
accept commissions for private profit. On the basis of 'if you can't
beat 'em, join 'em,' provision was made for the carriage of
private mail and the Postmaster General and his deputies,
the postmasters, were given authority to carry all letters.

The first royal messengers would requisition horses as
necessary but it soon became obvious that a reliable supply of
fresh mounts would ensure a more efficient service. The post road
was divided by posts into stages and it was accepted for horses
to be stabled at these posts under the control of Post Masters
whose duties were to provide horses, employ riders and post-boys
on foot and to ensure a safe and speedy passage for the mails.
The new Act required remaining foot-posts to be superseded as
soon as possible by horsemen in relay who, by travelling round the
clock, could increase the daily mileage from about 16 to 120 miles.

Along this stretch of the Great North Road posts existed at
Tuxford, Scrooby and Doncaster and in the early years of the
17th. century the Master of Posts for this stage was one William
Brewster, who had taken over the duties from his father. If Brewster's
claim to fame had depended upon his postal duties, efficient
though he may have been, it is highly unlikely that we would know
his name today; but William joined the Separatist movement
and helped to found the local congregation of the Pilgrim Church.

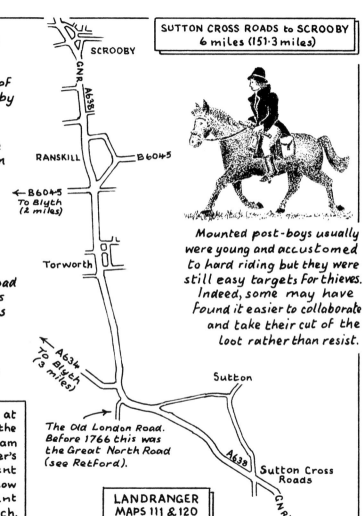

SUTTON CROSS ROADS to SCROOBY
6 miles (151·3 miles)

SCROOBY

GNR.
A638

RANSKILL — B6045

← B6045
To Blyth
(2 miles)

Torworth

↖ A634
To Blyth
(3 miles)

The Old London Road.
Before 1766 this was
the Great North Road
(see Retford).

Sutton

Sutton Cross
Roads

A638

GNR.

LANDRANGER
MAPS 111 & 120

Mounted post-boys usually
were young and accustomed
to hard riding but they were
still easy targets for thieves.
Indeed, some may have
found it easier to collaborate
and take their cut of the
loot rather than resist.

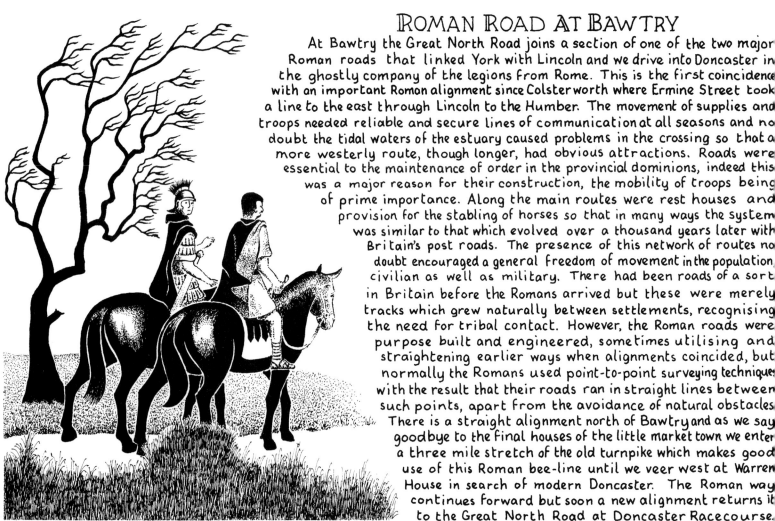

ROMAN ROAD AT BAWTRY

At Bawtry the Great North Road joins a section of one of the two major Roman roads that linked York with Lincoln and we drive into Doncaster in the ghostly company of the legions from Rome. This is the first coincidence with an important Roman alignment since Colsterworth where Ermine Street took a line to the east through Lincoln to the Humber. The movement of supplies and troops needed reliable and secure lines of communication at all seasons and no doubt the tidal waters of the estuary caused problems in the crossing so that a more westerly route, though longer, had obvious attractions. Roads were essential to the maintenance of order in the provincial dominions, indeed this was a major reason for their construction, the mobility of troops being of prime importance. Along the main routes were rest houses and provision for the stabling of horses so that in many ways the system was similar to that which evolved over a thousand years later with Britain's post roads. The presence of this network of routes no doubt encouraged a general freedom of movement in the population, civilian as well as military. There had been roads of a sort in Britain before the Romans arrived but these were merely tracks which grew naturally between settlements, recognising the need for tribal contact. However, the Roman roads were purpose built and engineered, sometimes utilising and straightening earlier ways when alignments coincided, but normally the Romans used point-to-point surveying techniques with the result that their roads ran in straight lines between such points, apart from the avoidance of natural obstacles. There is a straight alignment north of Bawtry and as we say goodbye to the final houses of the little market town we enter a three mile stretch of the old turnpike which makes good use of this Roman bee-line until we veer west at Warren House in search of modern Doncaster. The Roman way continues forward but soon a new alignment returns it to the Great North Road at Doncaster Racecourse.

BAWTRY'S market day is Sunday which tends to have the effect of making the place as busy on the Sabbath as on a weekday, quite understandable in a popular tourist centre such as York but here it is unexpected. Seekers of antiques will find something to interest them in the small Antique Centre. Though the A1 is now the A1(M), which passes nearly four miles to the west, Bawtry remains a busy focus for traffic with six A-class roads converging on the High Street. The A638 is the Great North Road and remains the direct route between Retford and Doncaster; in the old days High Street was where the coaches paused to avail themselves of the facilities provided by a number of coaching inns.

AUSTERFIELD, a mile from Bawtry, is the birthplace of William Bradford who was baptised in the local church in 1590. He was 23 years younger than William Brewster who, as a young man, he joined in the congregation at Scrooby. Bradford became Governor of Plymouth Plantation in America and it was he who provided the main documentation of the lives and movements of the Pilgrim Fathers.

Travellers who are interested in tracing the locations of the Pilgrim Fathers may opt to visit GAINSBOROUGH OLD HALL, some twelve miles to the east. The most convenient way of including Gainsborough in the itinerary is to take the A620 from Retford and rejoin the North Road by way of the A631, only a long mile north of Scrooby should you wish to go there. Gainsborough Old Hall is set amongst undistinguished modern housing but would certainly be worth a visit even without the Pilgrim connections and permanent exhibition. This large timber framed house was built in the late 15th. century. The great hall is superb and the original kitchens provide a window upon the servant's life in the late medieval period. Check with Tourist Information: you may find your visit enlivened by one of the special events which are a feature of the house.

SCROOBY to ROSSINGTON BRIDGE
6 miles (157·3 miles)

As we enter Bawtry we enter Yorkshire and will stay with the White Rose county for eighty miles, more than a fifth of our total journey to Edinburgh.

The River Idle is navigable from here to the sea (through the River Trent).

LANDRANGER MAP 111

DONCASTER

The fact that Doncaster's historic roots go back a very long way is evident when you consider that its Market Charter was first granted in the thirteenth century by King John. The market remains one of the largest in the north, part outdoors and part indoors within the old Corn Exchange. Yet there is not much to see in Doncaster that is an obvious link with any medieval past, apart from street names in the central area where stands the huge, cathedral-like church of St. George, a design of Sir George Gilbert Scott, completed in 1858 on the site of a medieval church which had been destroyed by fire. Grey Friars Road reminds us that the Franciscans arrived in the thirteenth century; many of the street names include the element 'gate' which is a sure indicator of antiquity, hereabouts usually derived from the Old Norse 'gata' meaning street. (Old English 'geat' also comes out as 'gate' but would refer to a gap or a gateway.)

Doncaster's market is as handy for Lincolnshire and Nottinghamshire as it is for its own native Yorkshire folk. The town's importance grew with the industrial revolution for it sits upon the Yorkshire coalfield. More industry meant more people who needed more houses and quickly the older architecture was swept away. The Great Northern Railway soon challenged the Great North Road as the major link with the south and in Race Week roads and railway bring in the racegoers.

To those racegoers (and surely to a majority of non-racegoers too?) Doncaster in the second week in September means the St. Leger, the oldest of the classic races, first run in 1776, four years before the first Derby. The Great North Road passes the racecourse and provides a fine view of the grandstand which, although altered and enlarged, is basically contemporaneous with the St. Leger itself.

The racecourse viewed across the Great North Road, from the football ground car park. (The perimeter fence has been removed, without authorization from the management.)

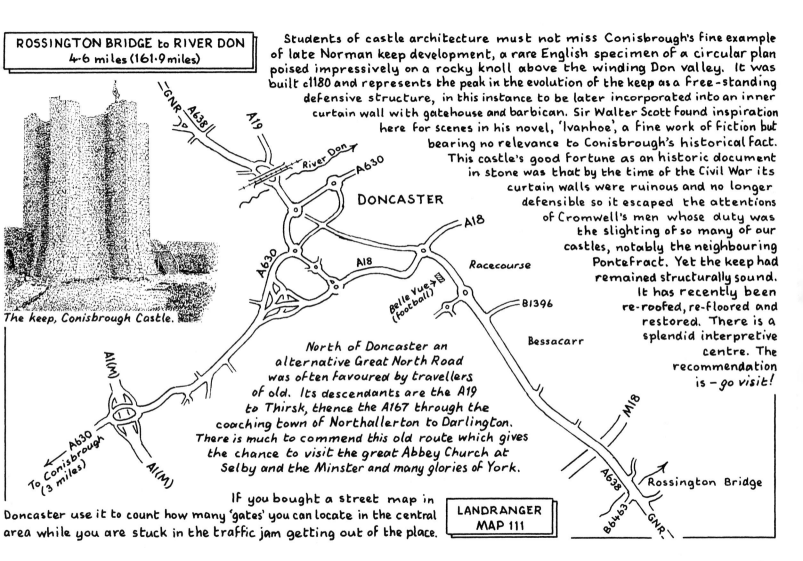

The keep, Conisbrough Castle.

Students of castle architecture must not miss Conisbrough's fine example of late Norman keep development, a rare English specimen of a circular plan poised impressively on a rocky knoll above the winding Don valley. It was built c1180 and represents the peak in the evolution of the keep as a free-standing defensive structure, in this instance to be later incorporated into an inner curtain wall with gatehouse and barbican. Sir Walter Scott found inspiration here for scenes in his novel, 'Ivanhoe', a fine work of fiction but bearing no relevance to Conisbrough's historical fact. This castle's good fortune as an historic document in stone was that by the time of the Civil War its curtain walls were ruinous and no longer defensible so it escaped the attentions of Cromwell's men whose duty was the slighting of so many of our castles, notably the neighbouring Pontefract. Yet the keep had remained structurally sound. It has recently been re-roofed, re-floored and restored. There is a splendid interpretive centre. The recommendation is – go visit!

North of Doncaster an alternative Great North Road was often favoured by travellers of old. Its descendants are the A19 to Thirsk, thence the A167 through the coaching town of Northallerton to Darlington. There is much to commend this old route which gives the chance to visit the great Abbey Church at Selby and the Minster and many glories of York.

If you bought a street map in Doncaster use it to count how many 'gates' you can locate in the central area while you are stuck in the traffic jam getting out of the place.

GNR
A638
A19
River Don
A630
DONCASTER
A18
Racecourse
A18
Belle Vue→ (football)
B1396
Bessacarr
A630
A1(M)
To Conisbrough (3 miles)
A1(M)
M18
A638
B6463
GNR
Rossington Bridge

LANDRANGER MAP 111

Brodsworth Hall

Brodsworth Hall and gardens were given to English Heritage in 1990 and opened to the public in 1995. Behind that statement lies a story of 18th. century legal caprice, Victorian aspiration and endeavour and 20th. century eccentricity.

The estate was purchased by Peter Thelluson whose unusual will was revealed to the world in 1797. After various bequests the major part of his fortune was to be held in trust to accumulate interest until his nine sons, grandsons and great grandsons had also died. Should there then be no one to inherit, the accrued monies were to provide help in paying off the National Debt! The will was contested, not surprisingly, but it was allowed to stand.

It was not until 1856 that the final grandson died and a court ruling declared that the fortune should be shared by two descendants, one of whom, Charles Sabine Augustus Thelluson, found that he now was master of Brodsworth. He thought it old-fashioned and chose to knock the place down and build a more up-date house, the one we have today.

Brodsworth Hall was a family home which survived with little change into the 20th. century. In 1931 it passed to Charles Grant-Dalton and his wife, Sylvia. After Charles' death Sylvia married again but became a widow once more in 1970 and continued to live there until her own death in 1988. Brodsworth had become Sylvia's responsibility. She lived for 56 years in a house that she never really took to her heart, struggling alone towards the end in her endeavour to fulfil a promise to keep the place going - a lady of character driven by memories and eccentric attitudes and determination.

The National Heritage Memorial Fund provided the finance which has enabled Brodsworth to retain the thousands of artefacts, from Victorian statuary and paintings to everyday objects, which mirror life in a family home over a period of 125 years. The increasing struggle against the odds in a situation of declining funds since the end of the war, when the house provided a billet for troops, led to increasing deterioration of the ageing grandeur of a once-great Victorian country house.

Although the house has needed extensive work to combat the ravages of time and the English climate, internally it has been preserved 'as found,' with only such attention as was needed to prevent further decay and to clean the contents. Herein lies its charm for the paying visitor. There is none of the untarnished perfection of renovation, just the lived-in clutter of a house that has been a home for over a century, with even evidence of the struggle to make ends meet. Look for the drooping wallpaper tacked back into place!

And don't forget the garden - it has charms of its own.

Brodsworth Hall.

You will find no water in Robin Hood's Well. The canopy was built to cover a spring presumed to have been used by Robin and his followers (in legend) when lodging in this part of Barnsdale Forest. It was designed, by tradition, by Sir John Vanbrugh who is decidedly more famous as the architect of Castle Howard and Blenheim Palace. The Earl of Carlisle may well have commissioned the tiny structure while Vanbrugh was engaged in his designs for Castle Howard (begun in 1701) but it is no longer on the site of the original well which was sealed when the spring became polluted by mining activity. The canopy was moved to keep it beside the highway where it presently sits on a lay-by formed by a loop of old road.

One ballad tells of the Bishop of Hereford and how Robin Hood *"took the Bishop by the hand and caused the music to play, and he made the old Bishop to dance in his boots, and glad he could so get away."* The oak around which the supposedly cavorted was between Robin Hood's Well and Skelbrooke.

Robin was native to the Forest of Barnsdale (let's assume he *was* based on a true historical figure) and he spent as much time in Barnsdale as in Sherwood's more famous glades. Here, between Robin Hood's Well and Barnsdale Bar (next page), we are in the very heart of Yorkshire's Robin Hood country.

Robin Hood's Well.

SCAWSBY to
ROBIN HOOD'S WELL
6 miles (167.9 miles)

It is worthwhile going on from Brodsworth to find Hooton Pagnell, an attractive village which straggles along the winding B6422 and is one of a chain of charming limestone villages shadowing the Great North Road in its progress across South Yorkshire. Hooton (the High Settlement) belonged to the Pagnell family, as lords of the manor, and indeed lies on a limestone ridge with the ancient All Saints Church keeping close company with Hooton Pagnell Hall.

Skelbrooke

Robin Hood's Well

SKELLOW
B1220

A638

A1(M)

Pickburn

Brodsworth

← B6422
To Hooton Pagnell (2 miles)

Brodsworth Hall

Site of Colliery

Line of Roman Road

ADWICK LE STREET

B1220

B6422

B6422

A635

A635

A1(M)

A638

GNR.

Scawsby

LANDRANGER MAP 111

Page 83.

PONTEFRACT

Most folk in West Yorkshire think of Pontefract in terms of coal mining and liquorice cultivation, both now largely a matter of history, but it would hardly cross their minds to offer the place as a tourist attraction. The castle? Just a few stones in a municipal park!

That may have been so for 100 years but archaeological exploration is beginning to reveal the real flavour of what must have been a truly magnificent fortress in its day. With knowledge of its history, it really should be visited. This was one of the great castles of the Middle Ages when the town could yet be styled by the name preserved in those liquorice sweets – Pomfret. For 250 years, until its demolition in 1649, it was a Royal Castle maintained as a stronghold and it still belongs to the monarch as part of the Duchy of Lancaster.

Pontefract Castle held a key strategic position where the east/west route through the Pennine Aire Gap reached the Great North Road and by the end of the 14th. century it was one of the chief administrative centres of the House of Lancaster, though Thomas of that line met his end here in 1322, beheaded in his own castle after defeat at the Battle of Boroughbridge. Richard II was held captive here until his mysterious death within the forbidding walls in the year 1400.

Medieval garden seat in the castle grounds.

Captives were brought for execution during the Wars of the Roses. Shakespeare's description, "bloody Pomfret", seems near the mark.

In the Civil War the castle three times faced siege tactics. After surrender in 1649 it was dismantled by order of Parliament, a decree supported by a petition from the townspeople of Pontefract who had had enough of its fearsome authority. It is significant that its very strength was its downfall - nearby Conisbrough was spared because it was no longer capable of defending itself.

Some of the Robin Hood legends are attached to Pontefract. It is told that he was first declared an outlaw here, accused of having taken one of the king's deer in the Forest of Barnsdale.

And in Southgate, Brother Adam de Laythorpe lived a frugal life in his two-roomed hermitage, a cell carved out of the solid rock and supplied with pure running water from an underground spring.

An impression of Pontefract Castle some 20 years prior to its demolition, based on a contemporary painting.

The A1 will hold little to delay you unless you wish to trace the old coach route through Wentbridge or pause at Darrington where the Church of St. Luke and All Saints attracted the attention of Nikolaus Pevsner who called it "one of the most satisfying village churches in the West Riding" (of Yorkshire). In the churchyard is an 18th. century dovecote.

The western variation can hardly claim to be tourist country, in the scenic sense, but there is much of historic interest in what was Yorkshire's coalmining heartland when the extraction of coal was still of real industrial importance in the United Kingdom. Mining is a difficult and dangerous business but, sadly for a population whose livelihood depended on it, the demise brought difficulties and stresses of a different nature for families when menfolk were made redundant.

At Barnsdale Bar the A639 branches away towards the north-west. This is the way the Romans marched from Doncaster to their fort at Castleford, a route which is occasionally obscure, notably where it is difficult to trace in the fields west of East Hardwick and especially when it is obliterated by the streets of Castleford. Otherwise the modern road tends to follow the same line. The route is named Roman Ridge hereabouts and for the colonists of nearly two thousand years ago it provided an alternative way north avoiding Ermine Street's crossing of the Humber. For those who wish to follow the tracks of the lads from Rome the route is shown on this and the following two pages until it rejoins the Great North Road at Hook Moor. All is plain sailing until you enter Pontefract at the top of this page where, despite any visual impressions to the contrary you will tread on ground known to kings of the land.

Outskirts of Pontefract

Darrington

Obviously, the village of Wentbridge took its name from the crossing of the River Went.

East Hardwick

Wentbridge

River Went

Roman Ridge

(Roman Road)

A639

A1

GNR

Barnsdale Bar

BARNSDALE BAR to DARRINGTON 5.5 miles (173.4 miles)

Apart from any Roman shadows lurking around Barnsdale Bar, the ghosts of Robin Hood and his Merry Men may also lurk amidst the equally spectral trees of the Forest of Barnsdale.

LANDRANGER MAPS 105 & 111

CASTLEFORD

Like Pontefract, Castleford is on the Roman way to the north; the name refers to their fort and the ford by which the River Aire had been crossed. Also like Pontefract, this is not a town that West Yorkshire folk regard as prime tourist territory and they may well be right! Coal and rugby have always been kings here and, with the cut-back in the mining industry, rugby has lost its consort. Together with neighbouring Featherstone the town provides a hotbed for Rugby League. In fact, when Featherstone's team has gone to Wembley the whole village has gone with it, and the same may be said of a large section of the population of Castleford when it is their team's day.

If you have taken the road to Pontefract you will touch down in Castleford, as did the Romans, but don't expect to see any remains. They are there, but beneath the ground. Industrial and residential development in the 19th. century went ahead with no respect for evidence of Roman occupation but, though modern redevelopment from the mid-1970s onwards has provided archaeologists with an opportunity to explore, Roman Castleford was re-sealed *in situ* for further investigation in the future.

However, archaeologists found a wealth of evidence to show that a major fort and *vicus* (small town) existed here. There are extensive remains of a splendid regimental bath house – and the granary, appropriately enough, is now beneath a supermarket. Roman Castleford (possibly *Lagentium* to the Romans) was south-west of the present bridge, which is 400 yards east of where the Romans crossed the river. Their ford, or bridge, was north of the parish church where traces of the road have been found. If you wish to know more, the story – as it stands at the moment – will be found in the town's museum.

Ferrybridge.

Tollbridge House.

The environs of the crossing of the River Aire look complicated on the map. Depart from the A1 and you will gain ample confirmation of this impression.

FERRYBRIDGE. The original bridge was of the 15th. century. The stylish replacement— now for pedestrians only—was begun in 1797 and finished in 1804, as dates on either parapet testify. The architects were Carr and Hartley. Traditionally, the foundations were set on bales of wool but this story may have been carried forward from the first bridge. The present A1 uses a functional structure of concrete.

At CASTLEFORD there is another grand old bridge, also by Hartley, built in 1804 when continuing need for repairs made it clear that the 14th. century bridge that preceded it had reached the end of its useful life.

The M62 links Hull with Liverpool and its crossing of the Pennines was the major British engineering achievement of its time. Notable among superlatives was the vast cutting at Deanhead where an entire hill was sliced through and deposited in the adjacent valley of Scammonden to make a tremendous earthen dam for a reservoir with the motorway sitting atop the embankment before diving under Britain's longest fixed-arch concrete bridge and through the deepest road cutting in Europe.

LANDRANGER
MAP 105

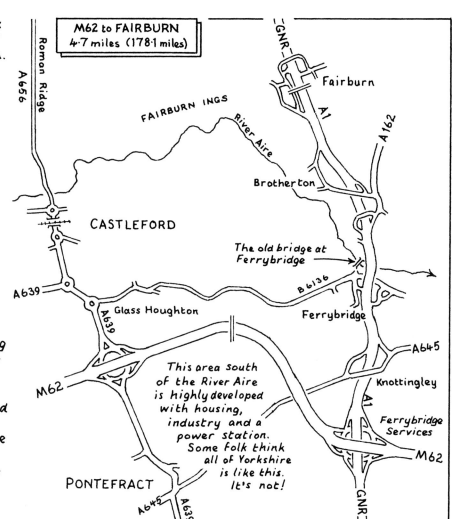

M62 to FAIRBURN
4.7 miles (178.1 miles)

Roman Ridge

A656

GNR

Fairburn

FAIRBURN INGS

River Aire

A1

A162

Brotherton

CASTLEFORD

The old bridge at Ferrybridge

B6136

A639

Glass Houghton

Ferrybridge

A639

A645

Knottingley

M62

Ferrybridge Services

This area south of the River Aire is highly developed with housing, industry and a power station. Some folk think all of Yorkshire is like this. It's not!

A1

M62

PONTEFRACT

A645

A639

GNR

FAIRBURN INGS

The area of small lakes and marsh reaching west from the A1 hereabouts looks natural enough to any casual observer whose eyes are drawn from the north/south highway by the glint of water. The names on the map seem to confirm this, for the common element in Newton Ings and Fairburn Ings refers to water meadows subject to seasonal flooding by an adjacent river. But these lakes are no longer seasonal. They are a permanent feature caused by modern mining subsidence, flooded by the River Aire. The shining mirrors attract migratory wildfowl and the Ings were declared a nature reserve in 1957 and specifically a bird sanctuary, by statute, in 1968. Over 250 species have been identified at the site which is managed by the R.S.P.B. Access is restricted for obvious reasons but there is a small education centre which may be open to visitors, usually at weekends. However, most of the reserve is visible from the by-road between Fairburn and Allerton Bywater (with a lay-by at the waterside) or from a footpath along the eastern limits close by the A1, so that anyone with a decent pair of binoculars may observe and not disturb.

Canada goose.

LEDSTON

This is a village tucked away amongst a network of byways and dominated by the Big House. Ledston Hall has been steadily evolving for seven centuries, having started life as a chapel, the undercroft of which remains. When Henry VIII dissolved the monasteries the Witham family gained the site and, around 1540, began the building that a succession of Lords of the Manor have been extending and altering ever since. Henry, one of the Withams, is recorded to have been "bewitched to death" and Mary Pannell was accused and convicted – and executed within sight of the scene of her "crime", since when the spot has been known as Mary Pannell Hill. This area has had a recent history of coal mining. Ledston Luck Colliery, now closed, was just up the road but the long term history has been agriculture. In 1976 a group of archaeologists found a couple of skeletons near Ledston Hall, believed to be the remains of an Iron Age farmer and his wife, surely long term enough for most folks.

LEDSHAM

Restored doorway in Ledsham's Saxon tower.

Here is an attractive village only a mile from the dust of the A1. The parish church of All Saints is soundly based on a nave, chancel and lower tower of the eighth century which makes it one of the most important Saxon churches in England. The belfry is Norman, there are additions and alterations of the 15th. century and, of course, the Victorians made their own alterations. Nearby is St. John's Hospital, almshouses founded in 1670 but now modernised as retirement homes. Another building of note is Lady Betty Hastings' Orphanage, three storeys high with striking octagonal chimney stacks. Farm buildings and cottages of character help to make this a village worth visiting but there is little parking space. The advice is to park elsewhere and walk in, so as to retain the peace of a quiet rural Yorkshire community.

The River Aire springs from the pristine limestone filter of Yorkshire's much-loved Craven District hills but the crystal clear becks of Malham would be ashamed to acknowledge any relationship with the murky industrial watercourse that approaches the Great North Road at Ferrybridge. Nor does the River Calder bring much joy to the flow at its confluence upstream of Castleford, despite its infant stirrings in the peaty Pennine hills and moors to the west. Pity the poor North Sea, the eventual recipient of these waters. And yet the quality *is* improving. Fish now survive where life would once have been miraculous. The sight of anglers along these banks is testimony to change and the lakes of Fairburn Ings are certainly good enough to support a thriving population of finned and winged wildlife.

The direct line of the A656 tells its own story. It is known locally as the Roman Ridge. Some time ago a cross section was taken while the road was closed for repairs and has proved the name to be accurate - it has its foundations on a Roman road of the first century.

Micklefield was another mining community until the industry collapsed. There are two settlements here, Old Micklefield and the Garden Village of New Micklefield. Both are happy to have the A1 as a bypass.

Collectors of abbeys will happily make the ten mile journey east from Selby Fork. The abbey was founded in 1069; construction in stone began c1100. The fine west door is Norman, the chancel has an east window which retains a quarter of its 1330 glass, the nave was built over a span of 100 years and shows a progression of styles from Norman to Early English. Certainly worth a visit.

LANDRANGER
MAP 105

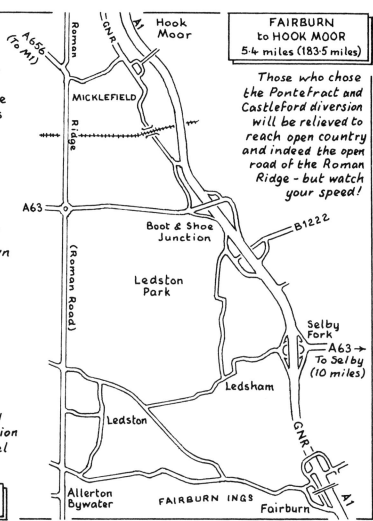

FAIRBURN
to HOOK MOOR
5·4 miles (183·5 miles)

Those who chose the Pontefract and Castleford diversion will be relieved to reach open country and indeed the open road of the Roman Ridge - but watch your speed!

ABERFORD

Here we are in limestone country and Aberford is a typical limestone village astride the coach road. An old inn displays evidence of coaching days in its stable yard with a covered entrance. However, the most memorable building in the village is a terrace of striking design, the Gascoigne Almshouses. The ornate assembly of gables, pinnacles and a central tower is quite austere in appearance as seen across the greensward flanking the Great North Road. This extravagance of Gothicism was built in 1844 by the Gascoignes of Parlington and Lotherton. The gatehouse, on the left, is a miniature in the same style. Aberford's stream, the Cock Beck, divides the village as it flows placidly towards its date with history at Towton. Cock Beck had an even earlier rendezvous with warfare. West of Aberford are the earthworks of Becca Banks which take advantage of the natural slope above the stream and are believed to be defensive in nature and of Iron Age date. There are further entrenchments east of the village.

The Gascoigne Almshouses.

BRAMHAM

Here is another charming village of limestone but whereas Aberford straddles the Great North Road as an informal linear community, west of the A1, Bramham spreads casually to the east of the modern dual carriageway. An unusual feature is the churchyard which is oval in plan so that the O.S. symbol for a church with a spire stares from the sheet like Cyclops in this odyssey of the Great North Road. West from the A1 is Bramham Park where the house defies local geology by being of sandstone. The 18th. century mansion and its French style gardens are open to the public during the summer months.

LOTHERTON HALL

The house, in its present form, was built in the 1890s. The original was purchased by the Gascoignes of Parlington in 1825 but the family did not transfer their affections to Lotherton for seventy years, after which they allowed the older house to fall into decay. It has now been demolished. In 1968 Lotherton was presented as a gift to the City of Leeds and is maintained as house, grounds, deer park and bird garden, open to the public. There is a Norman chapel beside the hall which, though restored in 1917, is worth a visit in its own right.

Lotherton Hall.

Barely three miles east of Aberford on Palm Sunday, 29th. March 1461, there took place an episode in the Wars of the Roses that has been described as the biggest, longest and bloodiest battle in Britain's history - Towton. The convenient title, "Wars of the Roses," was coined by Sir Walter Scott in his novel "Anne of Geierstein" but there is little historic foundation in the symbolism of the rose in this intermittent series of campaigns during which the monarchy was contested over a period of some forty years. At Towton 60,000 or more men were deployed, approximately equally divided on either side. After the battle nearly half of them lay dead, 8,000 Yorkists and some 20,000 Lancastrians. The latter's heavy losses occurred when they fled and were trapped in an attempt to cross the little River Cock where bridges of bodies formed and the river 'ran red with blood,' both here and at Tadcaster where the River Wharfe provided a similar barrier to the routed army. A cross commemorates those who perished in the conflict.

If you choose to visit Towton battlefield you'll pass Lead Church, situated near the site of the deserted medieval village of Lead. This early 14th. century chapel is eighteen feet long with a small bell cote and is surely one of the smallest in the land. It is dedicated to St. Mary, sits in pastures and is reached by a short field path. Though no longer in regular use it is still a consecrated building.

Lead Church.

At the Battle of Bramham Moor, south of Bramham, the Earl of Northumberland (father of Henry Hotspur who had died five years earlier at the Battle of Shrewsbury) led a rebel army against the supporters of Henry IV in 1408. He was defeated, captured, tried at York and executed. This is ground of ill omen for the Percys - the third earl fell at Towton 53 years later.

The small town of Tadcaster is home to two breweries named Smith-John and Samuel. The latter boasts its claim to be the county's oldest independent brewery. Long may it remain so!

LANDRANGER
MAP 105

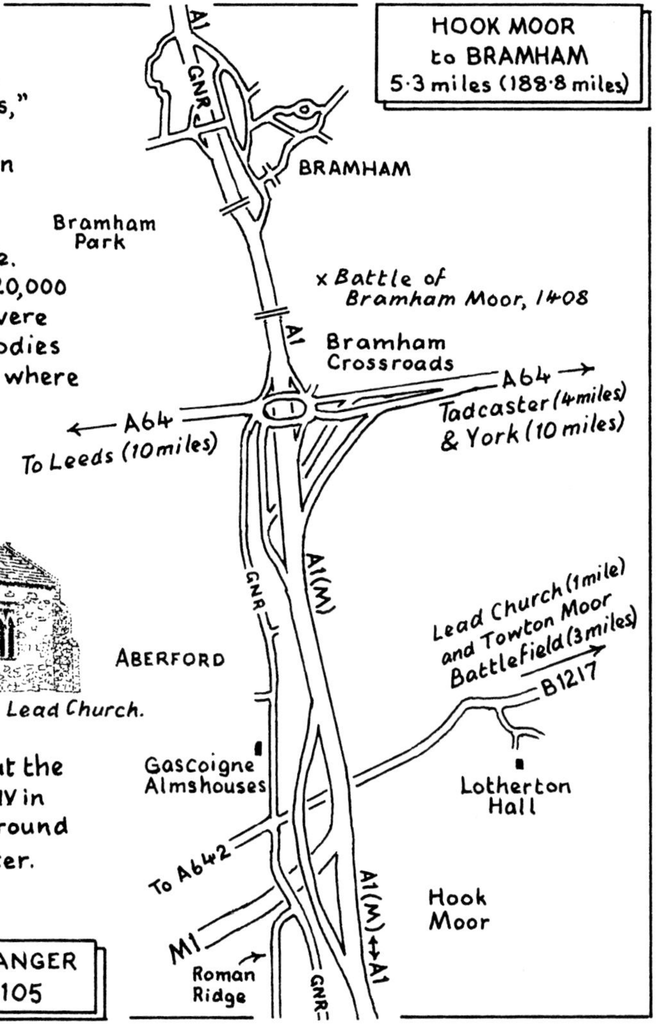

HOOK MOOR
to BRAMHAM
5·3 miles (188·8 miles)

BRAMHAM

Bramham Park

A1
GNR

x Battle of
Bramham Moor, 1408

Bramham
Crossroads

A64 →
Tadcaster (4 miles)
& York (10 miles)

← A64
To Leeds (10 miles)

A1(M)
GNR

Lead Church (1 mile)
and Towton Moor
Battlefield (3 miles)

B1217

ABERFORD

Lotherton
Hall

Gascoigne
Almshouses

To A642

A1(M) ← A1

Hook
Moor

M1

Roman
Ridge

GNR

THE CITY OF YORK

Why visit York? It is not on the modern Great North Road; but it was the destination of its Roman ancestor, Ermine Street, and the natural terminus of a major spur when medieval York was recognised as capital of the north. We can hardly pass so close to this magnificent city without indulging ourselves.

York's walls still almost enclose the ancient centre and two and a half miles of walking along this boundary are an excellent introduction to an extended stay. Within the walls is a web of narrow streets where every twist and turn reveals a new fascination. An archeologist can peel back the surface anywhere with optimism. The most famous example is in Coppergate where in 1976 excavations for a new shopping centre revealed remains of Viking Eoforwic (or Jorvik), a name which evolved into the modern York. The ruined streets of 1000 years ago are preserved in the underground exhibition of Jorvik Viking Centre.

Jorvik had used the same site as the Anglo-Saxons whom they replaced and indeed the Romans before them. This peninsular of land where the River Foss meets the Ouse was a fine defensive site with a good link to the sea for the transportation of goods by river. The early Roman fort of Eboracum was soon expanded to become a major fortress with a civilian vicus (settlement) outside walls which 800 years later would provide some of the foundations for the medieval perimeter we see today.

The walls are breached by four main gateways (bars, they are called) at the points of the compass. Micklegate Bar in the west was the main point of entry where, by tradition, all monarchs of England, except Henry VIII, have entered the city after travelling the Great North Road. Henry contradicted fashion by using Walmgate Bar in the south, the only gateway still retaining its defensive barbican. Monk Bar in the east is named after a monastery that once existed thereabouts and is the highest and best defended point of entry with a portcullis still in working order. In the north, Bootham Bar stands where the Romans had a gateway. If you have time for only a sample perambulation along the walls, choose the section between Bootham Bar and Monk Bar with its splendid views of the Minster and its environs. You will be walking where Roman centurions paced the perimeter of their great fortress. No Roman wall-work now remains here but you may seek it out in the museum gardens.

The Minster is York's crowning glory. The first place of worship to be built on the site was a wooden structure in 627 a.d. and here the bishop's throne (the cathedra) was set. It was replaced by a stone building which lasted for 350 years until it was destroyed by fire in 1069. The present church was begun in 1220, took two and a half centuries to complete and contains the finest display of medieval stained glass in Europe. See the Five Sisters Window in the north transept facing the Rose Window in the south; and the Great East Window holds the largest area of medieval coloured glass in a single window in the world. Though in fact a cathedral, this is historically a mission church which spread the Christian gospel and ministered to the surrounding region and for this reason has always been known as York Minster. It is the largest gothic church in England, showing a progression of styles to reflect the 250 years of its construction.

This page (this book!) could overflow with notes about places of interest worth visiting. Of so many consider the Guildhall by the river, the Merchant Adventurers' Hall, St. William's College, Barley Hall, the Castle Museum, the King's Manor and the tiny Holy Trinity Church off Goodramgate among the many religious houses deserving special mention. With the arrival of the age of steam York became a railway centre and you will find the National Railway Museum just outside the city walls. And see if you can find York's shortest street. According to local folklore Whip-ma-Whop-ma-Gate may have been a place where summary justice was meted out but its name lingers on long after the offenders have been forgotten.

Clifford's Tower.

Merchant Adventurers' Hall.

The Stonegate Devil.

The Shambles.

Micklegate Bar.

Walmgate Bar.

York Minster-
West Front

WETHERBY

At Wetherby the A1 is gradually creeping to the east as successive upgrades carry traffic ever further away but historically the Great North Road did not ignore the old market town. The approach from the south is over a bridge of six arches, two of which still contain medieval stonework. In 1378 pontage was granted to "the Good Men of Wetherby." Rights of pontage were often granted to those who built bridges to allow them to recoup some of the initial costs. In this case there was still a ford so, human nature being what it is, the payment was habitually evaded until after a year the Good Men decided that goodness and generosity did not necessarily go together and applied, successfully, for the grant to include the ford. The market charter was originally granted to the Knights Templar in 1340. It was never a large market but one of importance and it continues to be held on Thursdays in the small market place. The racecourse is beside the A1 and is one of the country's major venues for National Hunt racing. Wetherby was an important coaching halt on the road to the north but it was not until the early 19th. century that the village began to grow. Development had been hindered because the surrounding land was owned by the Duke of Devonshire, Lord of the Manor, but he chose to raise capital – to settle gambling debts, we are told – and in 1824 there was held the "Great Sale of Wetherby." From that time private owners were able to build houses and business premises and the town started to spread. Now, like many surrounding villages it is to a large extent a commuter community mainly serving Leeds and York; yet Wetherby remains proud of its own history and traditions.

BOSTON SPA

This village discovered its spa in 1744, originally Thorp Spa, the adjacent village across the River Wharfe. Until well into the 19th. century Boston Spa was plain Boston. Many of the finer houses date from those days when 'taking the waters' was the fashionable thing to do. Thorp Arch is smaller but it has its own village green and, at present, a claim to fame as home to the National Lending Library. A mile from Boston Spa, on the far side of the A1, is Dalton Parlours where a Roman villa was unearthed in 1854. An impressive tessellated pavement was found and is now in a York museum. The site has recently been researched but afterwards the remains were re-covered so don't go there expecting to see much more than green pastures.

Wetherby Bridge.

Once again we are close to the site of one of the significant battles of English history. At Marston Moor, half a dozen miles east of Wetherby along the B1224 (turn north at Long Marston) was fought one of the decisive campaigns of the Civil War where Cromwell's Parliamentarians broke the Royalist grip on the north and some 6000 troops died. A mile along the road leading from Long Marston to Tockwith an obelisk has been set up by the Cromwell Association. South of the memorial is a clump of trees on the skyline, still known as Cromwell's Plump and shown as such on the O.S. Landranger Map. This is the place where tradition has it that the Parliamentary leaders met to discuss tactics before the battle.

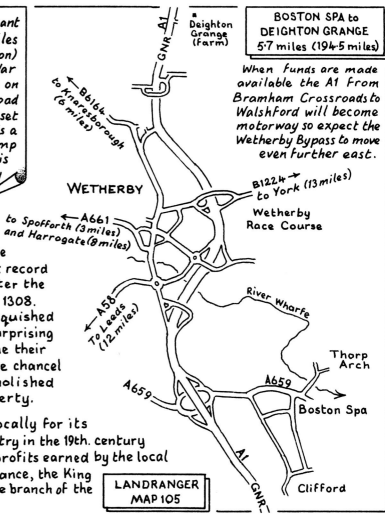

When funds are made available the A1 from Bramham Crossroads to Walshford will become motorway so expect the Wetherby Bypass to move even further east.

LANDRANGER MAP 105

SPOFFORTH. Collectors of castles may wish to drive three miles west from Wetherby along the A661 to find a minor example at Spofforth. It is a fortified manor house rather than a castle in the true sense of the term. The first record of a residence here places the original building soon after the Norman Conquest. Licence to crenellate was granted in 1308. It was renovated in 1559 but being small was soon relinquished in favour of greater castles to the north, which is hardly surprising for the owners were the Percy family and Alnwick became their main stronghold. The family coat of arms remains in the chancel of Spofforth church. Spofforth Castle was largely demolished during the Civil War. This is an English Heritage property.

CLIFFORD. This pleasant limestone village is noted locally for its splendid R.C. church. Clifford had a foot in the flax industry in the 19th. century and much of the money to build the church came from profits earned by the local mill, with contributions from the Pope, the Queen of France, the King of Sardinia, the Grand Duke of Parma and the Yorkshire branch of the Vavasour family. Quite an impressive pedigree!

ALLERTON PARK

On the eastern side of the road just north of the A59 are the grounds of Allerton Park where, perching on a gentle knoll, is the Palladian style Temple of Victory. It is believed to have been set up in the 1780s by Frederick, Duke of York, who owned the estate at the time. This was the duke whose inability to make firm decisions, particularly during the campaign against the French in 1793, gave rise to the satirical verse which generations of children have accepted as a traditional nursery rhyme. His Temple of Victory needed an artificial mound to set it above the surrounding parkland and folk like to suggest that this is the hill which the Grand Old Duke's 10,000 men spent their time marching up and down to no particular purpose. Beyond the Temple can be seen Allerton Hall. The Duke of York's house was altered and later, in 1848, largely rebuilt. By 1983 it was in a sad state of dereliction but was purchased by the American electronics millionaire Dr. Gerald Ralph who spent a fortune on its restoration. In the summer months it may be open to the public.

The Temple of Victory.

KNARESBOROUGH

"Blind Jack" Metcalf of Knaresborough, born in 1717, lost his sight at six years of age through smallpox but this proved no handicap to an adventurous life with the military and in commerce. His lasting claim to fame is in the design and building of roads and bridges in Yorkshire and Lancashire at the start of the turnpike era – for which he is noted here.

This market town, three miles west along the A59, has a much ruined castle but is better known locally for its Dropping Well and Mother Shipton's Cave. The former is a limestone petrifying spring whose calcareous content solidifies on a varying collection of old boots, teddy bears and the like which hangs below a small overhanging rock face to absorb a gentle trickle of lime-rich water.

Mother Shipton, who was born Ursula Southill in 1488, was a north-country Nostradamus whose prophesies included the Dissolution of the Monasteries and the accession of James I. She is also credited with foreseeing the invention of iron ships, aeroplanes, telecommunications and much else in the modern world – but there was considerable licence in later editions of her Prophesies, even the first not printed until nearly a hundred years after her death.

Knaresborough is a pretty place, nestling around a curve in the River Nidd where it cuts a deep gorge through the local limestone. The local guide book will tell you all about Blind Jack, the House in the Cliff, the Oldest Chemist's Shop; and everything else.

GREEN & KIRK HAMMERTON (3 miles east along the A59). It was once told that the Hammertons could ride from Bowland in Lancashire to York on their own lands all the way but their properties declined and in 1536 the family name was lost when Sir Stephen was hanged for participating in the Pilgrimage of Grace and his son Henry, last in the line, died of grief. The title survives as a placename in Green and Kirk Hammerton. At the latter is the church of St. John the Baptist which grew out of a 10th. century foundation originally dedicated to St. Quentin, which makes it one of England's oldest churches. It was altered in the 12th. century and enlarged in the 19th. century, yet the southern aspect is of a fine Saxon tower and nave (now the south aisle). At Green Hammerton the B6265 is Dere Street. This Roman road took over from Ermine Street at York (A59) though between Colsterworth and Boroughbridge neither equate with our own Great North Road.

The spa town of Harrogate, 7 miles west, was fictionalised by James Herriot as "Brawton."

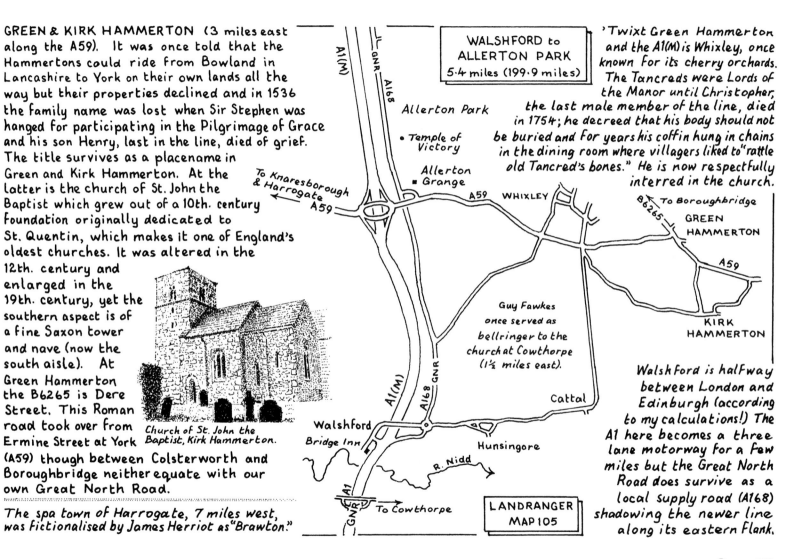

Church of St. John the Baptist, Kirk Hammerton.

WALSHFORD to ALLERTON PARK
5.4 miles (199.9 miles)

Allerton Park
• Temple of Victory
■ Allerton Grange

To Knaresborough & Harrogate
A59

A1(M)
GNR
A168

A59   WHIXLEY

Guy Fawkes once served as bellringer to the church at Cowthorpe (1½ miles east).

A1(M)
A168
GNR

Walshford
Bridge Inn

Cattal

Hunsingore

R. Nidd

GNR
A1
To Cowthorpe

LANDRANGER MAP 105

'Twixt Green Hammerton and the A1(M) is Whixley, once known for its cherry orchards. The Tancreds were Lords of the Manor until Christopher, the last male member of the line, died in 1754; he decreed that his body should not be buried and for years his coffin hung in chains in the dining room where villagers liked to "rattle old Tancred's bones." He is now respectfully interred in the church.

B6265   To Boroughbridge
GREEN HAMMERTON

A59

KIRK HAMMERTON

Walshford is halfway between London and Edinburgh (according to my calculations!) The A1 here becomes a three lane motorway for a few miles but the Great North Road does survive as a local supply road (A168) shadowing the newer line along its eastern flank.

BOROUGHBRIDGE

Here is another market town forsaken by the A1, which lures traffic towards the west. Yet Boroughbridge has a history which began at least 3000 years ago. Between the town and the A1 stand the Devil's Arrows, three lofty monoliths of millstone grit, the tallest reaching as high as 22 feet. A fourth failed to make the twentieth century, it having provided a source of stone for a nearby minor bridge.

Aldborough Roman Town (English Heritage) is along a byway on the eastern fringe and the remains include two mosaic pavements from a town house. Aldborough was a major settlement of the Brigantes, a powerful Celtic tribe of northern Britain and a thorn in Roman flesh until they came to uneasy terms with each other.

In 1322 Edward II was victorious in the Battle of Boroughbridge. The vanquished, Thomas Earl of Lancaster, was conveyed to his own Pontefract Castle where he was beheaded and his vast estates seized by the king – his cousin!

The Ure was first bridged by the Normans and in the 18th. century the river was considered wide enough to provide a trade route for nearby Knaresborough. The inns of Boroughbridge grew in importance until there were as many as twenty-two at the peak of the coaching era.

Today there is boating, fishing and pleasing walks beside the water. There is sense of the past to be found in the well-kept houses and in the cobbles of the old square surrounding an apparent market cross which is in reality a commemorative pump of 1875.

NEWBY HALL. On a visit to the south country we met a couple who enthused about a "house and gardens by a river somewhere near Ripon, the best stately home we have ever seen." This could only be Newby Hall. It is not the largest of houses but it has that indefinable quality of a home that has been loved and lived in by the same family for 250 years and, taken in conjunction with its gardens, is unforgettable. Here is a garden for all seasons whose cell-like structure has led to the comparison with Hidcote, though larger. Newby is halfway between Boroughbridge and Ripon. Whether or not you call at either you must not miss this home in its garden setting beside the River Ure.

The B6265 from Green Hammerton approaches Boroughbridge as a true Roman straight line. This is Dere Street on its way to the Roman Town of Svrivm (Aldborough). Beyond Boroughbridge the old Great North Road sits upon the Roman way. Dere Street came into being near the end of the first century a.d. as a supply route from York for armies occupying northern Britain, initially reaching into Scotland but mainly intended to provision garrisons along Hadrian's Wall. Our route is with Dere Street until Scotch Corner.

The River Ure, which we cross at Boroughbridge, rises in the high Pennines and carves the wide, green strath of Wensleydale – with Swaledale, the setting for so many of the James Herriot tales of veterinary adventure and humour. The curiosity is in the name. The old title of Yoredale was from an older spelling of the river's name but somewhere along the way Yoredale was lost and Wensleydale found. Wensley is a village on the tiny tributary of Wensley Brook, some way up the dale but proffers its name to one of the great valleys of the Yorkshire Dales.

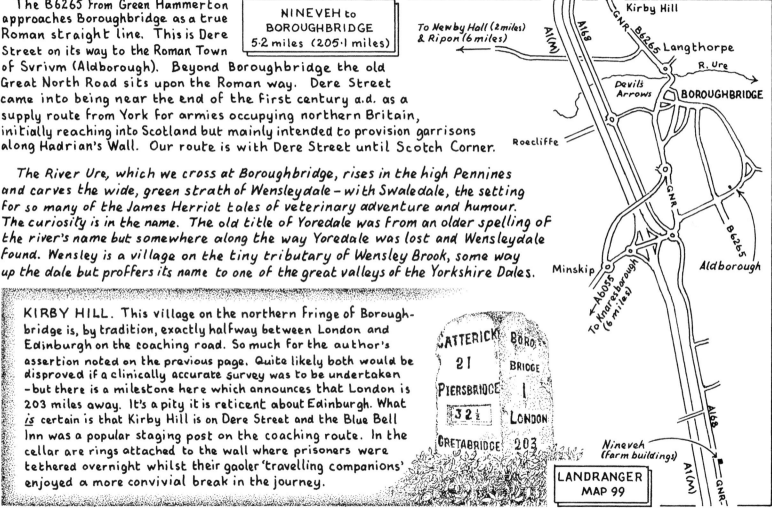

NINEVEH to
BOROUGHBRIDGE
5·2 miles (205·1 miles)

To Newby Hall (2 miles)
& Ripon (6 miles)

Kirby Hill

Langthorpe

R. Ure

BOROUGHBRIDGE

Devils Arrows

Roecliffe

Minskip

A6055

To Knaresborough (6 miles)

Aldborough

B6265

Nineveh (farm buildings)

LANDRANGER
MAP 99

KIRBY HILL. This village on the northern fringe of Borough-bridge is, by tradition, exactly halfway between London and Edinburgh on the coaching road. So much for the author's assertion noted on the previous page. Quite likely both would be disproved if a clinically accurate survey was to be undertaken – but there is a milestone here which announces that London is 203 miles away. It's a pity it is reticent about Edinburgh. What _is_ certain is that Kirby Hill is on Dere Street and the Blue Bell Inn was a popular staging post on the coaching route. In the cellar are rings attached to the wall where prisoners were tethered overnight whilst their gaoler 'travelling companions' enjoyed a more convivial break in the journey.

CATTERICK 21
PIERSBRIDGE 32½
GRETABRIDGE

BORO BRIDGE 1
LONDON 203

There is little to gain by staying with the Great North Road hereabouts unless fumes and traffic are your pleasure. If you have visited Newby Hall it is better to go forward to Ripon and Fountains Abbey. Rejoin the A1 along the A61 Thirsk road

RIPON

Ripon is distinguished by a cathedral built on the site of St. Wilfrid's minster of a.d. 670. The crypt of that original church survives below the present central tower - one of the earliest Christian places in England. This is not a particularly large church in cathedral terms but it makes the most of its 270ft length and has a stately presence that dominates this part of Ripon, being tightly contained by the road round its northern aspect. Approach from the market place to gain the full effect of the highly impressive west front.

The market place is large, rectangular and the focal point of Ripon, punctuated by the 90ft obelisk dedicated in 1781 to William Aislabie, for 60 years the local member of parliament. Much older is the Wakeman's house of the 13th. century where the Watchman lived with his wages paid by the householders who then expected complete recompense for any loss should they be robbed. The Town Hall of 1801 is inscribed with Ripon's motto:- "Except Ye Lord Keep Ye Cittie, Ye Wakeman Waketh in Vain." A 1000 year tradition is maintained each night when the Hornblower sounds a curfew for the mayor and at the market cross.

Fountains Abbey.

Ripon Cathedral.

FOUNTAINS ABBEY

These spectacular remains are three miles more beyond the A1 but should not be missed. The ruins stand in the exceptional park of Studley Royal where water features on the grand scale combine with mock temples, towers, banqueting house, grotto and other garden architecture, culminating in the abbey itself. Fountains Hall, begun in 1598, is Jacobean in style and its builders plundered stone from the abbey. A walk through Studley Royal's parklands will take time - but this is time well spent.

The abbey was founded in 1132 by Benedictine monks from York who sought to return to the basic principles in which they believed. They soon joined the Cistercian Order and after early years of austerity began to accumulate sheep farming estates across the north of England which became the basis of the abbey's wealth. Fountains Abbey is one of the finest and most important historical monuments in Europe and taken in association with its situation in the delightful glen of the little River Skell can hardly be bettered, certainly in England. It is owned by the National Trust but maintained by English Heritage.

As you drive back to the Great North Road along the A61 watch out for the first junction on your right past the River Ure, signposted Sharow. This is where the Rev. Charles Lutwidge Dodgson - better remembered under his nom-de-plume of Lewis Carroll - took the occasional holiday and met the little girl he later visualised as the best model for his Alice (of Wonderland fame). He brought a photograph of her to the notice of his illustrator, John Tenniel, though how far Tenniel used the likeness has been questioned. This young lady (not to be confused with Alice Liddell for whom the original story was written) was Mary Hilton Badcock, daughter of a canon of Ripon Cathedral. In Sharow, also, is the stump of Sharow Cross which is the last survivor of eight such crosses, all exactly one mile from St. Wilfrid's Minster and which marked the circle of sanctuary offered by the church.

Lewis Carroll.

Whilst in the region why not try some Wensleydale cheese? But certainly not the pre-packed supermarket concoction. A specialist will sell you the real, creamy, crumbly, honeyed cheese of the Yorkshire Dales, or even the piquant blue variety, if that's your fancy.

If you stay with the A1(M) you may note the junction at the end of the motorway section, signposted Thirsk (A168). This is the market town where the fictional James Herriot (in real life, Alf Wight) shared a veterinary surgery with Siegfried Farnon (Donald Sinclair). The old surgery is now a Herriot museum. Cricket enthusiasts may be more interested to learn that Thirsk is also the birthplace of Thomas Lord, founder of the headquarters of the game, Lord's Cricket Ground.

KIRBY HILL to
BALDERSBY GATE
5.5 miles (210.6 miles)

For travellers on the A1(M) Dishforth is an airfield but there is a quiet village hiding over a low ridge at the far side. It is now well and truly isolated by the vast Dishforth Interchange. Direct access is a thing of the past. You need to study the map to get there.

Baldersby Gate

(5 miles) To Ripon A61

GNR

Rainton

Rainton Services

A1

(11 miles) To Thirsk A168

Dishforth

Dishforth Interchange

Dishforth Airfield

Leeming Lane

A1 (M)

A168

Skelton Windmill

(5 miles) To Ripon B6265

A1(M)

A168

GNR

B6265

Kirby Hill

LANDRANGER MAP 99

An interesting collection of villages is divided by the Great North Road hereabouts, far more stimulating as an objective for exploration than the main highway. We have spent quite a few satisfying summer afternoons pottering about along these byways not so far from home, enjoying the pleasures of peaceful motoring with only local traffic to share the quiet lanes of the Vale of Mowbray (excepting the horrors of the A61). Use the O.S. map to trace a route and you may well find hidden corners not mentioned in the following notes. Houses referred to here are not necessarily open to the public.

WATH.
This village two miles west of the A1 can hardly have changed in centuries. The towered church has stone of Norman date. Nearby is the Jacobean hall of Norton Conyers, said to be the inspiration that gave rise to the house of Thornfield in Charlotte Brontë's 'Jane Eyre.'

KIRKLINGTON.
One mile to the west, the cottages are gathered around this village's green. The Church of St. Michael the Archangel has 600 year old origins; the Hall is not much younger and its mandatory ghost lurks behind a venerable gabled façade.

BALDERSBY & BALDERSBY ST. JAMES.
These villages are half a mile east for a crow fleeing from the noise and fumes of the A1 but for a mere human with the same idea some two miles of driving by way of the A61 is nearer the mark. Baldersby is a village linked to a great house but Baldersby Park (1720) is nearly another three miles south-east. Between them is Baldersby St. James whose soaring church spire is a landmark for miles around, its 160 feet high pinnacle a beacon to travellers on the Great North Road itself. Baldersby St. James is a Victorian estate village which, with its church, was commissioned by Lord Downe in the 1850s and designed by William Butterfield. This is, unusually, an example of Butterfield's work in the north, here listed for architectural merit and on the field study itinerary of many architecture students.

SKIPTON-ON-SWALE.
This settlement is a mile from Baldersby along the A61 and suffers the same problems of traffic on a busy route, here momentarily slowed by an old and narrow stone bridge from which there is no escape and from which cars are released like corks from a champagne bottle to the alarm of villagers beyond. Outside the Old Hall (currently a residential care home) is a cairn with a plaque beside a Canadian maple tree planted in memory of the R.C.A.F. squadrons who flew from the nearby Skipton-on-Swale airfield, one of whose bombers crashed on this site in 1944 with three fatalities.

PICKHILL.
It is hard to believe that this backwater village community once had an annual eight-day fair, was granted a Saturday market in 1307 and was a thriving village of shops and tradesmen until the beginning of the twentieth century. It is a charming place with a village green and a bubbling beck but it hides its charms on a loop of byway that leads to Pickhill alone.

The Church of Baldersby St. James.

Here the A1 is racing through the Vale of Mowbray centred on Thirsk, a wide and fertile plain between the Yorkshire Dales (west) and the North York Moors (east). The name is taken from the master of the lost castle of Thirsk, Roger de Mowbray. Two other ancient highways cross the Vale of Mowbray – the A19 to Tees-side (and beyond, to Tyneside) and the A168/A167 through the North Riding capital, Northallerton. Both are alternatives to the A1. The latter, less direct and single carriageway, possibly pre-dates our own route and it is fair to call it the Old North Road in Yorkshire.

At the junction with the B6267 we cross the line of a dismantled railway track, the Northallerton to Ripon and Harrogate line. Northallerton keeps its station because it is on the main line north; Ripon now has no railway connection at all. It is interesting to consider that the coming of the railway brought a steady decline in the public need for the stage coach from about 1840. In less than 50 years the coaches were out of business and it would have seemed that roads as major transport routes were no longer needed. But the internal combustion engine was invented. Now we have gone almost full circle; only main line rail routes are adequately supported and hundreds of minor lines like that to Ripon have vanished with only valiant railway preservation societies able to resurrect a few. One such group of enthusiasts is working hard to restore the Wensleydale line. We wish them every success.

The two national parks of the Yorkshire Dales and the North York Moors tempt the strongest willed of travellers so that only steely resolution or indecision over whether to turn east or west can be an excuse for continuing north. But if you do succumb, the finest way to get the flavour of such delectable country is to pull on a pair of boots and walk. Seek out the walking guides of Jack Keighley – they cover both areas.

LANDRANGER
MAP 99

BALDERSBY GATE to NEW INN FARM
5.2 miles (215.8 miles)

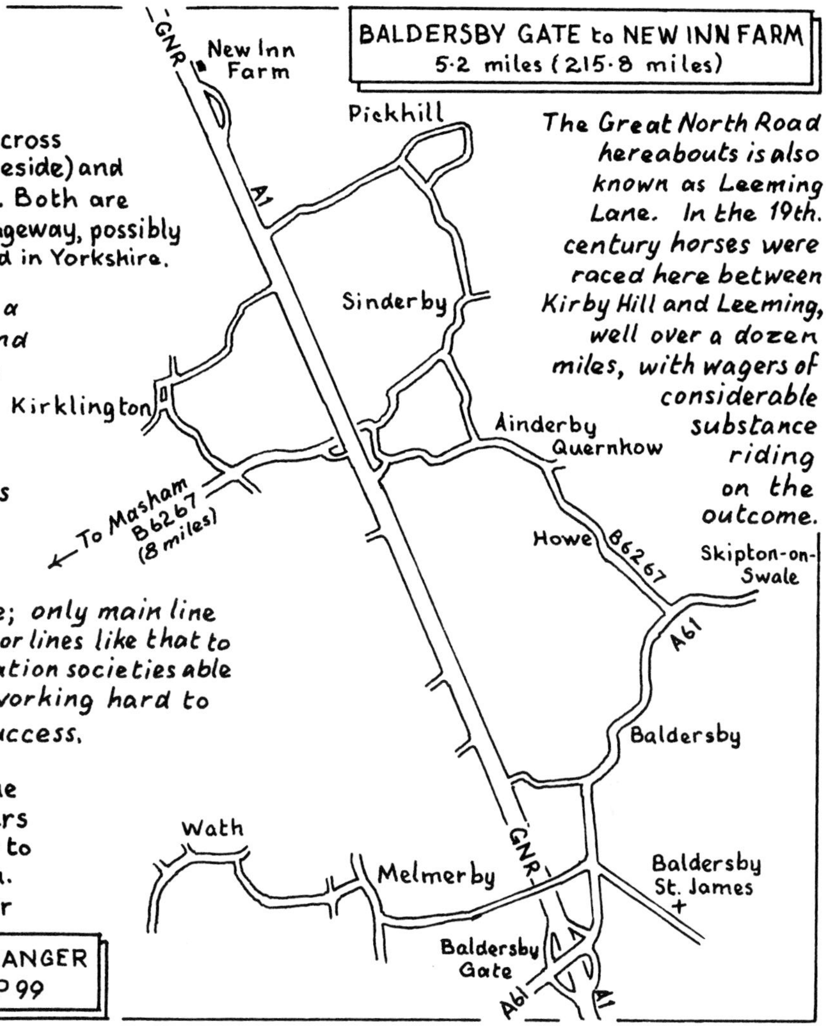

The Great North Road hereabouts is also known as Leeming Lane. In the 19th. century horses were raced here between Kirby Hill and Leeming, well over a dozen miles, with wagers of considerable substance riding on the outcome.

New Inn Farm
Pickhill
Sinderby
Kirklington
← To Masham B6267 (8 miles)
Ainderby Quernhow
Howe
B6267
Skipton-on-Swale
A61
Baldersby
Wath
Melmerby
Baldersby Gate
Baldersby St. James
GNR
A61
A1
A1

Bedale.

BURNESTON, SNAPE AND BEDALE

Leeming Bar is where the road from Northallerton into Wensleydale crossed the historic route to the north. But there is little to excite here so why not divert west through Burneston, Snape and Bedale? These settlements are generally thought of as being in Wensleydale but they are at the wrong side of an insignificant watershed; their streams feed the River Swale.

The battlemented church at Burneston has a neat tower crowned by a small witch's hat spire, like a big brother to the many pinnacles which decorate this delightful building. Inside is the squire's three-decker family pew. Across the road a row of almshouses, with a fine old sundial, faces a long red-brick barn.

Katherine Parr, the wife who survived Henry VIII, if only by a year, lived for a while at Snape Castle. The imposing building which is partly ruined, partly inhabited, has a restored chapel that now serves the village as a church.

Bedale's wide main street is the archetypal Market Place and the 14th. century market cross is its focal point. All roads in must negotiate this meeting of the ways.

At the top of the main thoroughfare, beyond the Georgian-style façades, Bedale Hall (now museum and council offices) faces the grand old church of St. Gregory, one of the gems of the Dales. The tower was a pele, a refuge against Border raiders. Portcullis grooves are visible in the doorway to the stair which gives access to the one time living space above.

In 1962 restorations revealed wall paintings which include St. George and the Dragon but the most immediately striking feature when you enter is the sense of light and upliftment. On a sunny day the range of clear-glazed windows in the Lady Chapel seems to bring the outside world of the Dales into the church. St. Gregory's alone makes this a diversion not to be missed.

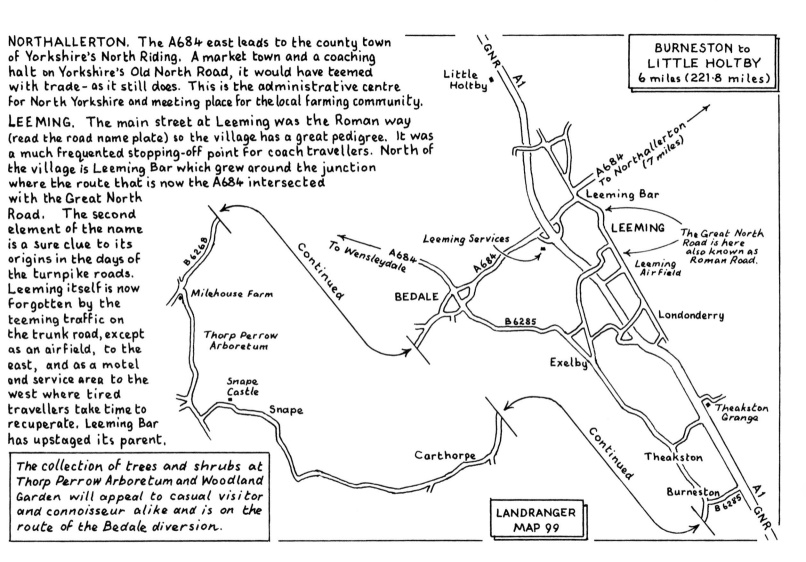

NORTHALLERTON. The A684 east leads to the county town of Yorkshire's North Riding. A market town and a coaching halt on Yorkshire's Old North Road, it would have teemed with trade—as it still does. This is the administrative centre for North Yorkshire and meeting place for the local farming community.

LEEMING. The main street at Leeming was the Roman way (read the road name plate) so the village has a great pedigree. It was a much frequented stopping-off point for coach travellers. North of the village is Leeming Bar which grew around the junction where the route that is now the A684 intersected with the Great North Road. The second element of the name is a sure clue to its origins in the days of the turnpike roads. Leeming itself is now forgotten by the teeming traffic on the trunk road, except as an airfield, to the east, and as a motel and service area to the west where tired travellers take time to recuperate. Leeming Bar has upstaged its parent.

The collection of trees and shrubs at Thorp Perrow Arboretum and Woodland Garden will appeal to casual visitor and connoisseur alike and is on the route of the Bedale diversion.

BURNESTON to
LITTLE HOLTBY
6 miles (221·8 miles)

Little Holtby

GNR · A1

A684 To Northallerton (7 miles)

Leeming Bar

LEEMING

The Great North Road is here also known as Roman Road.

Leeming Services

To Wensleydale

Continued

A684

A684

Leeming Airfield

BEDALE

Londonderry

B6268

Milehouse Farm

Thorp Perrow Arboretum

B6285

Snape Castle

Snape

Exelby

Theakston Grange

Continued

Theakston

Carthorpe

Burneston

B6285

A1 GNR

LANDRANGER
MAP 99

CATTERICK

The military presence at Catterick is well known – but that is Catterick Camp, nearly four miles west of the old village. The soldiers moved in soon after 1911 but they were only following the example of the Roman centurions who established a presence at *Cataractonium*, which became a substantial town on the line of Dere Street. That was beside the river, west of our own route and convenient for crossing the River Swale. Their bridge is, of course, gone but there are now three links, one the modern A1 span, the second a disused railway crossing and the third the historic Catterick Bridge used by the Great North Road. It dates from the 1420s but despite necessary repairs and widening the pattern of stone arches is unchanged. The strength

Catterick Bridge.

of the traditional design can be gauged by its performance in supporting the traffic of the main road until the A1 bypass was constructed and by the fact that until the alternative railway bridge was built in 1922 it also carried the railway track to Catterick Camp. What would the medieval masons have thought of the idea that rolling stock and engines of some 100 tons alongside cars and lorries would be supported by their handiwork 500 years after they had set their final stone? Long ago Catterick Bridge carried a chantry chapel where travellers could pray

THE RIVER SWALE occupies one of Yorkshire's most dramatic valleys, carved by glaciers in the last ice age, and with a reputation as possibly the fastest flowing major river in England. The upper reaches are deep, steep and remote with a hinterland of moors and fells where romantic ruins are in reality evidence of a harsh life in a long and grim history of industrial exploitation in search of lead, supplemented by subsistence farming.

and give thanks for safe passage on the bridge and along the road ahead after contributing to the alms box in which funds were collected for maintenance of bridge and chapel. Its ruins were removed in 1792 when the bridge was widened. This is also a natural site for a coaching inn and it is likely that an inn has accompanied the bridge since it was built. Catterick village is a mile south of the bridge and was an important coaching stop, well supplied with accommodation. It is a pretty place with three village greens. The racecourse keeps it on the map for followers of the turf but otherwise Catterick is invariably forgotten by birds of passage on the A1 bypass.

BROMPTON-ON-SWALE is not, strictly speaking, on the Great North Road but peripheral to it. Brompton grew up beside the Swale and the adjacent road (B6271). In fact the river has always been dominant as a force to be reckoned with especially in 1884 when one of Mother Shipton's prophesies (see Knaresborough) was realised: 'Brompton will wash away by Swale when God sees good.' Floods reached the upper storeys of riverside homes and roads were washed away.

This section of the way was a noted haunt of highwaymen. Coachmen hoped to gain a fair turn of speed along the straight and level line of Dere Street in their haste to reach the safe haven of Catterick but that would depend upon the season and the weather. Flat lands were always prone to mud and flood and to the coach driver's skill. The balance of the coach was a significant factor in ensuring a smooth, safe and swift passage and meant more than the careful distribution of goods and passengers. The rear horses, attached to the coach, (known as wheelers) had to be accurately paired for equal weight and stride to avoid pitching and rolling, otherwise accidents were likely if the speed was not checked; which would be playing into the hands of the 'gentlemen of the road'. It was all part of the coachman's craft. The fellow who excelled in his trade could give his clients a more comfortable journey with a better chance of getting them home intact.

A couple of miles down the River Swale from Catterick is Kiplin Hall, built by the founder of the American colony of Maryland in 1620. The First Lord Baltimore was granted by charter (in 1632) land that became one of the original thirteen states of the U.S.A.

If your car's wayward wheels should roll you into Bolton-on-Swale (two miles from the A1) look around St. Mary's graveyard and find Henry Jenkins' monument. His dates are: born 1500, died 1670: age 169 years! There is also a plaque within the church.

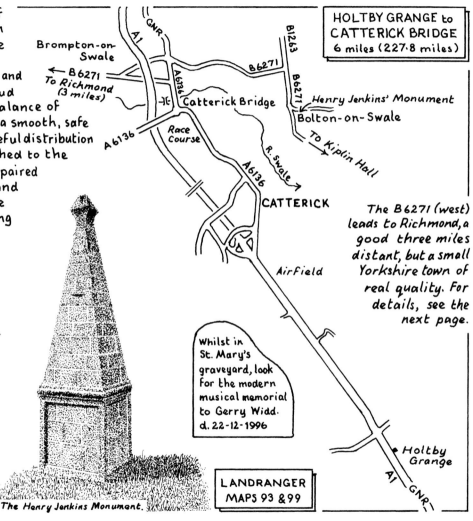

HOLTBY GRANGE to CATTERICK BRIDGE
6 miles (227.8 miles)

Brompton-on-Swale

← B 6271 To Richmond (3 miles)

Catterick Bridge

Henry Jenkins' Monument
Bolton-on-Swale

To Kiplin Hall

Race Course

A 6136

R. Swale

CATTERICK

A 6136

Airfield

The B6271 (west) leads to Richmond, a good three miles distant, but a small Yorkshire town of real quality. For details, see the next page.

Whilst in St. Mary's graveyard, look for the modern musical memorial to Gerry Widd. d. 22-12-1996

Holtby Grange

A1 GNR

LANDRANGER MAPS 93 & 99

The Henry Jenkins Monument.

RICHMOND

If the note on the previous page has tempted you to visit Richmond the chances are that you will arrive back at the A1 along the A6108 to Scotch Corner; otherwise it's not too late to change your mind for the town is less than five miles away. Richmond's charms are many. It is a castle town with a 100ft keep dominating a maze of streets and defending a large bailey above a wide sweep of the River Swale; but being set well away from the north/south communications axis of England, history has passed by and left it free from the discord of strife. Yet Richmond _is_ an historic town, deserving that tag infinitely more than so many of the 'historic' towns which countless signposts proclaim along the byways of England. The huge market place where cobbles still challenge the fashion shoe and where the medieval church is now a military museum is the hub of a complex of narrow ways and alleys. The gem hiding down Friar's Wynd is a splendid little Georgian Theatre, restored and re-opened in the 1960s after serving as a store for corn, for furniture and much else over the years. It retains its original boxes and gallery. Richmond's famous song was dedicated to Frances l'Anson in 1785. The 'Sweet Lass of Richmond Hill' was a Yorkshire lass from Leyburn who came to live here as a child at, appropriately, Hill House; there are hills a'plenty in Richmond.

On Richmond Hill there lives a lass
More bright than May-day morn,
Whose charms all other maids surpass,
A rose without a thorn.

MIDDLETON TYAS

We are only a mile from Scotch Corner but we might as well be in a different world. The road through Middleton Tyas is busy enough but it was never the Great North Road, just our chosen link with the old route. This is a village of byways with a couple of inns, two major houses and a church nearly half a mile distant along an avenue of lime trees. If you chance to stop here and go walkabout, look for the village wells.

The road through Middleton Tyas.

BARTON

The old road runs through the middle of the village, past the old cross, but the modern motorway has taken away much of the heavy through traffic. There is a 19th. century church, the old hall, a village green, the truncated cross and a picturesque footbridge across a winding beck with a shallow ford to accompany it — all the usual elements of the classic village scene. Barton is now commuterland to Darlington/Teeside.

The stump of the old cross at Barton.

SCOTCH CORNER & DERE STREET

The modern junction at Scotch Corner with its large scale roundabout over the A1 disguises the original crossroads where a choice of routes to Scotland was available – and still is if alternatives are needed. The A66 offers a road to Glasgow and western Scotland, setting out along a Roman alignment which branches from Dere Street here; or the Great North Road is the traditional east coast route; and there is a third way that leaves the A1 where the motorway begins, a good mile north of Scotch Corner, the B6275 – Dere Street – which connects with the A68 to lead over Carter Bar into Scotland. Dere Street continues the line of the north road straight and true out of Yorkshire's North Riding into Durham with few deviations until a mile beyond the A68 at the Royal Oak. Thereafter a little detective work with the O.S. Landranger sheets 99/88/87 is needed: for clues think of new alignments and consider Bishop Auckland (Binchester), Lanchester and Ebchester en route for Corbridge and Hadrian's Wall. Dere Street can further be traced into Scotland where it eventually reaches the Firth of Forth. Motorists can only drive short sections here but there are marvellous opportunities for walkers in the Northumbrian and Border Hills. Cars must turn left along the A68 through Jedburgh to Edinburgh (but near Corbridge the A68 and Dere Street do come together for a while). So you will see that Scotch* Corner is well named as the junction where you choose your route to Scotland.

*True Scots will tell you that the English don't know what they are talking about – you drink Scotch whereas 'Scots' or 'Scottish' is the adjective. In fact, at least one old map calls it 'Scots Corner.'

LANDRANGER MAP 93

North of Scotch Corner the A1 becomes the A1(M) but the motorway is the last thing we'll wish to use (you'll agree, of course?) Don't worry! The Great North Road heads for Darlington and has always done so.

— Don't miss this left turn (50 yards beyond the illustration on the facing page) or you'll find yourself travelling south in the tracks of the author!

The direct route to Darlington has gone. Choose either to go through Middleton Tyas or leave the A1 where the A1(M) begins. This traveller's preference is for the former.

The Scotch Corner Hotel – clad in its cloak of greenery.

DARLINGTON

We approach the largest town in County Durham across Blackwell Bridge. Darlington inevitably has its share of modern concrete development but this is a pleasant and compact town with much to see and enjoy. It began life as an Anglo-Saxon settlement and by the 12th. century had become a borough with a market which flourishes today. The High Street has buildings of the 1700s and the 1800s predating Victorian expansion. Its finest old building, indeed one of the gems of the north, is the Early English parish church of St. Cuthbert, completed at the outset of the 13th. century. It took longer to build than Durham Cathedral. Darlington's Town Arms feature the decapitated Sockburn Worm. We'll learn of its more famous cousin, the Lambton Worm, before we leave the county but that legendary beast did not command a monopoly in the terrorisation of the populace. Sockburn is beside the River Tees downstream from Darlington - which is actually on a tributary, the River Skerne. William Wordsworth met his wife-to-be at Sockburn. (Note: don't be confused by another Sockburn, a farmstead to the north of Darlington.

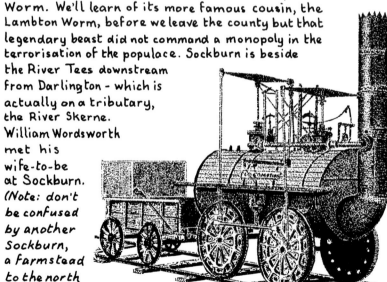

Locomotion. (Nº1)

PIERCEBRIDGE

This was the site of a Roman fort on Dere Street. Excavations have revealed some of the old stonework and also the abutments of the bridge which carried Dere Street over the Tees. The village is five miles west of Darlington along the A67 but the most attractive way of reaching it is along the B6275 (Dere Street) which branches from the A1 where the latter becomes a motorway. This approach brings you first to the George Hotel, separated from Piercebridge by The River Tees. An American, Henry Clay Work, visited the hotel in the 1880s and was inspired to pen a famous song about its grandfather clock, still there and still too large for the shelf. We've been singing about it ever since.

THE STOCKTON-DARLINGTON RAILWAY

Darlington is inevitably linked with Stockton, both historically and physically, by the railway. The early 19th. century textile industry needed a sound commercial connection with the sea and the nearest docks were at Stockton. Textile manufacturers Jonathan Backhouse and Edward Pease worked with George Stephenson as their engineer and the result was the world's earliest public steam railway which ran from Stockton through Darlington to Shildon. The first service for passengers and freight (coal) ran from Shildon to Stockton on the 27th. September, 1825, drawn by Engine Nº1, Locomotion. The engine is on display at the North Road Railway Museum.

The Great North Road and the Old North Road in Yorkshire become one again when the A167 reaches Blackwell, over the border in Durham and a mile from Darlington. This is the end of the variation which began its independent course just north of Doncaster where the A19 branches from the A1 to link with the A167 at Thirsk. The north Yorkshire capital of Northallerton was a major coaching stop. From here to Birtley the Great North Road is the A167, with minor diversions.

The River Tees is the historic boundary between Yorkshire and County Durham. It starts life in the wild Pennine hills where it soon becomes one of the finest rivers in the land, but here it is indulging in a series of irresolute meanders which become ever more devious as if it wishes to delay its inevitable fate in industrial Teeside. The contrast is unbelievable – from the dramas of Cauldron Snout and High Force, through the delicate beauty of riverside pastures where springtime wildflowers are a jealously guarded delight to a vast array of functional factory estates in 95 miles. Downstream Tees-side is being cleaned and polished but it will take time and those factories can never be pretty.

The road from Barton to Blackwell Bridge, where there is an old tollhouse, is the original route into Darlington.

BARTON to HARROWGATE HILL
6.7 miles (241 miles)

Harrowgate Hill

Railway Museum

Here begins the popular Carter Bar route to Scotland.

A68

DARLINGTON

(5 miles) To Piercebridge A67

Blackwell Bridge

A1(M)

A66(M)

GNR

Stapleton

GNR A167

Blackwell A66

Old North Road

R. Tees

A167

GNR Newton Morrell

BARTON

LANDRANGER MAP 93

Croft, south from Blackwell along the A167, was a spa in the eighteenth century but its main claim to literary fame is in its Lewis Carroll associations. That author's father, the Rev. Charles Dodgson, was vicar from 1843 until 1868 and his son enjoyed a happy childhood here.

*NOTE: The scale around Darlington is expanded in order to show detail.

Old Town Hall, Covered Market and Clock Tower, Darlington.

Old Tollhouse, Blackwell Bridge.

Page 111.

COUNTY DURHAM

So often the image of County Durham has been of pit spoil heaps and mining communities where existence mattered more than style in rows of unprepossessing cottages.   In the 1960s when I first drove through the county along the Great North Road it was on a wet and wintry afternoon and the impression of a gloomy, grimy backdrop predominated.   This was because the A167 - then the A1- together with the A19 and the railway provided lines of communication through an industrial heartland so that travellers saw the worst of Durham but it was not the complete picture. It took a motorway to reveal the truth. The A1(M) cuts through a wide green landscape, bypassing the brick of miner' houses and associated industry. The built-up ribbon remains but it now seems cleaner especially when the sun shines; and those old pit heaps are being landscaped away.   The towns and villages are learning to assume fresh identities as dependence on coal declines and other enterprises take over. And you don't have to go far from the old industrial communities to find a different scene. Away to the west is a land of dales and moors, long ago the location of lead exploitation, yet the technology of that age never allowed mining which would leave lasting, large-scale scars; to the east is a fine rocky coastline; and between is a pleasant green landscape of farmland cut by deep river valleys.   The whole is linked by a population of friendly folk, proud to claim their heritage in the only English county clearly labelled as such. County Durham is unique.

NEWTON AYCLIFFE is conspicuous by its absence when you study old maps of the area yet Aycliff and School Aycliffe may be found. The town was 'born' in 1948 as a post-war development beside the old village of Aycliffe, hence its name: New Town Aycliffe. It was the first of a series of new towns in County Durham and, in the now historic tradition of Welwyn Garden City, was carefully laid out with open spaces and green areas to form a pleasant environment for folk who would live in residential areas clearly separated from necessary workplaces which were none-the-less conveniently near.

AYCLIFFE straddles the Great North Road with its solidly towered 12th. century church (with Saxon antecedents) on one side and most of the rest on the other. The A167 now closely bypasses the original line which can be followed through Aycliffe, a minor diversion which is certainly worthwhile if you take the trouble to visit the village green which can easily be missed by motorists travelling north. The large green is set to one side through portals provided by the inn and the end of a row of cottages and in summer is not to be missed. This is not the bucolic scene of sheep and village cricket that you might expect on the typical English village green but the stage for a prize-winning floral display that is a delight to the eye. If you pass this way in summer enjoy it while you may.

Aycliffe Green.

COATHAM MUNDEVILLE, almost swamped by the motorway, the railway and the Great North Road, has few houses and its little red-brick church of 1865 is now St. Mary Magdalene House. The manor house, Hall Garth, is now an hotel.

SHILDON, west of Newton Aycliffe, is where George Stephenson's engine Locomotion (Nº 1) began its historic run to Stockton in 1825. The house where once lived Timothy Hackworth, superintendent of the Stockton and Darlington Railway and builder of the steam engine Royal George, is now part of a museum dedicated to his name.

KETTON HALL is a mile south-east of Coatham Mundeville. At the close of the 18th. century one Charles Collinge developed a strain of shorthorn cattle to compete with highly funded Dutch giants which farmers of the county admired and imported. Breeding for quicker fattening allied to satisfactory milk yield was the aim. If you find an inn hereabouts named the Ketton Ox, the Fat Ox or the Durham Ox, with a pictorial sign to match, you may be quite sure of the name's origins.*

* This note may mainly interest farmers and pub-crawlers but it fills an odd corner!

HARROWGATE VILLAGE to NEWTON AYCLIFFE
5.2 miles (246.2 miles)

St. Mary Magdalene House.

Shildon and Heighington ←

When James I (James VI of Scotland) travelled south to claim the English throne in 1603 he broke his journey at Walworth Castle, four miles west of Coatham Mundeville. That is not a great diversion from the Great North Road - or did he use Dere Street? He may have approached by the latter route through Bishop Auckland from Sunderland Bridge. It is also a more convenient link with the main way south. And by the side of Dere Street, a couple of miles north of Walworth, is the shaft of Legs Cross where, so the story goes, the new king sat and looked out in pride across the exquisite prospect of Teesdale which he called his "bonny land." Walworth Castle has succumbed to the temptations of trade in order to keep a roof resting upon its walls. Like others it is now an hotel.

LANDRANGER MAP 93

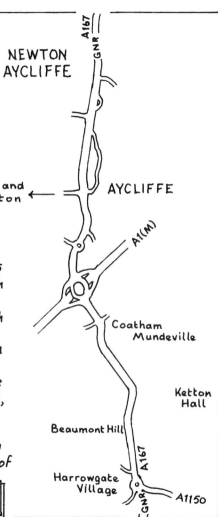

NEWTON AYCLIFFE

AYCLIFFE

A167
GNR
A1(M)
Coatham Mundeville
Ketton Hall
Beaumont Hill
A167
Harrowgate Village
GNR
A1150

BISHOP AUCKLAND

Though five miles off-route this town is important enough in the life of Durham to deserve a mention and a visit. The Bishop of Durham has had a residence here for over one hundred years; in fact the bishops have had a country retreat at Auckland since the 12th. century, originally shared with a palace at Bishop Middleham on the eastern side of the Great North Road, now more or less reduced to grass-covered mounds. Auckland is also a market town. Its town hall and parish church stand almost hand-in-hand as if in need of each other for confidence when faced by the fuss of the adjacent market place. The town's finest church, St. Andrew's, is a mile away at South Church, once supported by its own community and known as St. Andrew Auckland. But it is Bishop Auckland with its Bishop's Palace and Park which we think of in connection with the name Auckland. The Park is open to the public and approached through an impressive gatehouse surmounted by a clock tower. It is a pleasant open space where local folk may walk or enjoy a game of golf. It also contains a deercote of the 18th. century, a large stone-walled and arcaded enclosure with a tower which contained a small banqueting hall. The palace is separately enclosed within the park and is not open to the public though a tantalising glimpse may be seen through a crenellated gateway. As there is a West Auckland and a St. Helen Auckland within three miles it does seem important to distinguish Bishop Auckland with its full title.

WOODHAM

Woodham is just a small collection of houses beside the A167. All this land was forest of which only small patches remain. At the time of the Civil War woodland came close to the road and trees were cleared to make the place safer for the passage of troops and heavy equipment which would necessarily slow them down. Surprise attack would be far less likely with any adjacent cover removed. This clearance was probably prompted by military activity in the neighbourhood; there had been skirmishes on nearby Woodham Moor.

FERRYHILL

Until the Industrial Revolution this was a rural village with its manor house (now an hotel) but the extraction of coal and its use in local ironworks changed all that. Housing for colliery workers extended boundaries which have been pushed out even further with recent residential development. People who depended on coal for their livelihood now look in other directions for employment. The great spoil heaps from the mine which dominated the Great North Road have been smoothed and landscaped and the road in its cutting no longer seems as much under shadowed threat. Of course this is not the original road. Horses hauled carts and coaches through the village along a route that you may still follow if wish to be precise in observing the line. As to the name, it is told that the last wild boar in this area south of the Tyne was killed on a hill nearby in the 13th. century by Sir Roger de Ferie - hence 'Ferie Hill'. It may be true - or just a Ferie tale?

The Great North Road originally crossed the Rushyford Beck
by (surprise!) a ford. It was a well-used crossing because an
east/west route (now the A689) crossed here; a local track from
the south-west also linked with this nodal point. It may be appreciated
that this was a prime site for bridge building. The hamlet at the crossing
grew from estate workers' cottages serving the estate of Windlestone
Hall. An inn was opened to minister to the stage coaches, particularly
on the north/south route, with a place for stabling and a smithy to tend
to the horses - a fact borne out by the discovery of many used horse shoes in the
beck when the bridge was rebuilt. This inn was not the present Eden Arms Hotel
but another establishment, now private housing. The whole layout of the junction
suffered with the construction of the major roundabout. As is so often the case,
comparison with older maps of maybe only fifty years ago is revealing. It is certainly
a far cry from 14th. century shrub-cover when the menace of mud in the rushy
environs of the crossing reduced travellers to a slow and doubtful progress,
a perfect spot for an ambush. In 1317 the newly nominated Bishop of
Durham, Lewis Beaumont, was on his way to the cathedral for
enthronement accompanied by his retinue of cardinals and servants.
They were surprised by a band of kidnappers; all but the bishop
elect were robbed then released. Beaumont was a far greater
prize for exploitation. He was spirited away and held
until a hefty ransom had been extracted.

NEWTON AYCLIFFE
to FERRYHILL
5.1 miles (251.3 miles)

FERRYHILL

← B6287
to Kirk Merrington
(2 miles)

Cottages
by the Old Road,
Rushyford

CHILTON

to Bishop Auckland (5 miles)
(and Binchester)
← A689

RUSHYFORD

A689 →
to Sedgefield (5 miles)
and A1(M)

Woodham

BINCHESTER ROMAN FORT (Vinovia) is just north of Bishop Auckland, beyond
the Bishop's Park. Follow the minor road round the park and beside the River
Wear. Binchester was a military post for the control of the neighbourhood but
its position on the major Roman route of Dere Street gave it much the same
status as the coaching inns of the turnpike era and, indeed, the motorway
motels of the present day. But the customers would mainly be troops bound
to or from Hadrian's Wall. On view is probably the finest remnant example of
Roman military bathhouse in Britain and the remains of the commander's house.
You can also see a short stretch of Dere Street itself; all for a small fee.

NEWTON
AYCLIFFE

LANDRANGER
MAP 93

THINFORD

The crossing of the ways at Thinford is increasingly the province of industrial estates and little else but the industry is masked from the road by trees. As a crossroads it would have been well known to travellers of old by its inn. As a much frequented road junction it was the ideal spot for advertising the potential consequences of crime in a way common to many similar locations throughout the land. An instance in 1683 was of Andrew Mills, murderer of three children, whose executed body was hung in chains here so that all who passed by might take note.

> Before the Battle of Neville's Cross outside Durham in 1346 the English army had encamped on a ridge near Ferryhill while the Scots occupied Bearpark on the fringe of the city. The Scots sent out foraging parties (as did their opponents) and two skirmishes took place when the adversaries unexpectedly crossed paths in this area. They met near Sunderland Bridge and also clashed north of Thinford where the English outnumbered and took delight in 'butchering' the Scots. The site became known as Butcher Race and even quite recent maps indicated High and Low Butcher Race.

SUNDERLAND BRIDGE

The village of Croxdale, which grew up as a mining community around the junction of the present A167 and the B6288, continues into the tiny hamlet of Sunderland Bridge which largely hides down a byway to the east and is no doubt glad to be away from the rush of main road traffic. This little backwater does not advertise itself and makes no concessions to those who take the trouble to turn aside from the north road but it is neat, well kept and a delight to the discerning eye. Sunderland 'Bridge' distinguished this place from the much better known Sunderland which has dropped its 'by the Sea'. Across the main road is the medieval bridge which features in the hamlet's name. It is now an easily forgotten cul-de-sac settling in the shade of the modern A167 viaduct but for centuries it carried the Great North Road and the old Coach and Horses Inn played host to countless long distance travellers. It was not an easy bridge to approach, especially in winter when the bank down to the River Wear was a challenge to hooves and wheels. On one occasion a horse slipped on the camber of the bridge itself and the coach toppled towards the parapet throwing two outriders to their deaths in the river.

The old Sunderland Bridge.

The Land of the Prince Bishops

At the northern end of this map we are entering the first city of County Durham, seat of the Prince Bishops; for the benefit of tourists entering the county signboards proudly proclaim this to be "Land of the Prince Bishops." The county was a palatinate, a territory ruled by a prince, lord, earl, or in this case a bishop, who on behalf of the king exercised local rule, including responsibility for maintaining law and order. In the Middle Ages the Bishopric's semi-independent domain included other small northern regions, one between the Rivers Wansbeck and Blyth, another near the mouth of the River Tweed and an area around Yorkshire's Northallerton, all conveniently and significantly linked with Durham by the Great North Road. There were times when the King and the Lord Bishop were not in agreement and all administration reverted to the crown but local rule was soon enough restored. From the 17th. century the importance of the Prince Bishops declined until with the death of Bishop van Mildert in 1836 (the last of the 'Prince Bishops') the powers were relinquish but it was not until 1971 that the Courts Act of that year finally abolished the Palatinate Court and a unique era of English regional authority was officially terminated.

The A167 road between Farewell Hall and Pity Me (on the next map page) is variously named Darlington Road, Newcastle Road and Pity Me Bypass, the whole of this generally owning up to the alias of the Great North Road. Although in part based on older existing roads, elsewhere the route is modern and the alias a name of courtesy. The one and only, the true Great North Road, kept its appointment with the City of Durham.

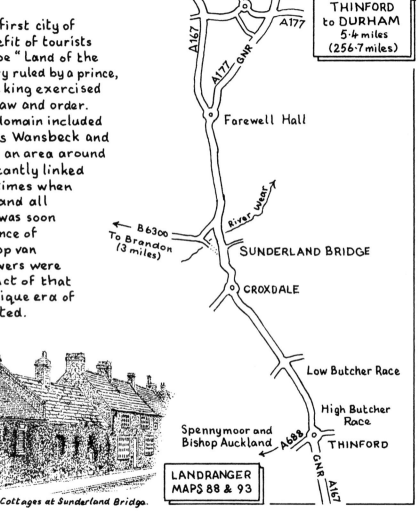

Cottages at Sunderland Bridge.

THINFORD to DURHAM 5·4 miles (256·7 miles)

Farewell Hall

River Wear

← To Brandon (3 miles) B6300

SUNDERLAND BRIDGE

CROXDALE

Low Butcher Race

High Butcher Race

Spennymoor and Bishop Auckland

THINFORD

LANDRANGER MAPS 88 & 93

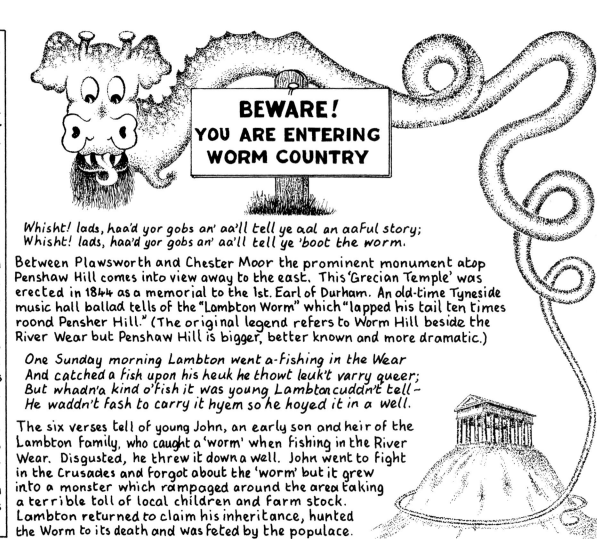

FINCHALE PRIORY is near enough to be worth a visit. It was built on the site of a hermit's cell, St. Godric having settled there from 1115 a.d. until his death fifty-five years later. When he died the place became a cell of the monastery at Durham and then a Benedictine Priory still attached to Durham from where the monks were able to take leave for three weeks at a time. Finchale Priory, an oasis of sylvan charm, rests in a loop of land surrounded on three sides by the River Wear, like a moated retreat. It seems remarkably secluded for a place so close to Durham's northern outskirts and housing estates; indeed an approach from the south, where there is a car park, is singularly unpromising. The north bank is reached by a woodland footpath which leads down to cross the river by a footbridge.

BEWARE! YOU ARE ENTERING WORM COUNTRY

Whisht! lads, haa'd yor gobs an' aa'll tell ye aal an aaful story;
Whisht! lads, haa'd yor gobs an' aa'll tell ye 'boot the worm.

Between Plawsworth and Chester Moor the prominent monument atop Penshaw Hill comes into view away to the east. This 'Grecian Temple' was erected in 1844 as a memorial to the 1st. Earl of Durham. An old-time Tyneside music hall ballad tells of the "Lambton Worm" which "lapped his tail ten times roond Pensher Hill." (The original legend refers to Worm Hill beside the River Wear but Penshaw Hill is bigger, better known and more dramatic.)

One Sunday morning Lambton went a-fishing in the Wear
And catched a fish upon his heuk he thowt leuk't varry queer;
But whadn'a kind o'fish it was young Lambton cuddn't tell—
He waddn't fash to carry it hyem so he hoyed it in a well.

The six verses tell of young John, an early son and heir of the Lambton family, who caught a 'worm' when fishing in the River Wear. Disgusted, he threw it down a well. John went to fight in the Crusades and forgot about the 'worm' but it grew into a monster which rampaged around the area taking a terrible toll of local children and farm stock. Lambton returned to claim his inheritance, hunted the Worm to its death and was feted by the populace.

If you wish to experience PITY ME you must leave Durham by way of Framwellgate but the direct road connection with this peculiarly named hamlet-within-a-city which once sat astride a busy Great North Road is no longer available. You must either find Front Street from the Dryburn Road roundabout or turn back from the A167/Durham Bypass when Pity Me is behind you. But there is not much out of the ordinary to see, just a straight road flanked by houses and the occasional shop. The strangeness is in a name whose origins are hardly what you might imagine. Apparently there was once a small lake here, a 'petit mere' whose corruption misleads the imaginative flow of at least one traveller; but if you think the idea of Durham pitmen spouting French is odd remember that long before the days of collieries Durham was a Norman city with the architecture of a great cathedral to prove it. If you wish to be true to the historic route then Pity Me is a place that must be visited.

Finchale (as in Finchale Priory, opposite) is, according to some sources, a descriptive name meaning 'a corner of land where finches nest' (Finca=finch; halh= corner of land or watermeadow). But Finchale is locally pronounced 'Finkle' and in the north of England streets of that name - and there are plenty of them - are rarely straight and if so you will usually find that at some point in the past it has been straightened out. A little research with a place-name book will soon reveal that 'Finkle' or 'Fenkel' in Middle English means 'corner' or 'bend' so that derivation seems obvious when you realise that Finchale Priory nestles in a protective bend of the River Wear with a Finchale Banks across the stream. As a northerner who married a Durham lass pleased to call the place 'Finkle' Priory I am happy to believe the name has its roots in this geographical feature.

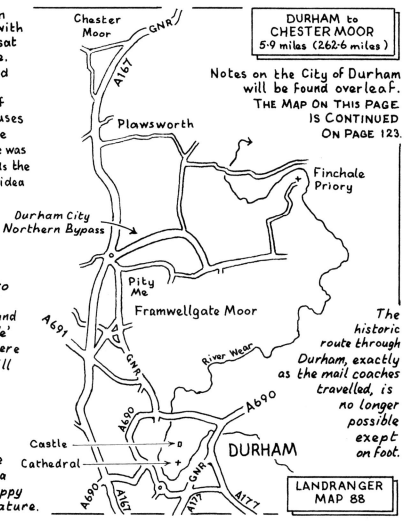

Notes on the City of Durham will be found overleaf.
THE MAP ON THIS PAGE IS CONTINUED ON PAGE 123.

Chester Moor

GNR

A167

Plawsworth

Finchale Priory

Durham City Northern Bypass

Pity Me

Framwellgate Moor

A691

GNR

River Wear

A690

Castle

Cathedral

DURHAM

A690

A167

GNR

A177

A177

The historic route through Durham, exactly as the mail coaches travelled, is no longer possible exept on foot.

LANDRANGER MAP 88

THE CITY OF **DURHAM**

The cathedral, castle and cluster of attendant buildings occupy an airy peninsular moated by a tight loop of the River Wear. The riverside walk around the almost-island is a fine prelude to an exploration of the city and should include a detour to South Street's classic view of Durham's pride.

Durham grew around its great church. The relics of St. Cuthbert were brought from Chester-le-Street (via Ripon) in 995 a.d. and his shrine led to the foundation of the cathedral. The present building was not begun until 1093 and was largely completed within forty years. Few can challenge the claim that this is the greatest Norman cathedral in Europe. At 470 feet long with a tower of 218 feet soaring imposingly high above the depths of the encircling gorge, here is a spectacle not to be missed.

The cathedral, cloister and Palace Green share the high ground with the castle, begun c1070 on the site of earlier fortifications and home to the Prince Bishops until 1837. It now houses the students of University College. Durham is fourth in age of England's universities, being established in 1833 after a number of false starts and the castle is but one of several colleges.

Medieval travellers arriving from the south would have crossed the Wear by Elvet Bridge and continued north over Framwellgate Bridge where the neck of the peninsular is at its narrowest. This route was never easy for heavy traffic and is now open only to those on foot. Durham's market charter was granted c1180 and the fine Market Place presided over by its Guildhall is the focal point of modern pedestrianisation. The trading centre sits neatly poised between access from the two old bridges.

It is not surprising that with space at a premium there was development beyond the bounds of the river from the earliest days. The Elvets, Old and New, barony and borough, grew at the eastern approach; indeed there was probably a settlement here before the Norman Conquest. The site of a Roman villa is evidence of Roman interest and there was an Iron Age fort even earlier. Little remains of these but don't dismiss The Elvets out of hand. A stroll along Old Elvet will reveal many buildings of note and the place has a character all its own. A little research will soon disclose an unsuspected history up to modern times.

Framwellgate was an early suburb where affluent merchants built their town houses but by the 19th. century these were becoming slum properties and most have now been cleared. In the 15th. century and for 200 years water from the Fram Well was piped across the river to the Market Place. Framwellgate and Framwellgate Peth (gate=way or road; peth=way or path; there's tautology here!) led to the well but also to the new Great North Road - our own A167 - the line of which although now straightened out, especially bypassing Pity Me at Framwellgate Moor, is much as it was when the original O.S. map was produced in the 1860s.

A good mile south along the A167 was Neville's Cross, near the crossroads of the A690, one of a series of medieval crosses which ringed the cathedral. This may have been the circle of sanctuary offered to fugitives seeking the security of the church. Traditionally the privilege was gained by grasping the sanctuary knocker on the north door but in fact Right of Sanctuary was granted by request. At Durham safe haven was for a period of 37 days, with specified conditions, after which the refugee was required to leave the country. The knocker is famous, magnificent, a work of art - but on the door, a replica. Neville's Cross also gave its name to a famous battle where the Scots were soundly routed by an English army led, coincidentally, by Ralph Neville.

Good stuff goes in small space, it is often said, and this is certainly true of Durham. If this is a first visit, enjoy it but you're sure to return. This is one of those places which leaves you with the feeling of having to go back and do it all again.

Castle Keep.

The Guildhall.

Bishop Cosin's Almshouses.

Framwellgate Bridge.

Durham Cathedral from South Street.

Page 121.

CHESTER-le-STREET

The 'Street' is the Great North Road, variously named Durham Road, Front Street and Newcastle Road as we proceed north. It was also a Roman road and there was a fort here as the 'Chester' of the name indicates. Chester-le-Street must be visited if the historic line of the old road is sought but in part it is now a pedestrian precinct so you'll have to park the car and walk. There is little to excite the imagination until you see the soaring spire that marks the historic church of St. Mary and St. Cuthbert which stands on the site of the fort. At nearly 190 feet it has been a call to worship across a wide expanse of the Durham lowlands for 600 years. The body of St. Cuthbert was brought to Chester in 883 a.d. and a small cathedral established which lasted 113 years until the monks moved on to find greater security, first at Ripon and finally at Durham. There is much of interest in this old church but many folk go away just remembering the array of fourteen stone knights, the supposed ancestors of the seventh Lord Lumley who had them installed in the late 16th. century. Attached to the church is the Anker's House, now a museum. An anchorite was a religious recluse who was sealed within his dwelling to live a life of prayer and contemplation. His (or *her* - but there was never an *anchoress* at Chester-le-Street) material needs were attended to through a hatch and in this case the anker was able to join in the church services through a narrow squint which enabled him to see the altar yet be unseen by the congregation. The house and exhibition are very much worth viewing and depend on visitors' donations for maintenance. Recommended!

The Church of St. Mary & St. Cuthbert. The Anker's House is to the left.

LUMLEY CASTLE is across the River Wear. It has a distinguished history and an imposing presence. The castle was built in about 1390 but has seen many changes over the centuries. When the Lumleys moved out in the year 1953 Durham University moved in – but it is now a most impressive hotel.

WASHINGTON is east of the A1(M). As a new town of the 1960s it was built to attract fresh industry as the decline in coal mining was foreseen. It has been developed around old villages, retaining existing features, and planned to eradicate all the dereliction of disused collieries by providing a congenial living environment with new industrial estates widely separated between residential areas. The town takes its name from one of the original villages: Washington, the very place from which the Washington family takes its name and though the branch which produced the first president of the United States moved from here long before he achieved fame across the Atlantic the village is justly proud of these links. The Jacobean Washington Old Hall is open to the public.

As you drive north from Birtley it is difficult to see where the early Great North Road went but the old maps reveal the truth. As the main road curves west towards the Angel Roundabout a minor road continues north; this is the start of the Long Bank but its progress is quickly halted by the modern A1 which cuts across it. To continue you must use the Angel Roundabout to cross the A1; the third exit connects with the Long Bank which leads on over the top, through Wrekenton High Street, to become the Old Durham Road.

THE BOWES RAILWAY.

Historic railway enthusiasts will wish to seek out the Bowes Railway Museum at Springwell by following the B1288 from Birtley. In Tyneside there was a network of small railways serving local collieries, linked to the main line systems. At Springwell the local railway carried coal from nine pits and indeed it was one of George Stephenson's early enterprises. It opened in 1826 and featured a number of rope-operated inclines. This stretch has been restored and as the only rope-hauled railway still in working order it is unique.

There was an old village of Birtley but the impression is of industry and modern housing. Don't linger – it's not pretty.

Expectation is high as the A1 is approached but do not let the Angel distract you from control of your car. Park and see it from close quarters.

The complications of Tyneside's road systems are imminent. A hint of what's in store can be gained from a glance at the spaghetti to the right. The coward's escape is the A1 and the Western Bypass, but you're made of better stuff than that, surely?

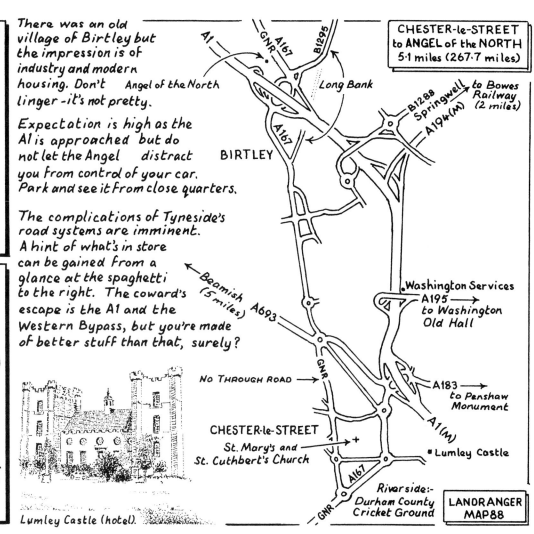

Lumley Castle (hotel).

CHESTER-le-STREET
to ANGEL of the NORTH
5.1 miles (267.7 miles)

Angel of the North

Long Bank

to Bowes Railway (2 miles)

Springwell

BIRTLEY

Washington Services
A195 →
to Washington Old Hall

Beamish (5 miles) A693

No Through Road →

A183 →
to Penshaw Monument

A1(M)

Lumley Castle

CHESTER-le-STREET
St. Mary's and St. Cuthbert's Church

Riverside:-
Durham County Cricket Ground

LANDRANGER MAP 88

GATESHEAD

Though it is largely a modern town Gateshead is proud to have a separate identity from its northern neighbour – Newcastle. At the start of the 19th. century it was still a modest village separate from other southbank communities which occupied niches on the hillside above – High Fell, Sheriff Hill, Wrekenton - all now absorbed in the encroaching suburban sprawl. Gateshead had its 'Great Fire' in 1854 and much of the historic core was destroyed; concrete modernity completed the job and the A167 (which was the A1) now strides across the centre on stilts. In 1990 Gateshead hosted the National Garden Festival, an event which helped to rejuvenate an industrial wasteland where the little River Team comes up gasping for air as it joins big brother Tyne. Close by is the mighty MetroCentre which attracts shoppers from all over the north - as many as 25 million a year and rising. A large proportion of them approach along Tyneside's Western Bypass (the A1) which seems a good reason for using the route in this book– but don't bank on it! The MetroCentre shares the same philosophy as all such American style centres by using a variant of the formula propounded by Dale Carnegie in "How to Win Friends and Influence People": make them feel happy in their surroundings and comfortable with you and they'll spend. It seems to work.

Until 1998 there was nothing specific to indicate that Gateshead was near but from the 15th. February of that year there has been no doubt; the landmark is there for all to see. The Angel of the North is a stark and dramatic guardian against southern invaders, standing exactly where the new A1 breaks away from the A167 which in turn had long ago escaped from the original Great North Road (The Long Bank). The controversial figure is 20 metres high, has a wing span of 54 metres, weighs 200 tonnes and is built to withstand winds of 100 m.p.h. Out of sight beneath the ground is a massive 150 tonne concrete block anchoring the figure to the solid rock of Tyneside from which it grows like the miners of old escaping the bondage of an underground workplace. It is constructed 'inside out' with its ribs on view to a gaping world, testimony to its towering strength. The sculptor, Anthony Gormley, has provided Gateshead with a landmark that tells the world that this is not a suburb of Newcastle and though some folk may object to having it in view from their front windows there is no doubt that it makes an impressive statement from its hilltop site. The ground in its shadow has now been landscaped and there is car parking so that visitors may wander round the feet of this steel giant. And there are those who are quick to take commercial advantage of a colossus on the doorstep. The Old Barn Inn is now the Angel View Inn!

It is worth an approach along the Old Durham Road, starting up the narrow lane of Long Bank from the Angel Roundabout. As you come down the hill from Wrekenton consider how the old time coaches and carts would have handled the muddy descent to the Tyne on a damp Durham day long ago; the ascent could hardly have been better. Perhaps you may manage a glance at the streets on the eastern margin of the road for an indication of when these terraces were built. Street names provide clues. Some such as Stavordale Terrace and Methuen Street may only interest historians but Baden-Powell and Kitchener Streets (and Mafeking Street around a corner) should provide a clear link with the South African Campaigns at the turn of the 20th. century.

High Street in Gateshead is hard to find in the constant flow of traffic which has a tendency to take wrong turnings when drivers are not familiar with the local geography. It was the original route with the Great North Road leading down to a crossing of the Tyne by the medieval bridge (on the site of the present Swing Bridge) when Gateshead was just a village. Down here near the river is the town's finest church. St. Mary's has 12th. century origins but is so often overlooked, in both senses of the word, as it sits in the shadow of the Tyne Bridge in (surprise!) Church Street.

Famous folk associated with Gateshead include Thomas Bewick the engraver and Joseph Swan, inventor of the incandescent lamp. Daniel Defoe also spent time in Gateshead during his travels round Britain and is believed to have penned part of 'Robinson Crusoe' during his stay.

Half a dozen miles downstream is Jarrow (A184/A185) famed as the town where in the 1930s lack of employment and poverty sparked the Jarrow Hunger March to Parliament. But go there to see St. Paul's and the remnants of the monastery where the Venerable Bede spent most of his scholarly life.

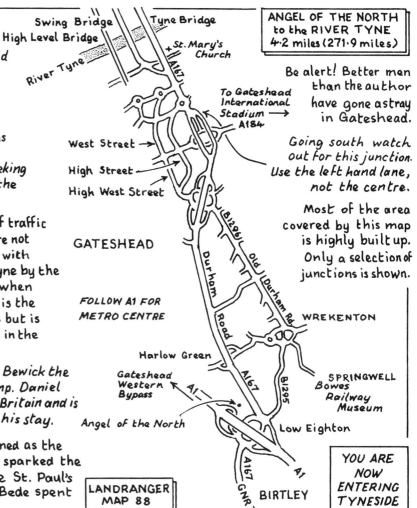

ANGEL OF THE NORTH to the RIVER TYNE 4.2 miles (271.9 miles)

Be alert! Better men than the author have gone astray in Gateshead.

Going south watch out for this junction. Use the left hand lane, not the centre.

Most of the area covered by this map is highly built up. Only a selection of junctions is shown.

Swing Bridge
High Level Bridge
Tyne Bridge
River Tyne
St. Mary's Church
To Gateshead International Stadium → A184
West Street
High Street
High West Street
GATESHEAD
FOLLOW A1 FOR METRO CENTRE
Durham Road
Old Durham Rd.
WREKENTON
Harlow Green
Gateshead Western Bypass
Angel of the North
SPRINGWELL
Bowes Railway Museum
Low Eighton
LANDRANGER MAP 88
A167
GNR
BIRTLEY

YOU ARE NOW ENTERING TYNESIDE

NEWCASTLE

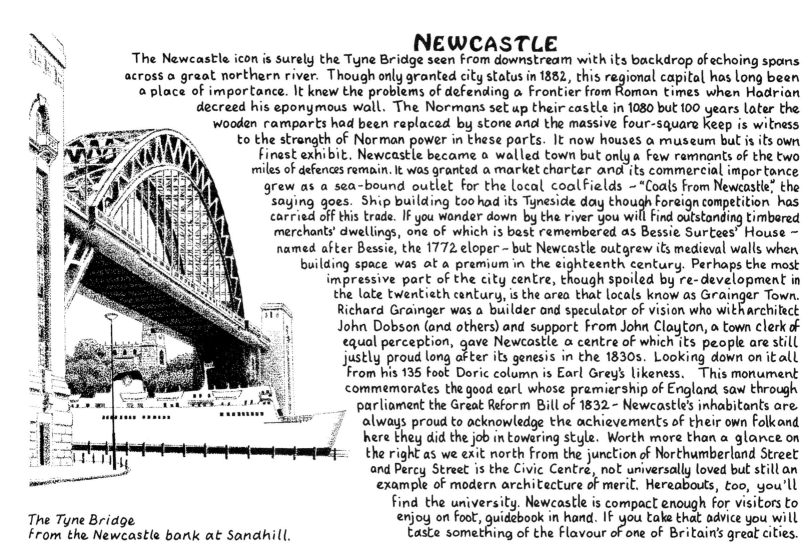

The Newcastle icon is surely the Tyne Bridge seen from downstream with its backdrop of echoing spans across a great northern river. Though only granted city status in 1882, this regional capital has long been a place of importance. It knew the problems of defending a frontier from Roman times when Hadrian decreed his eponymous wall. The Normans set up their castle in 1080 but 100 years later the wooden ramparts had been replaced by stone and the massive four-square keep is witness to the strength of Norman power in these parts. It now houses a museum but is its own finest exhibit. Newcastle became a walled town but only a few remnants of the two miles of defences remain. It was granted a market charter and its commercial importance grew as a sea-bound outlet for the local coalfields – "Coals from Newcastle", the saying goes. Ship building too had its Tyneside day though foreign competition has carried off this trade. If you wander down by the river you will find outstanding timbered merchants' dwellings, one of which is best remembered as Bessie Surtees' House – named after Bessie, the 1772 eloper – but Newcastle outgrew its medieval walls when building space was at a premium in the eighteenth century. Perhaps the most impressive part of the city centre, though spoiled by re-development in the late twentieth century, is the area that locals know as Grainger Town. Richard Grainger was a builder and speculator of vision who with architect John Dobson (and others) and support from John Clayton, a town clerk of equal perception, gave Newcastle a centre of which its people are still justly proud long after its genesis in the 1830s. Looking down on it all from his 135 foot Doric column is Earl Grey's likeness. This monument commemorates the good earl whose premiership of England saw through parliament the Great Reform Bill of 1832 – Newcastle's inhabitants are always proud to acknowledge the achievements of their own folk and here they did the job in towering style. Worth more than a glance on the right as we exit north from the junction of Northumberland Street and Percy Street is the Civic Centre, not universally loved but still an example of modern architecture of merit. Hereabouts, too, you'll find the university. Newcastle is compact enough for visitors to enjoy on foot, guidebook in hand. If you take that advice you will taste something of the flavour of one of Britain's great cities.

The Tyne Bridge
from the Newcastle bank at Sandhill.

NEWCASTLE'S BRIDGES

*Six river bridges link Gateshead with central Newcastle. They are, reading east to west:-

1. **The New Tyne Bridge:** completed 1928. Built in response to congestion on the High Level Bridge and the conflicting needs of river traffic at the Swing Bridge. The builders, Dorman, Long and Co., were already working on Sydney Harbour Bridge - note the family resemblance.

2. **The Swing Bridge:** 1876. The Roman Pons Aelius and the medieval stone arched bridge, replaced in 1771, occupied approximately this site so the Great North Road crossed at this point; therefore if you wish to be as authentic as possible you should enter the city here. This bridge answered the requirements of seagoing vessels bound for Armstrong's engineering works upstream.

3. **The High Level Bridge:** 1849. This is the oldest of the present bridges. It carries the railway on an upper deck and road traffic below.

4. **The Queen Elizabeth II Bridge:** 1980. Built for the Metro rail service which began in 1981.

5. **The King Edward Bridge:** 1906. This railway crossing made the working of Newcastle's Central Station easier as previously trains using the High Level Bridge had to reverse from the platforms in order to continue north.

6. **The Redheugh Bridge:** 1983. Connects Redheugh on the south bank with the western fringe of the city centre. It is the third bridge on this site.

Other crossings include the Scotswood Bridge and its adjacent A1 Western Bypass span. Until the bypass was completed the designated A1 for a time used the Tyne Tunnel which is the lowest crossing of the Tyne, apart from the foot ferry between North and South Shields.

CENTRAL NEWCASTLE
2 miles (273·9 miles)

North West Radial Road
A167

* 20·11·2000 Now seven! See notes on Gateshead Millennium Footbridge at end of book.

University of Newcastle-upon-Tyne

SCALE: 6 ins = 1 mile

Exhibition Park

The Radial Motorway is far more complicated than it appears here because in places it exists on two levels. 3-D representation would help!

There are many more streets than shown on this map. One way streets and pedestrian precincts are not indicated. Changes occur - alterations would cause confusion!

Don't try to drive around the city centre. Follow the one way system and car park signs to leave your car and go walkabout.

LANDRANGER MAP 88

GNR · A167(M) · Jesmond Rd. A1058 · A189 · GNR · Central Motorway · Civic Centre · St. Mary's Place · John Dobson St. · Northumberland Rd. · Durant Rd. · Percy Street · Eldon Square Shopping Centre · Northumberland St. · Blackett St. · Pilgrim St. · A187 · Newgate St. · Grainger Street · Grey St. · Market St. · Groat Market · Bigg Mkt. · Clayton Street · Westgate Road · Mkt. · Neville St. · Central Station · Dean St. · Castle · High Level Br. · Swing Br. · Tyne Bridge A167 · City Road A186 · Quayside · Tyne R. · A186

Town Moor

You can walk north from Newcastle's city centre and within a few minutes be on the fringe of wide grasslands where cattle graze. This is the Town Moor, over 1000 acres of historic common land where a sense of the countryside invades the heart of the city.

Control over this area was granted to the Freemen of Newcastle as long ago as 1357 and rights for the extraction of coal were granted even earlier, by Henry III in 1239, when bell pits were excavated. The grazing rights for cattle are still put to good use and horses, too, are regularly exercised.

Palace of Arts Building.

Such a wide and airy expanse of grassland in the midst of urban growth is a great asset to Newcastle and has always been a natural meeting ground for city events, the best known of which is the annual Newcastle Fair, one of the largest meets in the land. This is the descendant of a Temperance Festival (you would not think so now!) which had replaced the Race Week in 1882. The races moved to Gosforth Park which we pass three miles up the road.

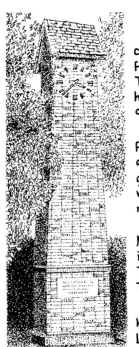

Queen Elizabeth II Coronation Clock Tower.

The Town Moor was once more extensive but there have been the inevitable encroachments here and there around the edges by civic, hospital and college building and by formal parkland. Lately Newcastle United Football Club has sought to extend its development at St. James' Park, so far without success.

In 1887 the Golden Jubilee of Queen Victoria's accession to the throne was celebrated in fine style by holding the Royal Jubilee Exhibition on the Moor, beside the Great North Road, an event which included the construction of a lake spanned by a two-thirds size replica of the medieval bridge across the Tyne. The bridge has gone but the lake and a bandstand remain, joined by a clock tower of 1953 built to commemorate the coronation of Queen Elizabeth II. In 1929 the North-East Coast Exhibition used the same site, now called Exhibition Park. Of this the Palace of Arts building stands, presently housing a Museum of Military Vehicles. Drivers on the old north road motor past in tight formation with neither time nor inclination to notice the park or moor beside them.

Residents of Town Moor

As you pass through Newcastle's northern suburbia of Gosforth and finally Wide Open, be ready to enter the vast landscape that is Northumberland. The name means 'Land North of the Humber.' The county is only a shadow of its historic self for in Saxon times land that is now Yorkshire, Durham, Westmorland, Lancashire and Cumberland was all included in the kingdom of Northumbria. This county of superb countryside is wide and green and full of the history of the borderlands – and you can see so much of it from the road.

Don't necessarily expect local people to be a fount of knowledge about their own neighbourhood. We had an example of this at Wide Open when we pulled off the road to check a note on the map about a bridge. A fellow out walking with his dog responded with a smile to a cheerful, "Good afternoon," so I followed this up with, "Is this Six Mile Bridge?"

"Not heard of it," he replied and nodding towards the adjacent stream volunteered, "This is Seaton Burn but there's a Six Mile Pub just up the road." He used the bridge to cross the burn and strode briskly to his house a mere fifty yards away. A glance at the bridge's parapet revealed an inscription, 'Six Mile Bridge,' clear for all to see.

There seems to have been a practice of using milestones as a source of inspiration for names hereabouts. There is a 'Seven Mile House' ahead and if you're alert to roadside features you'll have noted a couple of miles back another public house proclaiming that it is three miles north of the Tyne.

SIX MILE BRIDGE 1923

A quiet evening on the Great North Road at Seaton Burn.

Seaton Burn
Dudley
(Six Mile Bridge
Big Water Nature Reserve
Brunswick Village
WIDE OPEN
High Gosforth Park (Race Course)
Newcastle Western Bypass
Three Mile Bridge
Metro Station
GOSFORTH
WEST JESMOND
Town Moor Exhibition Park

The community of Wide Open is now bypassed by the A1. Most local settlements hereabouts, such as this and others like Dudley and Seaton Burn grew up around collieries. Maps of 100 years or more ago usually depict just the colliery and a small group of miners' cottages – and possibly an associated railway.

LANDRANGER MAP 88

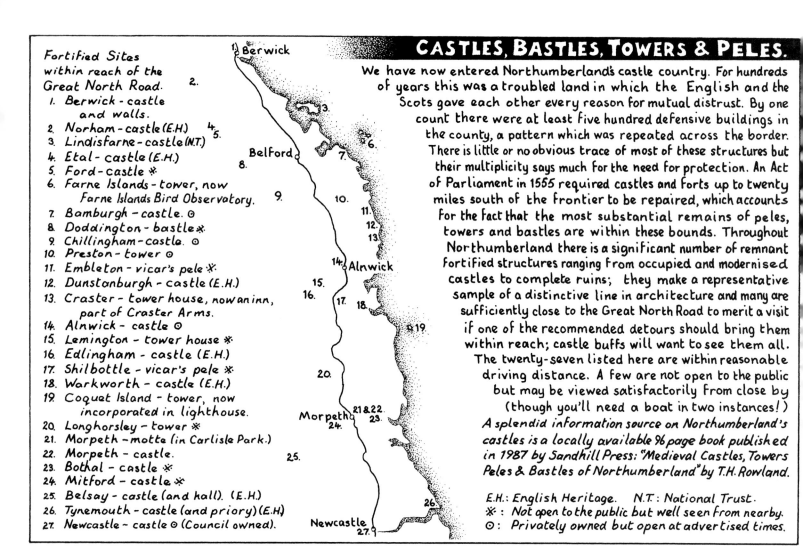

CASTLES, BASTLES, TOWERS & PELES.

Fortified Sites within reach of the Great North Road.

1. Berwick - castle and walls.
2. Norham - castle (E.H.)
3. Lindisfarne - castle (N.T.)
4. Etal - castle (E.H.)
5. Ford - castle ✳
6. Farne Islands - tower, now Farne Islands Bird Observatory.
7. Bamburgh - castle. ⊙
8. Doddington - bastle ✳
9. Chillingham - castle. ⊙
10. Preston - tower ⊙
11. Embleton - vicar's pele ✳
12. Dunstanburgh - castle (E.H.)
13. Craster - tower house, now an inn, part of Craster Arms.
14. Alnwick - castle ⊙
15. Lemington - tower house ✳
16. Edlingham - castle (E.H.)
17. Shilbottle - vicar's pele ✳
18. Warkworth - castle (E.H.)
19. Coquet Island - tower, now incorporated in lighthouse.
20. Longhorsley - tower ✳
21. Morpeth - motte (in Carlisle Park.)
22. Morpeth - castle.
23. Bothal - castle ✳
24. Mitford - castle ✳
25. Belsay - castle (and hall). (E.H.)
26. Tynemouth - castle (and priory) (E.H)
27. Newcastle - castle ⊙ (Council owned).

We have now entered Northumberland's castle country. For hundreds of years this was a troubled land in which the English and the Scots gave each other every reason for mutual distrust. By one count there were at least five hundred defensive buildings in the county, a pattern which was repeated across the border. There is little or no obvious trace of most of these structures but their multiplicity says much for the need for protection. An Act of Parliament in 1555 required castles and forts up to twenty miles south of the frontier to be repaired, which accounts for the fact that the most substantial remains of peles, towers and bastles are within these bounds. Throughout Northumberland there is a significant number of remnant fortified structures ranging from occupied and modernised castles to complete ruins; they make a representative sample of a distinctive line in architecture and many are sufficiently close to the Great North Road to merit a visit if one of the recommended detours should bring them within reach; castle buffs will want to see them all. The twenty-seven listed here are within reasonable driving distance. A few are not open to the public but may be viewed satisfactorily from close by (though you'll need a boat in two instances!)

A splendid information source on Northumberland's castles is a locally available 96 page book published in 1987 by Sandhill Press: "Medieval Castles, Towers Peles & Bastles of Northumberland" by T.H. Rowland.

E.H.: English Heritage.   N.T: National Trust.
✳ : Not open to the public but well seen from nearby.
⊙ : Privately owned but open at advertised times.

Page 130 .

A CASTLE GLOSSARY.

(Note that some descriptions are almost interchangeable. They came into being over many centuries to describe buildings similar in function and were used by local folk who never worried about precise terminology. All they were concerned with was security!)

BAILEY. A defensible enclosure around a castle or motte.

BARMKIN. A refuge in the form of a walled enclosure attached to or surrounding a tower or pele where livestock would be kept when the neighbourhood was under threat from raiders.

BASTLE. A strongly defended stone farmhouse where the base may have been a refuge for animals. The main hall would be on the first floor with further domestic quarters above, usually reached by a stairway within the wall. According to the 1970 "Royal Commission of Historical Monuments" the term bastle was in general use after 1541.

CASTLE. A large fortified building or complex of buildings with a surrounding curtain wall, frequently with a residential core and often used as a base for military activity. The term 'castle' may be used imprecisely to describe any large fortified building.

FORTALICE. The term was used to describe a lesser castle.

KEEP. The 'impregnable' core building of a castle to which all would retire if the main outer defences were breached.

MOTTE. A mound, artificial if a natural hill was unavailable, topped by a defensive structure, originally of wood. (Forerunner of the keep.)

PELE. A fortified tower with a protective enclosure. Like *motte* the name has French origins and in time was applied to the tower only. There would be a first floor hall and solar (the lord's retiring room), second floor bedchambers with wall walks and ramparts above. This was the basic arrangement but the pattern could be much more elaborate.

TOWER HOUSE. Similar in arrangement to the *pele* and effectively a miniature keep. The basement was used as a storehouse and often reached by way of a trapdoor in its ceiling. For defensive reasons the main access to the tower was by an outside stairway to the first floor.

SEATON BURN to CLIFTON
6 miles (284·9 miles)

CRAMLINGTON, to the east, is one of a pair of 'New Towns' (the other is Killingworth) though the old village remains at the core of the modern development. Old Cramlington was never interested in the Great North Road, being more concerned with the direct route to its own metropolis - Newcastle.

Note the increasing use of the word 'burn' for 'stream' in placenames as we travel towards Scotland.

A1 Clifton GNR

Badlington

Old Route

STANNINGTON

River Blyth

Stannington Bridge

Farewell Tyneside. Thanks for having us!

Seven Mile House

Cramlington

A1068

A19

B1318 GNR

SEATON BURN

LANDRANGER MAPS 81 & 88

MORPETH

We cross the River Wansbeck into Morpeth with a sense of having stepped on the doorstep of the real Northumberland with its hills, coast and history beckoning ~ indeed the name means 'the path (peth) to the moors'. It was always a bustling market town but being on the fringe of the coalfield much 19th. and 20th. century growth has accumulated round the earlier core obscuring its origins, yet it remains a good centre for the tourist. Although much of Morpeth is relatively new there is a sense of antiquity which begs closer examination. The Great North Road enters by Telford's bridge of 1831 which had a toll house though its function as such ceased in 1848; it survives, on the west side of the bridge. An older 13th. century hump-backed bridge carried the road prior to this but the Town Corporation chose a drastic means of avoiding the cost of maintenance in 1834: they had it blown up! The old abutments now support a footbridge. At the northern end of the older bridge a chantry was built in the 13th. century. In the ensuing years there have been many alterations to suit subsequent uses and in 1980-81 it was restored and currently houses the Tourist Information Centre, the Bagpipe Museum and a Craft Centre. Morpeth had two castles. The first was a motte and bailey with timber defences situated on Ha Hill south of the river; a little further south stands the 14th century gatehouse of a more substantial fortification. This, and a stretch of curtain wall, is all that was left after a 21 day siege in 1644 during the Civil War. Don't blame Cromwell this time though - it was the Royalists.

The Chantry.

THE NORTHUMBRIAN SMALL PIPES

Though the bagpipe is associated with Scotland this is one of the world's most ancient instruments and there is evidence that it arrived in Britain with the Romans and was popular in England before the Scots claimed it as their own. Shakespeare (Henry IV, Part 1) has Falstaff refer to 'the drone of a Lincolnshire pipe' as a simile for his melancholy. Other counties had their pipes but the English region which retains the bagpipe in regular use to the present day is Northumbria.

The Northumbrian Small Pipe differs from the Scottish Great Pipe in several respects. The air bag is inflated by bellows held under the arm and there are usually four drones, rather than the three of its Scottish relative. The chanter is stopped at the end so that when the finger holes are all closed there is no sound and staccato playing is possible. The pipes of Northumbria have a sweet and haunting quality whose gentle tone is quite suited to indoor playing. Visit the Bagpipe Museum in Morpeth to learn the history of the bagpipe and hear examples of its music.

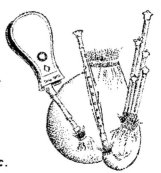

THE RIVER WANSBECK.

The Wansbeck is short, as rivers come and go, 27 miles from its source to Wansbeck Weir at its mouth. It traces a wavering line by the lost villages of West Whelpington and South Middleton. Only a few miles into its existence as a named river it reaches the National Trust property of Wallington Hall, worth a visit if you can find time. Mitford, not far upstream from Morpeth, has a castle, originally a motte and bailey but a shell keep was built on the motte. The ancient remains occupy a position of strength on a rocky ridge embraced on three sides by water at the confluence of the Wansbeck with a minor tributary, the Park Burn. As the river approaches close to Morpeth it passes the scant remnants of Newminster Abbey, once one of the richest establishments in the north whose wealth was in part gained from its pits, an early example of the local exploitation of coal. Downstream of Morpeth is yet another castle at Bothal where there is also a Saxon church. Ashington was the "largest coal mining village in the world" but football historians will know it as the birthplace of the brothers Jack and Bobby Charlton and their uncle, Jackie Milburn. From here to the North Sea it was coal all the way but in a changing world the environs of the river have been tidied with riverside paths, parks and woodland, collectively known as Wansbeck Riverside Park.

NOTE: THE CASTLES AT MITFORD AND BOTHAL AND ALSO NEWMINSTER ABBEY ARE CURRENTLY NOT OPEN TO THE PUBLIC.

When Thomas Telford built the new bridge over the River Wansbeck at Morpeth (designed by John Dobson) he re-aligned the approach from the south. Previously the Great North Road had hugged the hillside above the valley swamps. These were drained and the burn now flows in a culvert. The old route is still there as a narrow metalled lane and footway above the A197.

MORPETH
(CLIFTON to HEBRON HILL
5·7 miles (290·6 miles)

The east window of St. Mary's Church in Morpeth has fine medieval glass. If you are interested in Emily Wilding Davison, the suffragette (see next page) you will find her grave in the churchyard here.

Hebron Hill

GNR

A1

A697

Fair Moor

A192

B6343
MITFORD

B1337

A197 →
To Pegswood and Ashington (& Bothal)

River Wansbeck

A196 →
To Ashington (5 miles)

MORPETH

A192

A197

A1

GNR

Clifton

LANDRANGER MAP 81

Brinkburn Priory

The Norman doorway.

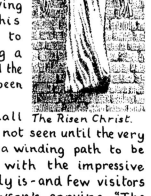

The Risen Christ.

A group of Augustinian canons chose a beautiful loop of the River Coquet for the site of a priory, c.1135. Little of their layout survives, in fact a manor house was superimposed on the refectory and the adjacent buildings after the Dissolution and the church gradually fell into disrepair. Sympathetic restoration was begun in 1858 so that we now have a church very close in appearance to the original building.

Being close to the Borders the canons of Brinkburn, despite living in a remote wooded glen, suffered as much as anyone in this troubled region. There is a legend that they were once so jubilant to have been missed by a party of marauding Scots that they rang a peal of bells in celebration; alas! the Scots were not far away and the chimes guided them to the spot. The bells are supposed to have been hurled into the Coquet where, it is told, they still lie.

A visit to Brinkburn Priory (English Heritage) does involve a small detour from the A1 but it is very much worthwhile. The church is not seen until the very last moment as you approach in the delightful sylvan seclusion of a winding path to be confronted by a classic Norman doorway. Inside you are faced with the impressive simplicity of a building that looks much larger than it actually is - and few visitors can fail to be moved by the majestic strength of Fenwick Lawson's carving, "The Risen Christ," which dominates the north transept.

EMILY WILDING DAVISON. A journey to Brinkburn may very likely take you through Longhorsley. One of Northumberland's tower houses stands here, a prominent building though in private occupation. But Longhorsley's fame rests securely in the person of the suffragette who threw herself in the path of the King's horse at the 1913 Derby.

Emily Wilding Davison was born here in 1872. After graduating from London University she joined the cause led by Emmeline Pankhurst and became a member of the more militant division of the Women's Social and Political Union. She interrupted debates in the House of Commons, horsewhipped an unfortunate clergyman whom she mistook for Lloyd George and when her activities - on more than one occasion - led to imprisonment her protests were maintained by hunger strikes, during which she suffered forced feeding. (As, of course, did her comrades.)

Emily died four days after that infamous Derby, from her injuries, and is buried in the graveyard of St. Mary's Parish Church in Morpeth. Her stand is not forgotten in Longhorsley. Look for her plaque outside the post office doorway.

Brinkburn Priory is barely five miles from Rothbury and the nearby Victorian splendour of Cragside. This "baronial style" mansion, now in the keeping of the National Trust, was built by Newcastle-born William Armstrong between 1864 and 1895. Elevated to the peerage as the first Lord Armstrong for his work as an inventor, specifically in the development of armaments, he put his inventive skills to use in the design of his house, the first to be lit by hydro-electricity.

The grounds are equally famous. A vast hillside was transformed by the creation of lakes, waterfalls, and miles of drives and pathways. Trees and shrubs were planted by the million. In the springtime the display of rhododendrons and azaleas is justly renowned.

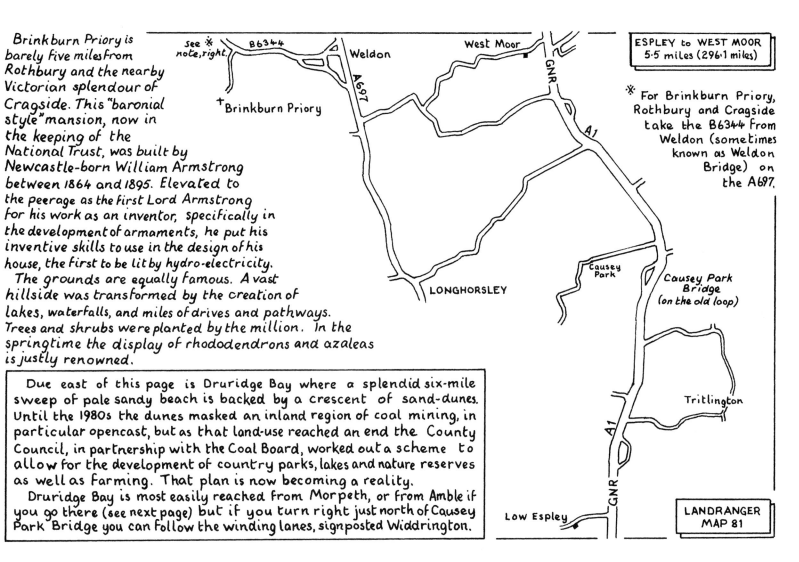

see ※ note, right.

B6344

Weldon

West Moor

GNR

A697

+ Brinkburn Priory

A1

LONGHORSLEY

Causey Park

Causey Park Bridge (on the old loop)

Tritlington

A1

GNR

Low Espley

ESPLEY to WEST MOOR 5.5 miles (296.1 miles)

※ For Brinkburn Priory, Rothbury and Cragside take the B6344 from Weldon (sometimes known as Weldon Bridge) on the A697.

LANDRANGER MAP 81

Due east of this page is Druridge Bay where a splendid six-mile sweep of pale sandy beach is backed by a crescent of sand-dunes. Until the 1980s the dunes masked an inland region of coal mining, in particular opencast, but as that land-use reached an end the County Council, in partnership with the Coal Board, worked out a scheme to allow for the development of country parks, lakes and nature reserves as well as farming. That plan is now becoming a reality.

Druridge Bay is most easily reached from Morpeth, or from Amble if you go there (see next page) but if you turn right just north of Causey Park Bridge you can follow the winding lanes, signposted Widdrington.

WARKWORTH

It is a serpentine diversion of some six miles to Warkworth but the journey should be undertaken, if only to compare the town with Alnwick, which appears on the next map. The links are strong. These are towns dominated by a castle, in each case a fortress of the Percy Earls of Northumberland, and here is the "daffodil castle." So frivolous a name may put the place into the realms of the fairytale rather than the military but you only have to visit in the springtime to see justification in the epithet.

Warkworth Castle is now a ruin, but an imposing one; the 14th century keep is one of the splendours of Northumberland. A study of the map will show how well sited is this stronghold. It sits astride the neck of a loop of the River Coquet, the little town being protected by the wide waters and the castle's defensive walls.

Such protection was surely needed. In 1174, before the castle reached full defensive power, a party of Scots burned the town and murdered 300 inhabitants who had trustingly sought refuge within the church. St. Lawrence's is beside the river with a clear view of the castle atop the hill at the far end of the wide main street. Mainly a Norman church, perhaps the best example in the county, it occupies the site of a previous Saxon building. There is much to repay a leisurely tour. The artless strength of the stone spire will linger in the memory.

The keep, Warkworth Castle.

The approach from the north was over a 14th century arched bridge with a gatehouse. A modern crossing alongside now takes the weight of today's traffic which must still negotiate the crowded peninsular of old grey stone houses.

Warkworth Hermitage is a cell carved in a rock cliff on the north bank of the Coquet and may be reached only by boat. Enquire at the castle.

The River Coquet reaches the sea at Amble. Its days of commercial prosperity as a port belonged to coal but fishing had its place too; this past industry has left the harbour with space for a fine marina and at least 250 berths for small boats. Offshore is the bird sanctuary of Coquet Island, home to eider ducks, terns and puffins. In 684ad amid the birds and the sea, St. Cuthbert met Elfreda, Abbess of Whitby, whose powers of persuasion were to lead him to the bishopric of Lindisfarne.

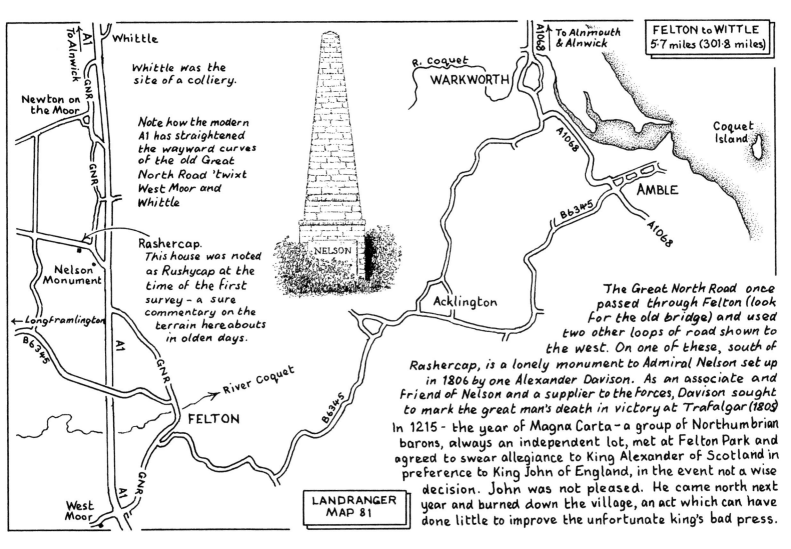

Whittle

Whittle was the site of a colliery.

Note how the modern A1 has straightened the wayward curves of the old Great North Road 'twixt West Moor and Whittle

A1
To Alnwick

GNR

GNR

Newton on the Moor

Nelson Monument

Rashercap.
This house was noted as Rushycap at the time of the first survey – a sure commentary on the terrain hereabouts in olden days.

← Longframlington

B6345

A1

GNR

River Coquet

FELTON

West Moor

A1

GNR

NELSON

R. Coquet

WARKWORTH

A1068
↑ To Alnmouth & Alnwick

A1068

A1068

B6345

AMBLE

Coquet Island

Acklington

B6345

The Great North Road once passed through Felton (look for the old bridge) and used two other loops of road shown to the west. On one of these, south of Rashercap, is a lonely monument to Admiral Nelson set up in 1806 by one Alexander Davison. As an associate and friend of Nelson and a supplier to the forces, Davison sought to mark the great man's death in victory at Trafalgar (1805)

In 1215 – the year of Magna Carta – a group of Northumbrian barons, always an independent lot, met at Felton Park and agreed to swear allegiance to King Alexander of Scotland in preference to King John of England, in the event not a wise decision. John was not pleased. He came north next year and burned down the village, an act which can have done little to improve the unfortunate king's bad press.

LANDRANGER MAP 81

ALNWICK

The adjective 'historic' is often used indiscriminately by those responsible for tourist publicity but there can be no criticism of its use in this case. When you pass through the Percy Gate of the Hotspur Tower, which straddles the old north road, you know immediately that here is a town with medieval roots. This is the remaining gate of the only walled town between Newcastle and Berwick, a form of defence deemed necessary in 1434.

Almost synonymous with Alnwick is the name of Percy, the family which has presided over Northumberland for nearly 700 years and whose family home is the twelfth century castle that surveys the northern approaches from a position of power above the south bank of the River Aln. It was the first line of defence against the Scots south of the Tweed. Lack of royal support in defence of the borderlands, especially in matters of finance, led to friction between the Earl of Northumberland and Henry IV. The Earl's son, 'Harry' Hotspur, marched in revolt but was defeated and killed at Shrewsbury in 1403.

The power of the Dukes of Northumberland remains immediately visible in the castle and in the extent of Alnwick Park. It was the influence of the Percys that caused the town to develop south and east from the castle and its parkland. Originally the town was centred round the Castle Square where there stood a cross but soon the commercial pivot came to rest at the village green which became the market place, now dominated by the striking, arcaded Northumberland Hall.

A walk around the Old Town well repays the effort. Narrow cobbled streets and inviting passageways hold fine old buildings of character, many of which now house craft or antique shops, art galleries, bookshops, restaurants and much else to attract the visitor.

If you happen to be there at the end of June you can hardly miss the annual street fair which lasts a week from the final Sunday of the month. The International Music Festival comes to town in August.

The Percy family emblem, a lion with a horizontal tail, stands high on the Percy Tenantry Column at the southern approach to the Old Town and it proudly guards the Lion Bridge which carries our route across the Aln on its way to Scotland.

Alnwick Castle from the Lion Bridge.

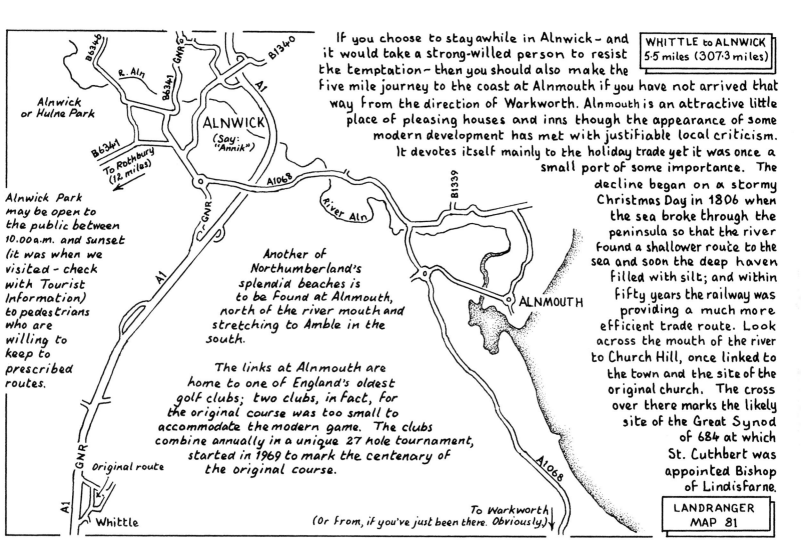

If you choose to stay awhile in Alnwick – and it would take a strong-willed person to resist the temptation – then you should also make the five mile journey to the coast at Alnmouth if you have not arrived that way from the direction of Warkworth. Alnmouth is an attractive little place of pleasing houses and inns though the appearance of some modern development has met with justifiable local criticism. It devotes itself mainly to the holiday trade yet it was once a small port of some importance. The decline began on a stormy Christmas Day in 1806 when the sea broke through the peninsula so that the river found a shallower route to the sea and soon the deep haven filled with silt; and within fifty years the railway was providing a much more efficient trade route. Look across the mouth of the river to Church Hill, once linked to the town and the site of the original church. The cross over there marks the likely site of the Great Synod of 684 at which St. Cuthbert was appointed Bishop of Lindisfarne.

LANDRANGER
MAP 81

Alnwick or Hulne Park

To Rothbury (12 miles)

ALNWICK
(Say: "Annik")

Alnwick Park may be open to the public between 10.00 a.m. and sunset (it was when we visited – check with Tourist Information) to pedestrians who are willing to keep to prescribed routes.

Another of Northumberland's splendid beaches is to be found at Alnmouth, north of the river mouth and stretching to Amble in the south.

The links at Alnmouth are home to one of England's oldest golf clubs; two clubs, in fact, for the original course was too small to accommodate the modern game. The clubs combine annually in a unique 27 hole tournament, started in 1969 to mark the centenary of the original course.

River Aln

ALNMOUTH

Original route

Whittle

To Warkworth
(Or from, if you've just been there. Obviously.)

DUNSTANBURGH CASTLE

The curtain walls at Dunstanburgh enclose a larger area than any others in Northumberland. These ruined walls, gatehouse and towers present a stirring sight on the castle hill, overlooking the sea and isolated from modern habitation where the Whin Sill reaches the coast. The northern defences largely rely upon basaltic cliffs but elsewhere the geology is less dramatic and the ruins present a greater impact on the eye. Behind the gatehouse, which also served as keep, is the small inner ward which was the focus of castle life. Dunstanburgh Castle was built primarily as a defended retreat for its owner, Thomas, the second earl of Lancaster, but he never used it as such. He was taken prisoner in 1322 at the Battle of Boroughbridge and put to death in another of his castles at Pontefract. Approach on foot from either Craster or, preferably, Embleton, finishing at Craster. The walk along the coast is worth the effort.

Dunstanburgh - the gatehouse/keep.

CHILLINGHAM CASTLE

Chillingham was a manor house but in the 14th. century licence to crenellate was granted and it is now a formidable castle with corner turrets. It became untenanted in 1933 but more recently was bought by Sir Humphrey Wakefield and restored. Many visitors are drawn by a wish to see the herd of Wild White Cattle for which Chillingham is famous. These animals have been enclosed in the park for 700 years and remain pure bred - a living link with the ancient wild cattle of Britain. Approach by way of Ros Castle from North Charlton; return through the attractive village of Chatton and along the B6348.

ROS CASTLE

This is not a medieval castle but an Iron Age hill fort of which only remnant earthworks may be seen. However as a viewpoint (on a clear day!) it is certainly worth the detour. Take the minor road west from North Charlton and in six miles, at the road summit, park on the verge with a hilltop on your right. The summit of this little peak is at 1034 feet (315m) but don't let that be a concern. You step out of the car at about 834 feet so the top is only two hundred feet higher, up an initially steep but obvious track through the bracken. You'll be rewarded by a splendid panorama. Seawards, look for the real castles at Dunstanburgh, Bamburgh and Lindisfarne, and the Longstone Light on the Farne Islands. To the west, Chillingham Castle and Park are close by with the distant Cheviot Hills beyond. All this is fine walking country, very tempting if you have the appropriate gear and walking boots (which should really be on your feet, anyway).

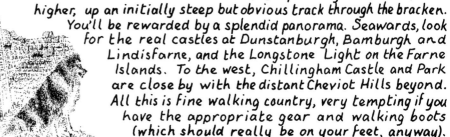
Ros Castle summit.

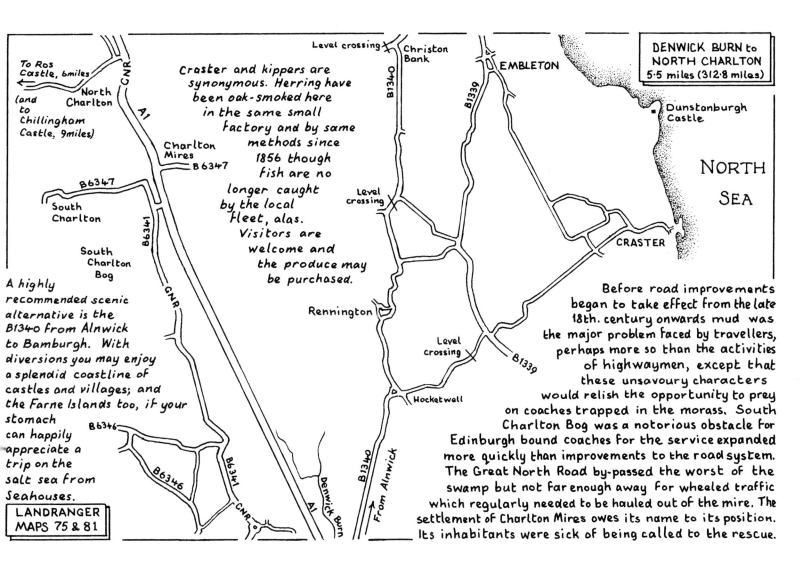

To Ros Castle, 6miles

(and to Chillingham Castle, 9miles)

North Charlton

Charlton Mires

B6347

B6347

South Charlton

South Charlton Bog

Level crossing

Christon Bank

EMBLETON

Dunstonburgh Castle

NORTH SEA

Level crossing

Level crossing

Level crossing

CRASTER

Rennington

Hocketwell

B1340

B1339

B1339

B1340

A1

GNR

GNR

B6341

B6341

B6346

B6346

Denwick Burn

From Alnwick

Craster and kippers are synonymous. Herring have been oak-smoked here in the same small factory and by same methods since 1856 though fish are no longer caught by the local fleet, alas. Visitors are welcome and the produce may be purchased.

A highly recommended scenic alternative is the B1340 from Alnwick to Bamburgh. With diversions you may enjoy a splendid coastline of castles and villages; and the Farne Islands too, if your stomach can happily appreciate a trip on the salt sea from Seahouses.

LANDRANGER MAPS 75 & 81

Before road improvements began to take effect from the late 18th. century onwards mud was the major problem faced by travellers, perhaps more so than the activities of highwaymen, except that these unsavoury characters would relish the opportunity to prey on coaches trapped in the morass. South Charlton Bog was a notorious obstacle for Edinburgh bound coaches for the service expanded more quickly than improvements to the road system. The Great North Road by-passed the worst of the swamp but not far enough away for wheeled traffic which regularly needed to be hauled out of the mire. The settlement of Charlton Mires owes its name to its position. Its inhabitants were sick of being called to the rescue.

THE FARNE ISLANDS

This group of islands spans over three miles from one and a half miles off-shore. The isles are the last visible sign of the Whin Sill as it dips into the sea. The National Trust is the major landowner. Permission to land on Inner Farne and Staple Island is granted at stated times in spring and summer (but not in the breeding season) when the designated boatmen are satisfied that weather conditions are safe. Make enquiries at Seahouses harbour. But even if there is no chance of landing, the possibility of a trip around the islands should be gratefully accepted, with every chance of seeing seals amidst the multitudinous seabird life and of identifying the place where Grace Darling and her father performed great deeds (see overleaf). There are perhaps 28 islands, but at high tide and with a high sea running only 15 are visible. St. Cuthbert meditated in a hermitage on Inner Farne for six years until he was persuaded to become Bishop of Hexham and later of Lindisfarne in 684. After two years he returned to Inner Farne and three months later he died there.

> *THE WHIN SILL* or Great Whin Sill is a series of basaltic rocks known as dolerite which has resisted erosion and is evident right across Northumberland, often in the form of crags on which our ancestors found ideal sites for military and defensive architecture. Castles and pele towers often point to the presence of the Great Whin Sill – and the Romans must have rubbed their Mediterranean hands with glee when surveying the line of the wall that the Emperor Hadrian had decreed.

PRESTON TOWER

The tower at Preston was a small rectangular tower house or hall with turrets at the corners but by 1860 this had become ruined to the extent that only the south front and two turrets remained. A new wall was built along the north side of the remnant to preserve the remains, which then became a clock tower in the gardens of the adjacent more modern hall. It is open to the public in summer, usually at weekends, and is certainly worth looking at if you are in the vicinity. Explore the old chambers and enjoy a fine view of the surrounding countryside from the top.

BEADNELL

The large village of Beadnell is hardly unique in having a fine beach – that is really par for the course around here. It also has its own miniature harbour, which turns its back on the North Sea and was a safe haven for the fishermen in the days when the harvest of the sea provided a reliable livelihood.

Preston Tower.

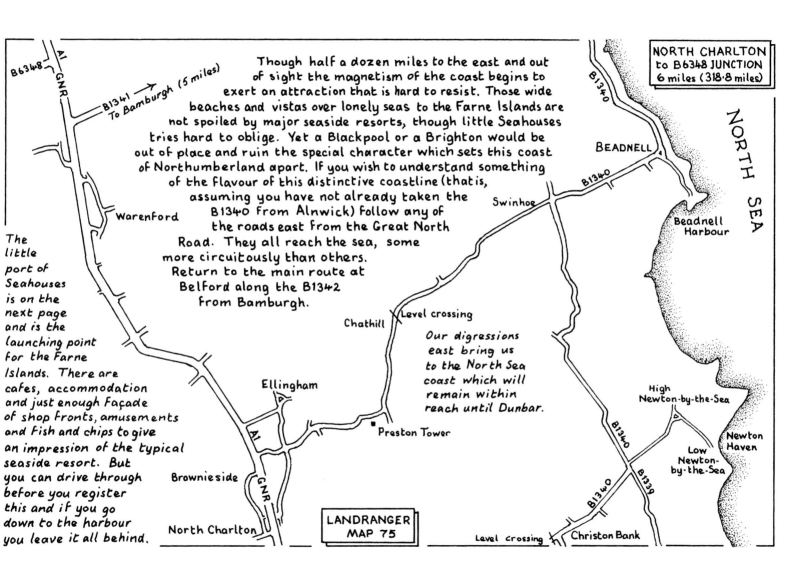

B6348

A1
GNR

B1341 →
To Bamburgh (5 miles)

B1340

NORTH SEA

BEADNELL

B1340

Beadnell
Harbour

Swinhoe

Warenford

Though half a dozen miles to the east and out
of sight the magnetism of the coast begins to
exert on attraction that is hard to resist. Those wide
beaches and vistas over lonely seas to the Farne Islands are
not spoiled by major seaside resorts, though little Seahouses
tries hard to oblige. Yet a Blackpool or a Brighton would be
out of place and ruin the special character which sets this coast
of Northumberland apart. If you wish to understand something
of the flavour of this distinctive coastline (that is,
assuming you have not already taken the
B1340 from Alnwick) follow any of
the roads east from the Great North
Road. They all reach the sea, some
more circuitously than others.
Return to the main route at
Belford along the B1342
from Bamburgh.

The
little
port of
Seahouses
is on the
next page
and is the
launching point
for the Farne
Islands. There are
cafes, accommodation
and just enough façade
of shop fronts, amusements
and fish and chips to give
an impression of the typical
seaside resort. But
you can drive through
before you register
this and if you go
down to the harbour
you leave it all behind.

Chathill

Level crossing

Our digressions
east bring us
to the North Sea
coast which will
remain within
reach until Dunbar.

Ellingham

High
Newton-by-the-Sea

B1340

Preston Tower

Newton
Haven

Low
Newton-
by-the-
Sea

Brownieside

A1
GNR

B1340

B1339

LANDRANGER
MAP 75

North Charlton

Level crossing

Christon Bank

BAMBURGH CASTLE

It is very likely that the strong defensible position of the crag overlooking and defying the North Sea was used before history was written. Pottery finds show that the Romans were there, and surely they were not the first, but the fortress as we know it began to take shape when the Normans came. For 400 years the keep and defensive bulwarks provided a stronghold, impregnable to attack, favoured by kings and princes and feared by the prisoners who were brought there; but the development of the cannon caused this to become the first major stronghold in England to succumb to the force of artillery. After 200 years of neglect Bamburgh was partly restored and became a school, an infirmary and a hostel for seamen. Its position also made it the obvious location for a lighthouse. In the late nineteenth century it was bought by Lord Armstrong who restored it on a massive scale so that, while from the outside this one is certainly among the most exciting castles in Britain, within the walls much of the Norman work has been lost to provide comfortable accommodation in keeping with a modern world.

Bamburgh

GRACE DARLING

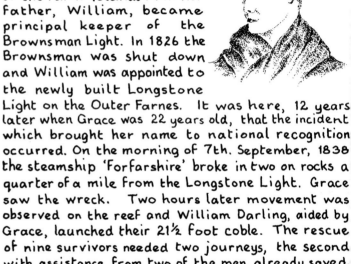

Grace was born in Bamburgh in 1815 but before she was a year old her parents took her to the Farne Islands when her father, William, became principal keeper of the Brownsman Light. In 1826 the Brownsman was shut down and William was appointed to the newly built Longstone Light on the Outer Farnes. It was here, 12 years later when Grace was 22 years old, that the incident which brought her name to national recognition occurred. On the morning of 7th. September, 1838 the steamship 'Forfarshire' broke in two on rocks a quarter of a mile from the Longstone Light. Grace saw the wreck. Two hours later movement was observed on the reef and William Darling, aided by Grace, launched their 21½ foot coble. The rescue of nine survivors needed two journeys, the second with assistance from two of the men already saved. Grace became a national heroine for the story appealed to the Victorian sense of values and duty. There has been much exaggeration in the telling of the tale, often with the suggestion that she was the driving force behind the decision to attempt the rescue. However, her father was his own man and one of great bravery, as he displayed in other rescues. Yet Grace, too, showed courage in volunteering her help, without which the outcome may have been uncertain. Grace died of tuberculosis in 1842.

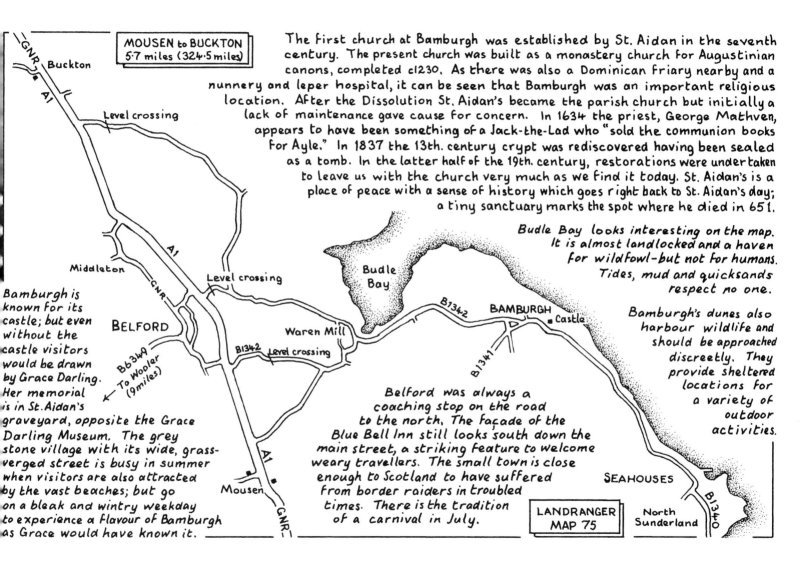

Buckton

GNR
A1

Level crossing

A1

GNR

Middleton

Level crossing

BELFORD

Bb349
To Wooler
(9 miles)

B1342   Level crossing

A1

GNR

Mousen

Budle
Bay

Waren Mill

B1342

B1341

BAMBURGH

Castle

SEAHOUSES

B1340

North
Sunderland

The first church at Bamburgh was established by St. Aidan in the seventh century. The present church was built as a monastery church for Augustinian canons, completed c1230. As there was also a Dominican friary nearby and a nunnery and leper hospital, it can be seen that Bamburgh was an important religious location. After the Dissolution St. Aidan's became the parish church but initially a lack of maintenance gave cause for concern. In 1634 the priest, George Mathven, appears to have been something of a Jack-the-Lad who "sold the communion books for Ayle." In 1837 the 13th. century crypt was rediscovered having been sealed as a tomb. In the latter half of the 19th. century, restorations were undertaken to leave us with the church very much as we find it today. St. Aidan's is a place of peace with a sense of history which goes right back to St. Aidan's day; a tiny sanctuary marks the spot where he died in 651.

Budle Bay looks interesting on the map. It is almost landlocked and a haven for wildfowl-but not for humans. Tides, mud and quicksands respect no one.

Bamburgh's dunes also harbour wildlife and should be approached discreetly. They provide sheltered locations for a variety of outdoor activities.

Bamburgh is known for its castle; but even without the castle visitors would be drawn by Grace Darling. Her memorial is in St. Aidan's graveyard, opposite the Grace Darling Museum. The grey stone village with its wide, grass-verged street is busy in summer when visitors are also attracted by the vast beaches; but go on a bleak and wintry weekday to experience a flavour of Bamburgh as Grace would have known it.

Belford was always a coaching stop on the road to the north. The façade of the Blue Bell Inn still looks south down the main street, a striking feature to welcome weary travellers. The small town is close enough to Scotland to have suffered from border raiders in troubled times. There is the tradition of a carnival in July.

LANDRANGER
MAP 75

HOLY ISLAND

When St. Aidan came to Lindisfarne from Iona in 634 a.d. he set up a small oratory and his dynamic personality powered his teaching from a site which became the missionary focus of Christian Northumbria. Thirty years later St. Cuthbert arrived, soon to lead a solitary life off-shore on St. Cuthbert's Isle. He moved to a tiny hermitage on the Farne Islands but returned six years later as Bishop of Lindisfarne. His ministry lasted for two years until he went back to the Farnes to die. Holy Island will forever be linked with St. Cuthbert and the Lindisfarne Gospels. This famed illuminated manuscript was begun eleven years after St. Cuthbert's death and remained on the island some 200 years until continuing threats of Danish invasion caused the monks to leave. The Gospels spent many medieval years at Durham Cathedral but may now be found at the British Museum. The priory ruins are of Benedictine origin and date from 1093 when the name 'Holy Island' was adapted. This was a cell of Durham and in some respects the ruined church displays a family resemblance to the cathedral there. Perhaps the most remembered feature is a solitary remaining supporting rib of the departed central tower which, with its zig-zag moulding, earns its popular name of the 'Rainbow Arch'. From the mainland the Holy Island landmark is Lindisfarne Castle. The hundred foot crag on which it rests, yet another outcrop of the Whin Sill, is a cornerstone of the island. The castle was built in the mid-16th. century after an Order that all northern harbours should be defended against the Scots. After the Union of Thrones it was of less importance but soon continental threats brought the need for repairs and improvements. It is smaller than appearances suggest and was essentially a fort which held two batteries of guns. Considering the dramatic situation, commanding aspect and perfection of scale, it is not surprising that it is always referred to as a castle. At the beginning of the twentieth century Sir Edwin Lutyens was engaged as architect when it was re-designed as a private house. In 1944 it was handed over to the National Trust. There is so much to see on Holy Island that the period between the tides is not long enough for a visit. The suggestion is that if the tide timings are convenient to plan being stranded and enjoy the island without the coach parties and between-tide visitors. Half the place closes down, the streets are suddenly empty and you get some slight impression of what Holy Island might be without tourists.

The 'Rainbow Arch' in the Priory.

Lindisfarne Castle.

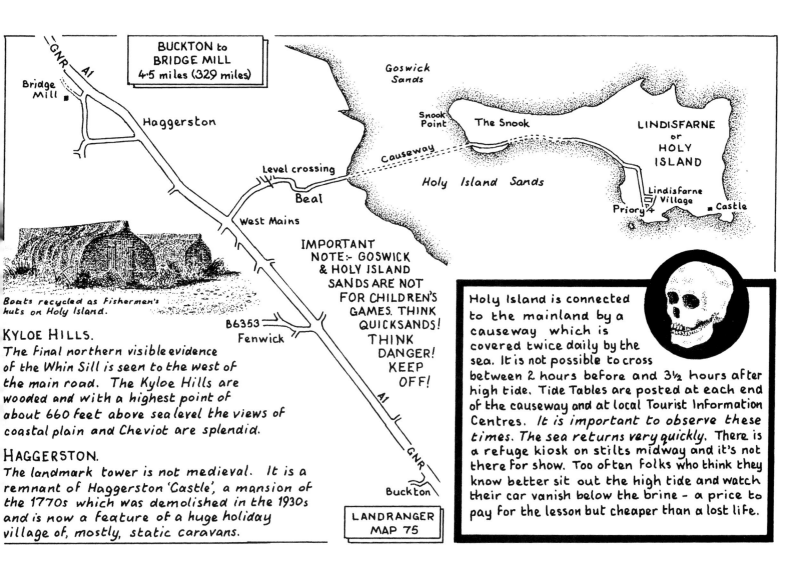

BUCKTON to BRIDGE MILL
4·5 miles (329 miles)

Bridge Mill

Haggerston

Goswick Sands

Snook Point

The Snook

LINDISFARNE or HOLY ISLAND

Causeway

Holy Island Sands

Level crossing

Beal

West Mains

Lindisfarne Village

Priory

Castle

Boats recycled as Fishermen's huts on Holy Island.

IMPORTANT NOTE:- GOSWICK & HOLY ISLAND SANDS ARE NOT FOR CHILDREN'S GAMES. THINK QUICKSANDS! THINK DANGER! KEEP OFF!

KYLOE HILLS.
The final northern visible evidence of the Whin Sill is seen to the west of the main road. The Kyloe Hills are wooded and with a highest point of about 660 feet above sea level the views of coastal plain and Cheviot are splendid.

HAGGERSTON.
The landmark tower is not medieval. It is a remnant of Haggerston 'Castle', a mansion of the 1770s which was demolished in the 1930s and is now a feature of a huge holiday village of, mostly, static caravans.

B6353
Fenwick

Buckton

LANDRANGER MAP 75

Holy Island is connected to the mainland by a causeway which is covered twice daily by the sea. It is not possible to cross between 2 hours before and 3½ hours after high tide. Tide Tables are posted at each end of the causeway and at local Tourist Information Centres. *It is important to observe these times. The sea returns very quickly.* There is a refuge kiosk on stilts midway and it's not there for show. Too often folks who think they know better sit out the high tide and watch their car vanish below the brine - a price to pay for the lesson but cheaper than a lost life.

TWEEDMOUTH

We reach the Border river at Tweedmouth which deserves a separate identity though it is now effectively a suburb of Berwick. Before crossing the river consider a short there-and-back detour past the old shipyard and Tweed Dock to Sandstell Point to enjoy an aspect of the river's mouth that usually only the locals see. On the way along the riverside you'll see the lifeboat station – don't pass it! We drove round here late on a sunny autumn afternoon and parked on Carr Rock Quay beside the lifeboat house to eat our sandwiches with only a couple of young fishermen for company. From the quay there is a splendid view of the three Tweed bridges, seen as a well-composed group that demands a photograph when the sun is in the right position. The tide was on the turn and we were fascinated by a group of cormorants fishing for their dinners and a couple of grey seals diving with obvious success, more so than the anglers who packed up and went home. Round the corner from Sandstell Point with its fine sands is Spittal where local folk enjoy the seaside from a small promenade. Beyond this is the coastal path which was a route to the south in olden times.

Norham – the keep seen through the curtain wall.

Alternative route south from Spittal at Cheswick Dunes.

NORHAM CASTLE

Although Norham is some seven miles distant, castle enthusiasts will find the A698 an irresistible road. The ruins of this fortress, built in the twelfth century by a bishop of Durham, still dominate a bend in the River Tweed. The pattern is of the classic motte and bailey converted to and consolidated by massive stone defences. The plan is of a quadrant with the motte situated at the pivotal right-angle and defended from the outer bailey by a deep ditch. There is no doubt that its impressive strength was due to the proximity of Scotland and its garrison must have believed the position impregnable – until the Scots James IV organised its defeat and partial destruction in 1513. Norham is one of the unsung castles of Northumberland but consider its praises set to an heroic tune now!

The village of Norham looks up to its castle; indeed the castle is some distance away but as you stand on the fringe of the triangular green with the old market cross on your right you feel a sense of a village at one with its own stronghold. The church is an essential part of the group. It also has Norman origins; and what dedication could be more appropriate in this part of the North Country? St. Cuthbert, of course!

THE DEVIL'S CAUSEWAY. The Romans, as ever, were here first. They built a road from Corstopitum (Corbridge) near Hadrian's Wall to the mouth of the River Tweed. This bears no geographical relationship to our own road. The Roman forerunner lies more to the west but the routes do come together just south of the Tweed where the built-up area of Tweedmouth begins. There are few signs of the Devil's Causeway on the ground. It is better to trace it on the map by reference to various road, bridleway and footpath alignments and it is fascinating to follow the line on O.S. maps (75, 81 and 87). When the soldiers of Rome had gone it was not maintained and from medieval times the Great North Road became more important. The Roman way was lost by neglect.

BRIDGE MILL to TWEEDMOUTH
5·5 miles (334·5 miles)
The original line of the Great North Road continues in a straight and obvious line through Scremerston to Tweedmouth as the A1167.
Sandstell Point
TWEEDMOUTH
Spittal
A1
A698
A698
B6354
GNR
A1167
By-pass
B6354
Scremerston
GNR
Line of the Devil's Causeway
Cocklawburn Beach
An older and now forgotten route south continues as a track through the dunes (as noted on the opposite page).
B6525
Cheswick Buildings
A1
GNR
Bridge Mill
LANDRANGER MAP 75

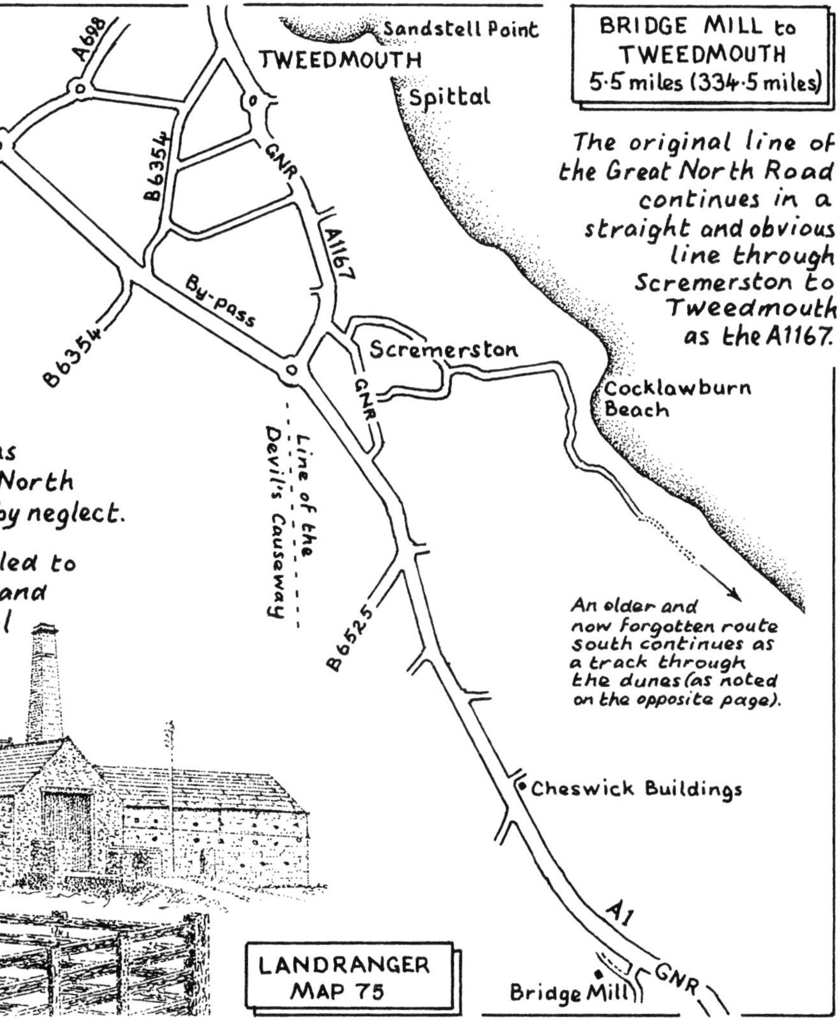

THRESHING MILLS. The advent of steam power led to some mechanisation in farming and with Tyneside's and Scotland's coalfields not far away many substantial farmsteads in the Borders turned to steam to power their threshing mills. A feature of many large farms is a tall chimney, now redundant and seemingly out of place in a rural and peaceful landscape. The example at Cheswick Buildings appears to be in a fragile condition at the time of writing.

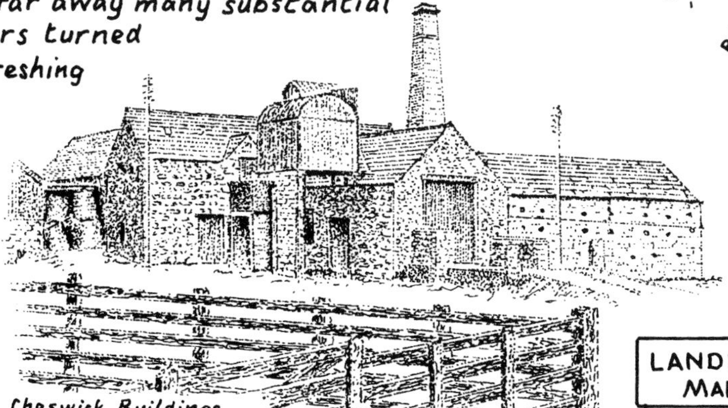

Cheswick Buildings.

BERWICK-UPON-TWEED

Berwick is the northernmost town in England but it has stood on Scottish soil many a time during its long and exciting history. The River Tweed is the natural frontier but Berwick was Scottish and English in turn as the national boundary was re-drawn some fourteen times during 200 years of conflict between the 13th. and 15th. centuries. Though now English, Berwick has always had an essential affinity with Scotland which is sensed on crossing the Tweed, yet the political boundary is now almost three miles further north. Pevsner calls Berwick 'one of the most exciting towns in England' and it is easy to see why. This is a walled town, the walls being substantially Elizabethan fortifications designed for the use of artillery as a study of the various bastions makes clear. The Elizabethans did not complete the project and the riverside section has remained from the earlier defences constructed in the days of Edward II, largely rebuilt in the mid-18th. century. Within the walls is a town built on a medieval street pattern but because of those years of strife little of the older housing has survived. Rebuilding in the 18th. and 19th. centuries, when prosperity returned to Berwick, produced a wealth of fine architecture and it is well worth the purchase of a guide book to bring the buildings to life during a perambulation of the old streets.

THE TWEED BRIDGES

There was certainly a bridge over the Tweed before 1199 for history records that it was destroyed by floods then. Berwick Bridge (the Old Bridge) occupies approximately the same site because building took place alongside a current wooden bridge used until its stone replacement was completed in 1624. The wooden crossing was used by James (6th. Scotland/1st. England) during his stately progress south after Sir Robert Carey's epic ride with the news of Elizabeth's death. James remembered this weak link between the administrative capitals of the united countries so monies were made available for a replacement, begun in 1611. Adjacent is the 1920s bridge which carries the road over four reinforced concrete arches. It was a fine answer to the needs of increasing traffic yet romantic souls will prefer the Jacobean design that it tries to dominate - but you can't dominate history! Railways also need bridges, hence the Royal Border Bridge of 1850 which soars across the Tweed on 28 spectacular

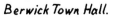

Berwick Town Hall.

arches. The latest bridge carries the A1 Berwick bypass a couple of miles upstream and from which only the railway viaduct is visible. It is a functional span that we cross with speed, hardly realising that it's there.

Berwick Old Bridge.

LAMBERTON

This tiny community, the first in Scotland, is now by-passed. The hamlet has an importance quite out of proportion with its size for it was here that Princess Margaret Tudor, daughter of Henry VII of England, was in 1503 met by the Scottish Commissioners as she crossed the border. She was betrothed to Scotland's James IV at Lamberton's tiny kirk before going on to Edinburgh for formal marriage. This union produced the Scottish line of succession which led to James VI and the Union of Crowns. Margaret's brother became Henry VIII whose childless successors left no direct heirs after the death of Elizabeth I, hence the historic ride south of James VI - through Lamberton - exactly 100 years after his great grandmother had journeyed in the opposite direction. As James I of England he reigned for 22 years and returned to his homeland just once. Lamberton Kirk is now a roofless ruin which might appear to be a large sheepfold on a small hill were it not for the tottering gravestones surrounding it - and the unlikelihood of any farmer building a sheepfold in what is already a small enclosure, the old graveyard.

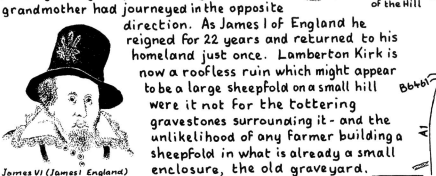

Margaret and James IV

James VI (James I England)

BERWICK-upon-TWEED to LAMBERTON MOOR 5.7 miles (340.2 miles)

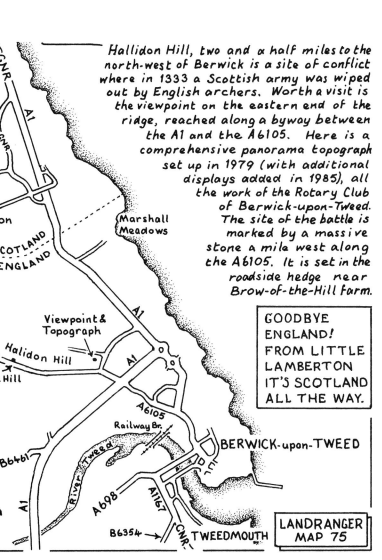

Hallidon Hill, two and a half miles to the north-west of Berwick is a site of conflict where in 1333 a Scottish army was wiped out by English archers. Worth a visit is the viewpoint on the eastern end of the ridge, reached along a byway between the A1 and the A6105. Here is a comprehensive panorama topograph set up in 1979 (with additional displays added in 1985), all the work of the Rotary Club of Berwick-upon-Tweed. The site of the battle is marked by a massive stone a mile west along the A6105. It is set in the roadside hedge near Brow-of-the-Hill farm.

GOODBYE ENGLAND! FROM LITTLE LAMBERTON IT'S SCOTLAND ALL THE WAY.

LANDRANGER MAP 75

At Burnmouth we have a choice: continue with the A1 or turn north along the A1107. The former is more direct and follows the valleys of Eye Water and Pease Burn to Cockburnspath. There is splendid valley scenery but to sweep along a busy trunk road with a main line railway in attendance is not the way to appreciate it. If there is no need for haste (surely not!) the choice is clear - it must be the A1107, the scenic coastal route.

EYEMOUTH

This is a fair sized town which had a good reputation as a fishing port, especially in the 19th. century. But in 1881 an extreme storm caught the fishing fleet at sea and one half of Eyemouth's men (129) were lost together with sixty others from this coast. The disaster is commemorated by a fifteen foot tapestry sewn to mark the centenary and on view in Eyemouth's small museum.

Coldingham and the road to Coldingham Moor.

COLDINGHAM

Coldingham had a religious foundation as early as 635 a.d. but various monastic buildings suffered destruction by fire, plunder and finally Cromwell. Today only part of the choir remains: as the parish church. The importance of Coldingham declined with the loss of the priory but it is still a pleasant village, popular with holiday makers who enjoy the small sandy beach. Coldingham of a century ago is photographically documented through the discovery of glass negatives in a retired market gardener's shed. A fine collection of prints from these is displayed locally, named after the original photographer as "The John Wood Collection."

COLDINGHAM MOOR. Between Coldingham and Cockburnspath the post boys of old met the lonely expanse of Coldingham Moor where their route peaked at 740 feet (226m) above the nearby sea. Here the transportation of the mail was surely a duty fraught with peril, many miles beyond the reach of help in case of accident or attack. Post boys were always vulnerable and in 1688 guards on horseback were assigned to the Edinburgh/Berwick road, being stationed at Tranent, Haddington, Broxburn (near Dunbar), Coldingham and at Berwick to ride with the mail. No doubt the post boys were glad to have company when crossing what was then a wasteland, not enclosed until halfway through the next century. A contemporary traveller was Daniel Defoe who obviously had no love for the place since he reported being impressed only by the barrenness of the wide moorland.

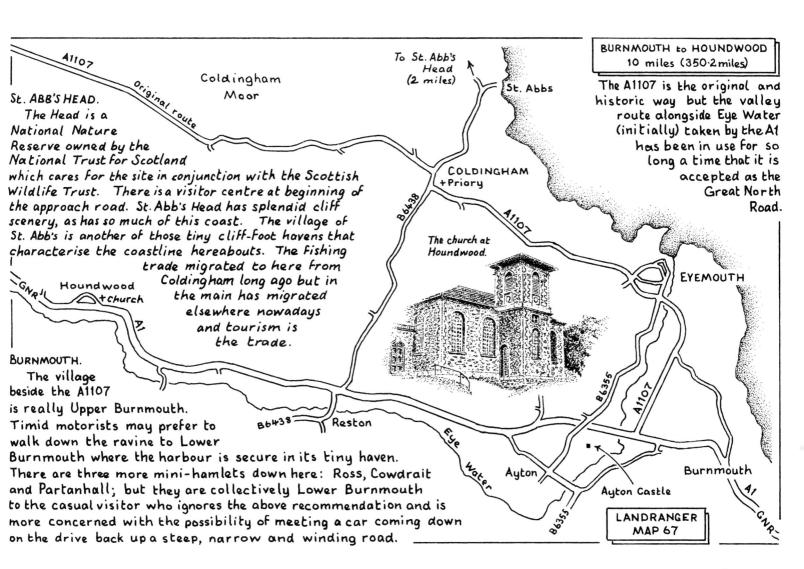

A1107

Coldingham
Moor

Original route

To St. Abb's
Head
(2 miles)

St. Abbs

COLDINGHAM
+ Priory

B6438

A1107

The church at
Houndwood.

EYEMOUTH

GNR

Houndwood
+ church

A1

B6355

A1107

The A1107 is the original and
historic way but the valley
route alongside Eye Water
(initially) taken by the A1
has been in use for so
long a time that it is
accepted as the
Great North
Road.

St. ABB'S HEAD.
The Head is a
National Nature
Reserve owned by the
National Trust for Scotland
which cares for the site in conjunction with the Scottish
Wildlife Trust. There is a visitor centre at beginning of
the approach road. St. Abb's Head has splendid cliff
scenery, as has so much of this coast. The village of
St. Abb's is another of those tiny cliff-foot havens that
characterise the coastline hereabouts. The fishing
trade migrated to here from
Coldingham long ago but in
the main has migrated
elsewhere nowadays
and tourism is
the trade.

B6438   Reston

Eye Water

Ayton

Ayton Castle

Burnmouth

A1

GNR

BURNMOUTH.
The village
beside the A1107
is really Upper Burnmouth.
Timid motorists may prefer to
walk down the ravine to Lower
Burnmouth where the harbour is secure in its tiny haven.
There are three more mini-hamlets down here: Ross, Cowdrait
and Partanhall; but they are collectively Lower Burnmouth
to the casual visitor who ignores the above recommendation and is
more concerned with the possibility of meeting a car coming down
on the drive back up a steep, narrow and winding road.

LANDRANGER
MAP 67

COCKBURNSPATH

Cockburnspath is no longer on the Great North Road, being bypassed by the A1. Yet it would be a shame to ignore the signpost which urges this tiny diversion. The mercat cross was set up around 1503 to celebrate the marriage of James IV to Margaret Tudor. It is the focal point of the village square and now marks the end of the Southern Upland Way which walkers follow from Portpatrick, 212 walking miles away on the west coast. The pleasing parish church of St. Helen is built of glowing warm sandstone and visitors will go away with a memory of its narrow cylindrical tower set centrally in the south gable.

In 1603 a postmaster was established at Cockburnspath - King James was quick to recognise the need for sound communications when he acceded to the English throne. The village was considered to be an important station on the post road to the Border, trapped between the Lammermuir Hills and the sea and coming before the perilous Pass of Pease and the difficult crossing of Coldingham Moor. This postmaster also had responsibility for customs dues on goods coming in at little Cove harbour. By the mid-eighteenth century the importance of the postmaster here was declining.

DUNGLASS

A collegiate church was one which had a college, or collective body, of ministers and priests in the same way as a cathedral. Dunglass Collegiate church was endowed as such in 1450. The church is now a shell, but an impressive one despite being used as a barn and for stabling in the 18th. century. It is reached along the old road that was the A1 before the bypass was built. Dunglass Burn is well bridged at this point. Apart from the old and new A1 bridges and the railway viaduct, there is the old post road bridge nearer the sea. Another old packhorse bridge at the mouth of Bilsdean Burn about a mile north is known as Prince Charlie's Bridge.

COVE

Cove is the 'port' of Cockburnspath, if so grandiose a title may be allowed to describe the relationship between the two villages. The tiny harbour was begun in the mid-18th. century and work continued spasmodically until 1831. The earliest surviving evidence is an access road and a tunnel driven through the cliffs which still provides an interesting approach. The only way in is on foot ~ cars must be parked at the cliff head.

The Mercat Cross, Cockburnspath: mercat = market. Most surviving crosses post-date the Reformation and rather than being cruciform have commemorative or other origins. They are the focus of trade and ceremony in many villages and towns.

PEASE BRIDGE. When Cromwell saw Pease Dene he realised its potential as a defensive barrier on the north road. "Ten men to hinder are better than forty to make their way," was his assessment. That was before the gorge was bridged in 1786. As you drive the narrow roadway across these towering A-listed* arches, once claimed as the world's highest bridge at 130 feet above the burn, there is no opportunity to realise the depths of the ravine but it is possible to park nearby and walk the footpath down the bank where trees strive to maintain a tenuous hold on vertiginous slopes. They also obscure the view when the leaf canopy is in the full flush of summer fecundity. Pease Bridge was a relief for travellers but it came almost too late. A better road was imminent. The A1 is the newer road which follows the valleys of the Upper Pease Burn and Eye Water, the sort of route avoided before swampy ground prone to seasonal flooding was systematically drained, woodland cleared and careful routing made it possible for the mail coaches to pass.

* *Historic Scotland lists buildings in three categories:-*
 A- of national importance; B- of regional importance; C- of local importance.

GRANTSHOUSE. This tiny settlement is on the A1 - the 'New Post Road'- where there is an inn and little else. The hamlet was originally known as Bankhouse but was re-named, according to one tradition, when Tommy Grant opened the inn after working as a navvy on this new route between Burnmouth and Cockburnspath. This minor entrepreneur no doubt saw his opportunity to cash in on his own labours when a majority of traffic diverted from the wilder route over Coldingham Moor. The place and its inn have been Grantshouse in memory of old Tommy ever since.

GRANTSHOUSE
to DUNGLASS
6.5 miles (356.7 miles)

Dunglass

Dunglass + Collegiate Church (ruin)

COCKBURNSPATH

Cove Harbour

Cove

NORTH SEA

GNR A1

Pease Bridge

A1107

Original route

A1107

I have heard Cockburnspath pronounced as Co-burn-spath or alternatively as Co-path, however never as it is spelt: Cock-burn-spath.

Howpark

A1

GNR

LANDRANGER MAP 67

Grantshouse

A6112

DUNBAR

In the wake of our scenic, indeed historic introduction to Scotland this page is something of an anticlimax. The nuclear power station at Torness dominates the seascape, inevitably, but it tries to compensate with a visitor centre. Industry is not new on the approach to Dunbar for the cement works also makes an impression on the landscape. The only change here is that the trunk road has switched from north to south of the works, but rejoining the original route past the old fishing port of Dunbar. Oliver Cromwell had a hand in the building of this harbour which became a herring port and it also had a whaling fleet in the 18th. century. The great days have gone but a little inshore fishing survives. The scant remains of the old castle perch apologetically above the harbour reminding visitors that the old town had troubles of a military kind, culminating in Cromwell's battle of 1650. Now there is provision for holiday visitors. The East Beach is popular for the usual seaside reasons. The Dunbar Underground is not a railway system but a museum of local archaeology. On the approach from the east the most obvious landmark is the parish church, large, gothic, pinnacled and on a rise above the sea maximizing its undoubted size. If it looks pristinely clean there is no mystery - it was destroyed by fire in 1987 but was rebuilt to stand as before and be back in service by 1992.

OLDHAMSTOCKS

This pretty village is off-route but should not be missed. There is a mercat cross and a village pump on the village green and the churchyard has a watch house set up to give shelter to the lookout appointed to guard by night against bodysnatchers. Oldhamstocks' major claim to fame in the wider world is a local family, the Broadwoods, whose son went to London to make his name as a piano maker.

INNERWICK

If you visit Oldhamstocks it is likely that you'll rejoin the North Road along byways that will take you through Innerwick. There is a farmstead, Temple Mill, with a threshing mill chimney; and watch out for the toll house with its clock, sundial and inscribed tablet.

O'ER EVERY HOUR THATS BRIGHTEST
A SHADOW CREEPS
AND HE WHOSE LAUGH IS LIGHTEST
FULL OFTEN WEEPS
O LOOK WE FOR THE MORROW
WHICH HATH NO NIGHT
WHEN LOST IS EVERY SORROW
IN GOD'S OWN LIGHT

SIC TRANSIT GLORIA MUNDI
SO PASSES AWAY THE GLORY OF THE WORLD

Tollhouse and sundial inscription, Innerwick.

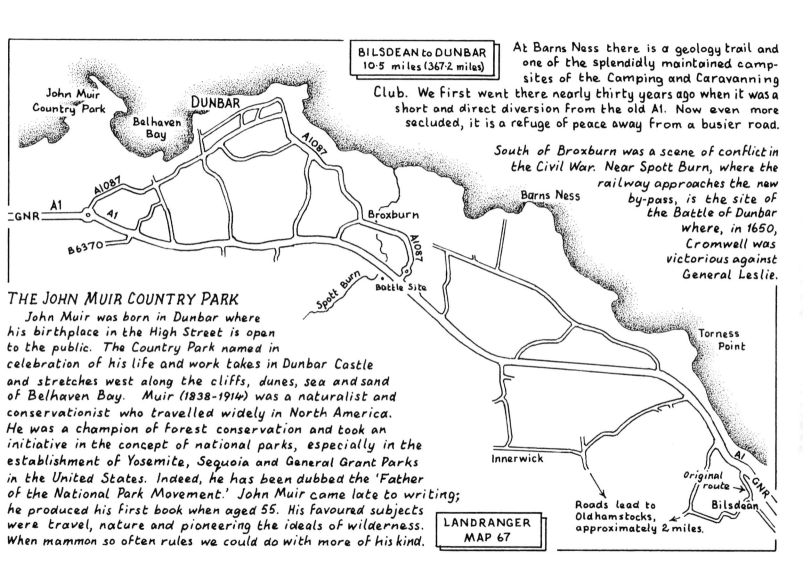

At Barns Ness there is a geology trail and one of the splendidly maintained camp-sites of the Camping and Caravanning Club. We first went there nearly thirty years ago when it was a short and direct diversion from the old A1. Now even more secluded, it is a refuge of peace away from a busier road.

South of Broxburn was a scene of conflict in the Civil War. Near Spott Burn, where the railway approaches the new by-pass, is the site of the Battle of Dunbar where, in 1650, Cromwell was victorious against General Leslie.

John Muir Country Park

DUNBAR

Belhaven Bay

A1087

A1087

GNR   A1   A1

B6370

Barns Ness

Broxburn

A1087

Spott Burn   Battle Site

Torness Point

Innerwick

Original route

A1

GNR

Bilsdean

Roads lead to Oldhamstocks, approximately 2 miles.

THE JOHN MUIR COUNTRY PARK

John Muir was born in Dunbar where his birthplace in the High Street is open to the public. The Country Park named in celebration of his life and work takes in Dunbar Castle and stretches west along the cliffs, dunes, sea and sand of Belhaven Bay. Muir (1838-1914) was a naturalist and conservationist who travelled widely in North America. He was a champion of forest conservation and took an initiative in the concept of national parks, especially in the establishment of Yosemite, Sequoia and General Grant Parks in the United States. Indeed, he has been dubbed the 'Father of the National Park Movement.' John Muir came late to writing; he produced his first book when aged 55. His favoured subjects were travel, nature and pioneering the ideals of wilderness. When mammon so often rules we could do with more of his kind.

LANDRANGER MAP 67

EAST LINTON & PRESTON MILL

It is 'East' here to differentiate from the West Linton south of Edinburgh. This one is a large village closely bypassed by the A1. Our own visit was abruptly curtailed by an excited convention of marauding wasps but we did have time to note the elaborate cast iron fountain at the village centre before hastily retreating in the direction of Preston Mill.

The mill is a rare survival, a tiny working rural corn mill with a kiln. It dates from the early 18th. century but by the 1960s it was in a serious state of disrepair. The rescue was largely due to the support in terms of cash and expertise of an international milling company, Rank-Hovis-McDougall, Ltd., a case of the elephant coming to the aid of the tiniest of mice. The delightful waterside setting of this homogeneously pleasing group is one which Constable would have been delighted to set on canvas. If you go nowhere else on this page don't miss Preston Mill – and its neighbour, the charming Phantassie Doocot.

Preston Mill.

TRAPRAIN LAW

The facts are these: the hill is 725ft (221m) high and the site of a bronze age hill fort which persisted as a fortified hill-top town through the Roman occupation. Excavations have revealed many finds, including Roman silverware. But forget the facts – just climb it. You may reach the top in ten minutes (if you're fit!) from the car park in an old roadside quarry beneath the sharp northern flank but it is better to approach by the lane from Hailes Castle. The view is superb, from the Lammermuirs to the sea and Bass Rock and with Edinburgh's Arthur's Seat beckoning in the west.

HAILES CASTLE is in the care of Historic Scotland.

The ruins, nestling in a secluded curve of the River Tyne, are best approached from East Linton. This is a fine spot for lunch, unless you save the sandwiches for the top of Traprain Law.

In Scotland dovecote = doocot (pronounced approximately 'dook't' with a short 'oo'). Before refrigeration fresh meat was a rare commodity in winter and for those who could afford it pigeon meat was an answer to the need.

TYNINGHAME.   If you turn off the A1 along the A198 to get a closer look at the Kirklandhill Standing Stone it is worth continuing to the first turning left for the return to Preston Mill and East Linton. By doing this the village of Tyninghame will be included in the itinerary. This estate village of the adjacent Tyninghame House was begun in the 18th. century and constructed mainly between then and the mid-19th. century. These cottages provided homes for retainers and workers on the Earl of Haddington's estate. The result is a pretty village without a long line of history.

KIRKLANDHILL
to HADDINGTON
7·5 miles (374·7 miles)

To Tantallon Castle
(5 miles)

Tyninghame

B1407

B1377

Preston Mill

EAST LINTON

River Tyne

A198

Kirklandhill
× Standing Stone

A1

GNR

The Kirklandhill Standing Stone, presumed to date from the Bronze Age, is eleven feet tall but on private land so it must be viewed from the nearby road to the disadvantage of its true height.

At the time of writing (1999) a Tourist Information Kiosk is installed at the Pencraig Wood lay-by.

Pencraig
Wood

The A198 to Tyninghame (above) also leads to Tantallon Castle, well off-route but in a spectacular cliff top location above the surge of the sea. A pair of binoculars would come in handy should you wish to contemplate Bass Rock across a mile and a half of waves.

B1347

GNR

A1

A199

River Tyne

Hailes Castle

Traprain Law

HADDINGTON

Just when Tyneside seems a distant memory here is another River Tyne for us to follow, from East Linton to Haddington, but any Geordie met here will be either a fellow tourist or an immigrant.

PENCRAIG WOOD is noted on the Ordnance Survey's Landranger Map as both picnic site and viewpoint. In the latter case the description is accurate for there is a splendid and tempting outlook over the Valley of Tyne to Hailes Castle and Traprain Law but only a masochist would choose to eat sandwiches with the main road so near. Far better to note the view and go to the castle or even climb Traprain Law to enjoy your packed lunch.

LANDRANGER
MAPS 66 & 67

Haddington

Haddington must qualify as one of the five finest towns or cities along the Great North Road* It was designated as a Royal Burgh in the 12th. century and its medieval street plan is still the framework upon which it is stretched. The structural base is a triangle, built over in the 15th. century, but Market Street, Hardgate and High Street still outline the original pattern. Townsfolk were allocated plots of land called tofts where they would build their houses and businesses; and behind the buildings were riggs which reached to the town walls and where smallholdings were developed – rather like the burgage strips of English towns such as Alnwick. These plots have gradually been infilled with housing but with little damage to the original basic structure. The North Road bypassed Haddington in the 1920s and this has minimised the sort of damage so many ancient towns have suffered in the name of road improvement in the 20th. century. The town has received a European Architectural Heritage Year Civic Trust Award for architectural conservation which indicates that here is a place where the townsfolk are proud of their town and are willing to do something about preserving its heritage – without the place becoming merely a museum piece. 284 buildings have been listed for historical and architectural reasons and it is worth buying the booklet 'A Walk Around Haddington' if you wish to get the most out of your visit.

*A subjective list will appear at the end of the book.

St. Mary's Collegiate Church interior – looking east to the restored choir.

The Lamp of Lothian

St. Mary's Collegiate Church, Haddington, is a building of cathedral-like proportions, larger than Edinburgh's "cathedral", the High Kirk of St. Giles. The name 'Lamp of Lothian' which dates from the 13th. century, was originally borrowed from a nearby friary church of grace and light but now it refers to the spiritual light of this church of distinction. The siege of Haddington, 1547-48, rendered the transepts and choir roofless and so they remained for 400 years, with a wall to seal off the ruins so that the nave became the parish church. In the 1970s restoration gave Haddington its complete church back. The weather-worn walls were too weak to bear the full weight of a stone vaulted roof but the authentic style has been preserved by using fibre glass, the first time the material had been used on such a scale. You would never notice unless you compare the new roof with its supporting walls which betray the weathering of the centuries.

HADDINGTON to MUSSELBURGH
10 miles (384·7 miles)

THE BATTLE OF PRESTONPANS. Between Tranent and Prestonpans, at Meadowmill beside the A198, is an artificial hill rather like a Norman motte.* On the summit is an impressive interpretive display overlooking the field of a famous battle. An older monument of stone inscribed 1745 stands ¾ mile west at a road junction. On 20th. September of that year Bonnie Prince Charlie's supporters having marched east from Edinburgh met the troops of Sir John Cope who had landed at Dunbar. The Jacobites took advantage of high ground at Tranent while the government forces settled for a defensive position facing south from behind marsh and ditch. However, the intervening terrain proved difficult for both armies and the Jacobites moved east to face the left flank of Cope's line which re-formed to confront the new direction of threat. At dawn on the 21st. the Highlanders charged with fearsome war cries and much waving of weapons, a spectacle which proved too much for the opposition. The majority fled, soon to be followed by most of the rest who found time to fire only a single round. It was a stunning victory for the supporters of Charles Edward Stuart, the Young Pretender, early in his unsuccessful campaign to seize the throne.

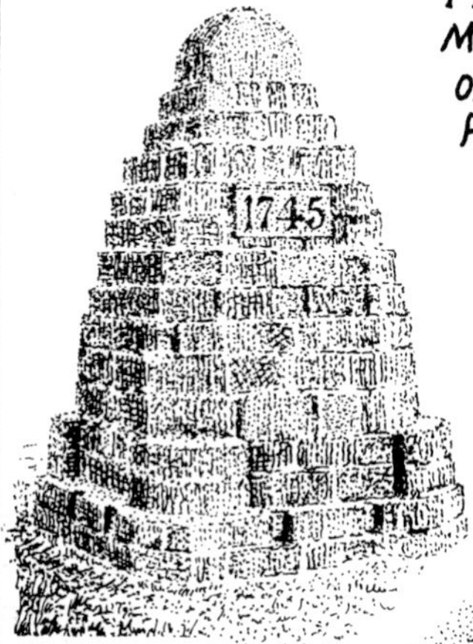
1745

Prestonpans Monument.

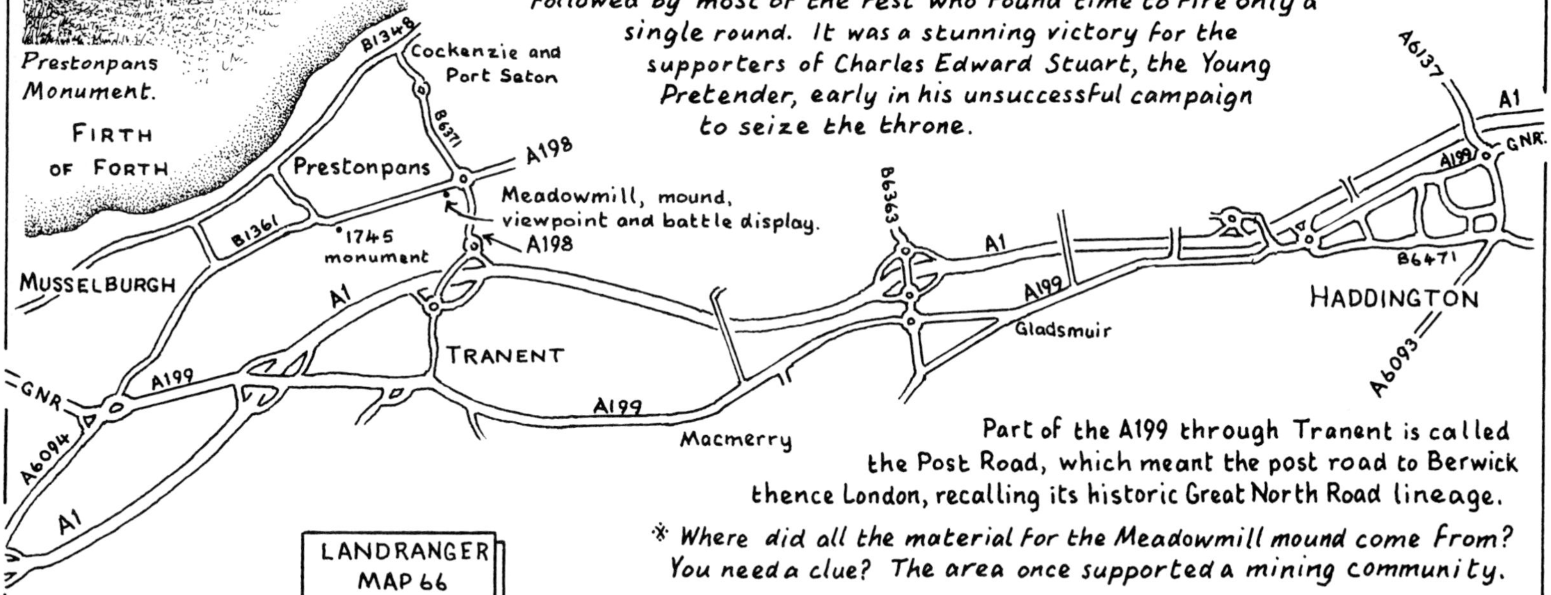
B1348
Cockenzie and Port Seton
B6371
A198
Prestonpans
FIRTH OF FORTH
B1361
1745 monument
Meadowmill, mound, viewpoint and battle display.
A198
MUSSELBURGH
A1
TRANENT
GNR
A199
A6094
A1
A199
Macmerry
B6363
A1
A199
Gladsmuir
A6137
A1
GNR
A199
B6471
HADDINGTON
A6093

Part of the A199 through Tranent is called the Post Road, which meant the post road to Berwick thence London, recalling its historic Great North Road lineage.

* Where did all the material for the Meadowmill mound come from? You need a clue? The area once supported a mining community.

LANDRANGER MAP 66

JOURNEY'S END

The Head Post Office in Edinburgh, as with the G.P.O. in London, is no longer housed in the same building that was used when this book was planned. Yet these points remain the extremities of the A1. Edinburgh's first post office was in a house near the Mercat Cross on the Royal Mile which would have been the logical termination of the post road from London; the post boys would have ridden up Canongate (where at a later date the postmaster had his office) and into High Street, which is the axis of Old Edinburgh. However the modern Head Post Office was until recently established in a grandiose building in Waterloo Place, close by the corner junction with North Bridge where Princes Street begins and the A1 ends, and this must also be the end of our journey.

There can be no mistaking Edinburgh. The architecture of good Scottish stone fits functionally and easily into the scene of a city built on hills so that there are frequent vistas of townscape, country, hills and sea. There is a clear divide between the romantically unplanned growth of the Old Town and the elegant design of the Neo-Georgian New Town, begun in 1770 as the result of an inspired collaboration between Lord Provost Drummond, leader of the Town Council, and his architect James Craig. Until then the waters of the Nor'Loch filled valley now occupied by Princes Street Gardens and where Waverley Station is the terminus of the railway line from London. It marked the northern limits of the Old Town that started life in the seventh century as the powerbase of Edwin, King of Northumbria, whose settlement around the castle rock grew from Edwin's Burgh to become the Edinburgh of today. But Edinburgh, like London, has a fascinating story for which there is no space on one tiny page, a story that you must find and read for yourself.

392 miles ago we ate sandwiches in Postman's Park. If the weather is fine there are plenty of places here where a picnic is possible but I'll be taking my sandwiches to the top of Arthur's Seat to find a quiet belvedere away from the summit, there to look out over one of the finest cities in the world and contemplate with satisfaction a journey well completed and consider candidates for future exploration. Journey's End, indeed!

The old head post office building where the Duke of Wellington's likeness overlooks the end of the Great North Road.

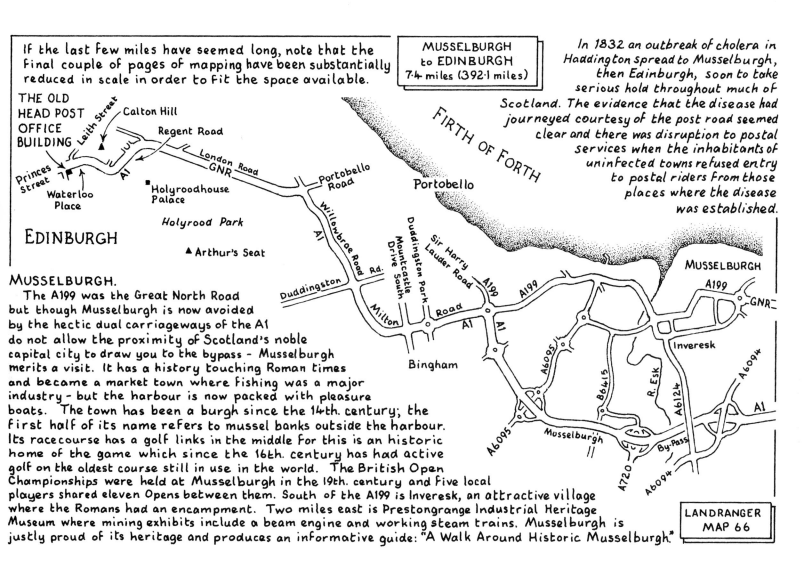

If the last few miles have seemed long, note that the final couple of pages of mapping have been substantially reduced in scale in order to fit the space available.

In 1832 an outbreak of cholera in Haddington spread to Musselburgh, then Edinburgh, soon to take serious hold throughout much of Scotland. The evidence that the disease had journeyed courtesy of the post road seemed clear and there was disruption to postal services when the inhabitants of uninfected towns refused entry to postal riders from those places where the disease was established.

THE OLD HEAD POST OFFICE BUILDING

Calton Hill

Leith Street

Regent Road

Princes Street

London Road GNR

Waterloo Place

A1

Portobello Road

Holyroodhouse Palace

FIRTH OF FORTH

Portobello

Holyrood Park

EDINBURGH

▲ Arthur's Seat

Willowbrae Road

Duddingston Rd.

Duddingston

Milton

Mountcastle Drive South

Duddingston Park Road

Sir Harry Lauder Road

A199

A199

MUSSELBURGH

A199

GNR

Inveresk

A6094

A1

A6095

B6415

R. Esk

A6124

A6094

A1

Bingham

A1

A1

MUSSELBURGH.
    The A199 was the Great North Road but though Musselburgh is now avoided by the hectic dual carriageways of the A1 do not allow the proximity of Scotland's noble capital city to draw you to the bypass - Musselburgh merits a visit. It has a history touching Roman times and became a market town where fishing was a major industry - but the harbour is now packed with pleasure boats. The town has been a burgh since the 14th. century; the first half of its name refers to mussel banks outside the harbour. Its racecourse has a golf links in the middle for this is an historic home of the game which since the 16th. century has had active golf on the oldest course still in use in the world. The British Open Championships were held at Musselburgh in the 19th. century and five local players shared eleven Opens between them. South of the A199 is Inveresk, an attractive village where the Romans had an encampment. Two miles east is Prestongrange Industrial Heritage Museum where mining exhibits include a beam engine and working steam trains. Musselburgh is justly proud of its heritage and produces an informative guide: "A Walk Around Historic Musselburgh."

Musselburgh

A720

A6094

Musselburgh By-Pass

A6095

LANDRANGER MAP 66

INDEX

POSTSCRIPT: a closing letter to the reader.

This has been a labour of love, a pleasurable way of recording so many of the places visited — usually with my wife — over many years. In fact the first drawing I ever made of a structure beside the Great North Road (hereafter to be referred to as the GNR to save space and time) was done over thirty years ago. That was of Robin Hood's Well, part of a proposed itinerary of places in Yorkshire that came to nothing. Yet it may be regarded as the genesis of this book, begun after several false starts some twenty years later.

As the project developed I gradually came to realise that I was showing the 'pretty' face of the GNR. There is an ugly face too, which should be recognised. Much of the ugliness is the traffic, particularly south of the Tyne, but being part of the flow we can hardly complain. Yet we don't have to be harnessed to the traffic of commerce. Take the hints of the suggested diversions and get away from it all whenever you can; indeed, use the splendid publications of the Ordnance Survey and devise variations of your own. Show enterprise, have fun.

Some diversions on foot come highly recommended, by the author at least. Those who know me will not be surprised to find that I encourage the reader to finish the itinerary by climbing to the summit of Arthur's Seat in Edinburgh, not the only ascent of a minor hill to be suggested, which emphasises a liking for the heights of England and Scotland; and when you get to Lindisfarne a stroll around the coast of this Holy Island is urged. If the weather is bright, sunny and breezy and you think your legs are up to it there can be few better places for a short day's gentle exercise. Study the tide tables so that you can be cut off from the mainland for a few quiet hours to share the island with a few like-minded individuals and the long-suffering local folk.

The seascape and historic locations of Holy Island provide fine walking but even in cities, towns and villages you should get plenty of exercise. Park the car, buy the local guide and use it to explore the historic core of the old townships. There is more to even the smallest village than immediately meets the eye. By getting away from the car you'll get the real flavour of a place, it's building materials, the vernacular architecture, the history, geography and the people living there. Don't expect to learn about the diverse character of the GNR with all its regional variations if you just sit in your car or merely visit museums, open houses, castles and exhibitions.

I suppose many of the subjects noted and drawn may seem quite trivial in the context of a route of nearly 400 miles. Some folk may query the importance of a little local lock-up at Eaton Socon, for instance, or Robin Hood's Well in south Yorkshire? The answer may well be, 'Not a lot,' in terms of relevance to the GNR but things like these caught my attention and were attractive (and easy to draw!) so they are there. The drawings are, in some part, the reason for the book. I enjoy pen and ink drawing but can always use practice and here was the perfect opportunity - but look on these impressions simply as illustrations, not as works of art. They were never intended as that.

The subjects are quite selective, chosen as uncomplicated scenes which I thought would be effective on paper, with the intention of decorating the text rather than as a record of the GNR. The scenes may look remarkably unpopulated and roads unnaturally free of vehicles. Obviously people and cars are not favourite subjects. They clutter the scene, take time and need practice! It's not that they won't keep still. That was never a problem because I travel with a camera and draw from photographs in the comfort of home.

The first pages were produced some eight or nine years ago but were discarded as I searched for the best way to tackle the project. Initially they were set out portrait style, that is vertically, but it soon became obvious that while such a layout would be perfect for a strip-map of the GNR for most of the way to Scotland this would be less convenient across the border where the route's bearing is switched to east/west. And a possible follow-up book, 'The Holyhead Road,' would be mainly east/west too so a landscape alignment seemed more logical.

Even then pages were jettisoned for the slightest error until I realised that aspirations of perfection were unrealistic. Nor were they produced in geographical sequence. The first page to avoid rejection and make it to the book was begun on the 18-2-1993 and finished on the 1-3-1993. Often several pages would be worked on at the same time. The first page actually completed was filed on 24-2-1993 having been started two days earlier. Others, begun around that time, saw the final application of ink several years later, especially if they contained road maps, these usually being left until the end.

It has been a time consuming task, sometimes worked on with commendable regularity, sometimes sporadically. Some may suggest that it would have been more sense to produce the book in the traditional way of typesetting or even, in this age of electronic technology, by the use of computing techniques. That would have been too easy. Let's show that the older technology of pen and ink has not died. Think of this as a personal notebook, a record of my travels that I have no objection to you sharing.

There will inevitably be errors. Some I am well aware of, for example the careless use of the term 'medieval'. The middle ages should be the period from about 1000 a.d. until the 15th. century but critical eyes will find examples of its use as an inaccurate synonym for old, ancient; referring to olden times only approximate to the medieval period. Naughty! But I did become more precise as time progressed yet saw no reason to make alterations to earlier work, especially as this might mean redrafting whole pages. Pedantic readers will have to put up with it and anything else which may catch their eyes. There may be examples of repetition. When a task is spread over some eight years it is easy to provide the same information twice. Put it down to absent-mindedness. There will also be descriptions that are out-of-date, places closed, roads re-routed, buildings altered or even demolished. Insert your own comments and alterations to bring the book up to date, by all means. A brief note in the margin should do the trick. Neatly, of course!

Buildings have even appeared. It was frustrating to have written about the six bridges across the River Tyne only to learn that a seventh was about to be added. On the 20th. November, 2000, an arch of innovative design was swung into place downstream of the Tyne Bridge to link the Newcastle bank with Gateshead Quays where the Baltic Centre for Contemporary Art is emerging from the shell of a disused grain warehouse alongside a brand new concert hall. Here will be a south bank to visit, a highlight of the Tyne. The Gateshead Millennium Bridge is for the use of pedestrians and cyclists and is unique, being described as a rotating bridge. Its arc pivots to allow for the passage of ocean-going vessels. It is the first opening bridge to be built across the Tyne for some 100 years and they had to put it there just after I had completed page 127 to my satisfaction!

On page 160 I promised to reveal my selection of five finest towns/cities on the route. That has been a difficult choice to make. Newcastle, even without Gateshead, is a city of great interest and history and is overwritten by much modern work of style. Yet inevitably, in a regional capital of size, there is a great deal of dross amidst the quality and away from the historic central area the spread of urban development sullies the overall impression. Newcastle is good and would certainly be in a top ten, possibly even coming in at number six, but perhaps not good enough to make the top five.

London and Edinburgh, despite their urban sprawl, would be front-running candidates but the self-imposed mandate is to nominate places en route which, as terminal points, they obviously are not. That's a relief! In any case, I could not possibly include Edinburgh since I spent many childhood weeks there every year, especially in the summer holidays, because my grandparents lived there. It became a second home and remains high on a very short list of favourite cities and its inclusion would certainly give rise to justified claims of prejudice. York and Lincoln are enthusiastically described in the text but they are not on the modern GNR though they may have been on the route at some stages in its history.

Some of the criteria for a final selection, admittedly very much a personal choice, are simple enough to list although an inventory does little justice to all that is good in the quality of a town. However, here are just some of the points which influenced the listing of five firm favourites.

i.   Historic buildings; i.e., religious houses, castles, palaces, mansions, etc., not forgetting smaller structures of outstanding interest or intrinsic curiosity (ruined or not!)

ii.   Good vernacular architecture.

iii. An obviously historic town plan.

iv.   Links with interesting people of local, national or even international importance.

v.   An historic past allied to an historic placement on the G.N.R.

vi.   That indefinable quality which we call character.

These six provide a good framework for the final choice. Places like Highgate, Peterborough (but it's a few miles east of the route proper), Grantham, Newark, Retford, and Morpeth, among many, have reasonable claims for a final place; however my top five - in alphabetical rather than merit order - are Alnwick, Berwick-upon-Tweed, Durham, Haddington and Stamford.

It's a personal selection and if there seems to be a bias towards the north, I apologise. All the good southern towns seem to be bypassed. I don't intend to use any more space in justification. Just visit each, give an honest critical assessment and see if you agree. It is interesting to note that when I asked my wife to make a selection independently of my own choice she came up with the same five, even including Newcastle as a probable number six. It's nice to have my assessment backed up in this way. We don't agree about everything!

A point intended for the introduction is that one historical aspect of the GNR is its importance as a line of communication when various factions were at odds with one another. It is hardly surprising that many significant battles took place within easy reach of the road. Armies marching to meet an opposition would take the easiest, most obvious route and where their paths intersected an engagement would ensue. Perhaps this assertion is rather simplistic, yet consider the list of battles that took place on or near the GNR. In chronological order, here are a few, some mentioned in the text: Lincoln, 1141;

Boroughbridge, 1322; Hallidon Hill, 1333; The Standard (between Thirsk and Northallerton), 1338; Neville's Cross, 1346; Bramham Moor, 1408; Towton Moor, 1461; Losecoat Field, 1470; Barnet, 1471; Marston Moor, 1644; Dunbar, 1650; Prestonpans, 1745.

And never forget the year 1066 when Harold rode north to defend his crown against Harold Hardrada at Stamford Bridge on 25th. September. He won that encounter but two days later William of Normandy embarked on his fateful crossing of the Channel. The North Road provided a direct route in both directions but even so it was not until about the 6th. October that Harold returned to London with his cavalry to regroup and continue to his destination with fate at Hastings. The question arises – and is unanswerable – did the North Road have a significant influence on Britain's ruling lineage?

As I write, the daily paper informs me that the A1 is to be Europeanised (can there really be such a word?) as the E15 which will connect Edinburgh with Gibraltar. Not in this book! It will not be re-written for the benefit of Europe. But does it really matter? London to Edinburgh will always be the Great North Road and the truth is that the journey is always more important than the road. Enjoy it and take care for yourself and for those around you, your fellow travellers. In the words of an old T.V. jingle advertising a well known brand of petrol: "Happy motoring!"

Frank Goddard

Beeston,
Leeds,
2003.